# Puppies

*To Bernard*

*and our two "little wolves"*

See page 239 for Table of Contents

English translation © Copyright 1997 by Barron's Educational Series, Inc.

© Éditions Nathan, Paris, France, 1995.
Published originally under the title *Les Jeunes Chiens*

*All inquiries should be addressed to:*
Barron's Educational Series, Inc.
250 Wireless Boulevard
Hauppauge, NY 11788

International Standard Book No. 0-8120-6631-6

*Library of Congress Catalog Card No. 97-8732*

**Library of Congress Cataloging-in-Publication Data**
Bulard-Cordeau, Brigitte.
    [Juenes chiens.  English]
    Puppies / Brigitte Bulard-Cordeau.
            p.    cm.
    Includes bibliographical references  and index.
        ISBN 0-8120-6631-6
        1. Puppies.  2. Dogs.  I. Title.
    SF429.B92513    1997
    636.7'07—dc21                                          97-8732
                                                                   CIP

Printed in Hong Kong

987654321

# Puppies

BRIGITTE BULARD-CORDEAU

BARRON'S

As soon as he's born the baby pup crawls, clumsily, onto his mother's belly, and with a light tap of her paw she helps him to get to a nipple. He sucks away sightlessly. He's deaf. But he keeps up a constant squeaking! It sounds something like mewing. At ten days, he barks, in company with his brothers and sisters, who make use of this concerto in "Wah" major in season and out. He'll find out what it sounds like in four days' time.

Now this is progress! His birth weight has doubled in a week. He's used to human hands now. He sniffs at them, with his sense of smell that's a hundred times better than ours. At twenty-one days, the smell of a human being is his ultimate quest, and stroking reassures him. This is the time of assimilation. A big moment in his doggy life.

He plays like a crazy dog, carrying off handkerchiefs and socks in his catch-all mouth, growling and struggling that's what it's all about for a child of the pack, always in a gang. His master's presence will make him choose the camp of the human beings, his allies.

And yet at two months, fear suddenly sets in. The master, after having been his friend, makes him anxious, bothers him. Noises intimidate him, movements scare him out of his wits. A week earlier, he had become a big boy, cutting his milk teeth, weaned and autonomous, ready to take off on his own. Who would have thought him independent? The puppy still has everything to learn.

No other baby animal so much needs human beings to grow up successfully. Time is short. At six months, a Cocker is already at 80% of its adult size, and any dog already has his personality set. Socialization, training, health, feeding. . . nothing may be neglected.

We'll follow the baby pup step by step, hour by hour, from his intrauterine existence to birth, with supporting photographs. Day after day, from the first age to the second age, week after week, let's help him grow up. With firmness and patience, let's assist him when halfway through his growth he experiences both ravenous hunger and the urge to run away, signs of adolescence. And in just a year, or sometimes a year and a half, depending on whether he's a Pekingese or a German Mastiff, the young dog has become an adult. What an amazing feat! It takes human beings 20 years to get there.

This book tells the whole secret behind this performance: the start of a dog's life with his mother, his pack, and his master; his place in the family, his role in society; his games and what he's not allowed to do; his tastes in food and his health. The story of a young dog under his owner's influence: without human beings, this animal is lost.

*How could anyone help wanting to pet this Cocker?*
*A puppy's arrival in the home brings joy to the whole family.*

# A Sweet Little Puppy

*Shy, awkward, the baby-dog touches our very hearts. An unfocused gaze, harmless milk teeth, a promise of affection. And he feels so good in our arms! Any child wants to make a friend of him, any adult wants to make him a companion. That's how a sweet little puppy ends up being always on our minds and becoming indispensable to us.*

*The picture of innocence!
Three tiny American Shepherds
look as good as gold.*

## INSTINCT REVEALED
### Mothering

Tiny, flat on the ground, lost in a new world, the baby dog is a touching little thing. We bend down to stroke him, to hug him: we want to protect him, pet him. Man or woman, we find ourselves mothering him. He has yet to take his first steps, and already he's calling us, imploring. Where would he be without us? Barely conscious, he places all his trust in human beings. A murmur reassures him, a pat soothes him, and given the slightest encouragement, he responds to our efforts. You would think he was meant to be with human beings.

### Domestication

It's the voice of memory: our friendship has survived for millennia. The dog shares our life, despite our evolution. He is always there, always faithful. This canine has only one thing on his mind: making his master happy. The young dog's gaze could not lie: you can see he loves us.

### The Children's Friend

Having a puppy as companion is a dream come true for a child. He strokes the dog, talks to him, cuddles up to him, and finds consolation when he's sad. And the puppy is always ready to play. The house, the playing field, the yard, the woods, whatever the place it's always good for a game. Muscles are developed, energies are let loose, laughter blends with barks. If the young dog goes too far, sinks his fangs in the ball, or chases wildly after strangers, the human youngster plays the grown-up, scolds the offender, and grows more sure of himself. He gives orders, the pup obeys. The hierarchy establishes itself automatically. The toy dog is a thing of the past! A real friend is here.

### Taking Him in Hand

Crazy and full of vitality, the puppy is "a bit of a mess." Left to his own devices, it's total anarchy. Not just around him, but in his innermost self. Contradictions, ignorance… . How can one sort out what's going on in his young brain? It will take some method and a lot of patience. The first task will therefore be education. The puppy, to be loved, must be perfectly integrated into society.

## A COMMITMENT TO BE KEPT
### A Long-term Companion

Love at first sight for a puppy is only the beginning of a long love story. The little dog is going to grow up, have his place in the household, be an integral part of the family. He comes into our lives for over ten years, maybe twelve. Every Christmas, every birthday, every party, he'll be included in the celebrations. He too will have a right to a planned vacation. That calls for some thought. The commitment is a serious one, even though it is not easy to foresee the future. The decision is not one to be made on a whim: afterwards it is too late to backtrack. The puppy lives only for his master: he has to be able to count on him.

### A Brat to Be Brought Up

There can be no question of letting him do as he pleases. He jumps on people, licks their faces, runs into the street, shows his fangs. What impudence, what a nerve! He must be started on the right road early: a puppy must have a strict upbringing. That's the only way he'll be appreciated by everyone, strangers as well as family members. The more disciplined he is, the better he is accepted into society. But bringing him up will require time, perseverance, and a lot of vigilance. He can't be taught just anyhow. A method that fits his psychology must be used.

### A Sports Lover to Be Walked

A puppy requires us to be very available. A minimum of twice a day, he has to be taken outside the house. He must relieve himself, and he also needs to stretch his legs, especially if he's of the athletic sort. No puppy can get by without wearing down his nails and working his muscles. The yard may seem ideal, but watch out for the flowerbeds! He is sure to prefer a master who likes to walk and who will take him outside, on the street,

*She's on her bicycle, he's trotting alongside! The outing's a joy for both of them. In the woods or elsewhere, going out is essential, whatever the breed of the young dog, who must relieve himself, and also wear down his nails, exercise his muscles, and thus begin his socialization.*

## Little Scrap of a Dog

He plays, he barks, he gesticulates. The puppy is a veritable antidote for boredom. On the street, he attracts attention, causes people to meet, sweeps shyness away, starts conversations. With him, there's no more loneliness, he's the key to new places and new people. All by himself, he's a whole world.

# A Formal Marriage

The formalities have to be strictly observed with dogs: it should always be the female who goes to meet her intended mate. If neither of the animals have mated before, you may have to offer some assistance. However, this is not recommended unless the animals are having severe problems.

The union of purebred dogs is not always synonymous with impregnation: a 20% failure rate is observed in bitches in which ovulation takes place outside the normal dates. But diagnostic tests permit reliable planning of a meeting of male and female. Using a single drop of plasma or serum, the measurement kit defines the progesterone rate and indicates the optimum period for impregnation.

along the byways. It's not all that difficult, and meeting people of all sorts is a good way of becoming socialized.

## A New Baby to Be Settled In

A puppy in the family gladdens children and adults alike. But his presence can also cause some friction. Some offer him tidbits, others won't give him any. One day he'll find people glad to take him for a walk, the next day he runs into refusal. It's best to establish a consensus from the beginning. From a practical standpoint, sharing out the tasks should perhaps be considered: walking the puppy, grooming him, buying his food, playing with him. There must also be full agreement as to the principles of his upbringing. There is nothing worse for a puppy's mind than being filled with contradictions.

## A Character to Be Mastered

Things have to be very clear. For the dog to know his place, the master must show it to him. The man is the boss: he's the one who gives orders, not this stubborn little creature who coolly settles in the master's armchair or stretches out on the bed. You have to react at once and assert yourself, using voice and gestures. In a dog's mind, the rules made by the family have the same value as those in force in the pack. They are his reference, the framework of his life.

## An Expensive Friend

Doghouse, basket, dishes—even before his arrival, the dog represents a certain investment. You can't receive him empty-handed. In addition to the accessories there is the actual purchase price of the puppy: next to nothing for a little mongrel, but the price is high for a little purebred. The amount varies between $150 and $1000, depending on whether the little dog is in fairly plentiful supply or is a rare gem. Though it may be tempting to purchase on credit, the price won't be any lower! And there's no way to hold down other expenses while the monthly payments are being made. Food, healthcare, identification tattoo—you can't be stingy about these. Food alone costs a fair amount: it cannot be just table scraps. It must be perfectly suited to the dog's growth, to his breed. If you choose a dry "growth" food suitable for the puppy for the whole period from 2 to 14 months, you can expect to spend between $50 and $100 a year to feed a little dog such as a Pomeranian, between $250 and $500 a year for a medium-sized dog such as a Beagle, and between $750 and $1,500 for a big dog such as a German Mastiff. But if you opt for canned or home-prepared food the cost goes up.

Whatever his breed or size, the puppy must be protected by vaccination, which means, after the initial first-year vaccinations ($100–$150 including tattooing), the annual boosters ($50–$75). You also have to face worming treatments, anal sac draining, and other visits to the veterinary office in the event of illness, accidents, etc. (between $150 and $500 a year). Let's not forget the cost ($100–$150 a year) of grooming, the frequency of which depends on hair type. Lastly, and depending on individual lifestyle, vacation time kennel costs must be taken into account, and insurance, especially if you have a watchdog or guard dog. On average, the foreseeable annual budget is from $500 for a small dog to $2,000 for a large dog.

## HOW DO YOU GO ABOUT IT?
### The Bitch and Her Babies

Being present at the birth of dog babies, then helping the mother to raise them are exciting experiences. It's the simplest solution and at the same time the most interesting. But first of all, it's essential to know if the mother is fit for reproduction: for that, the estrus calendar is observed. This occurs twice a year (or even once only, as in the case of the Basenji). It begins as early as the age of 5 months, in the most precocious bitches, and up to 18 months for the slower ones—it depends on the breed—and the first time it is not followed by impregnation.

When she is ready to mate, the bitch is a little disoriented: she has eyes only for the door and one thing on her mind: going on the loose. As soon as anyone strokes her back, she arches it; her vulva is swollen; in addition she leaves bloodstains on sofas or carpets: it's impossible to be unaware of her condition.

All that does not mean that it's time for the bitch to meet the male. That, incidentally, is a difficult moment to determine: you have to choose between the 9th and the 14th day after the onset of estrus. So there is a margin. However, vaginal smears make it possible to specify the ovulation date. The date of whelping can thus be determined, scheduled 64 days after mating.

## Receiving a Dog Baby

Alternatively you can patiently wait for your puppy, after reserving him from a private party or from a breeder, if you want a purebred. Things simply cannot be hurried along! This is no cradle-snatching. The pup must remain in his "nest" up to a specific age.

## How Old?

It would be unwise to take a puppy before he's 6 weeks old: until then, the dog baby isn't weaned and hasn't been vaccinated. If he were to become sick, deprived of his mother, he would be too fragile. The 8th and 9th weeks should also be avoided: that is the age at which fear makes its appearance, and strong emotions may be imprinted in him and upset him. So there is no point in hurrying events: between 10 and 12 weeks, the dog baby will be ready to leave the cradle of his birth and his environment. It is even entirely possible that he

*What more could any child want? It's so nice to have a puppy to cuddle. And when they are both bigger, they'll stay the best of friends.*

## Canine Sperm Banks

How can canine beauty be perpetuated? The extinction of certain breeds be avoided? Anything can be hoped for thanks to canine sperm banks, located on the premises of the veterinary schools and breeding kennels across the country. There sperm is stored, deep-frozen at −320°F (−196°C), and the use of the flakes is a matter of the goodwill of the donor dog's owner.

11

may associate the image of his master with the period of socialization.

## Male or Female?

What kind of dog do you want to live with: male or female? The question is of importance only if you are thinking about breeding your pet. As far as behavior is concerned, it's about the same for either. The male is considered to be more independent perhaps, and the female gentler. But the latter is not entirely reliable when the time for love comes around: all she has on her mind is absconding.

## Mongrel or Purebred?

The issue of breed, on the other hand, requires mature reflection. A mongrel? He has everything in one. A bit like a Retriever, a hint of Pointer, plus a slight resemblance to the Dalmatian. He has charm, that much is certain. His particular trait is that he was "born in the gutter" and has no pedigree. He ranks with the "non-standards," and is just as smart as any other and equally winsome. Moreover, buying him won't ruin anyone. But he doesn't have the good looks of a Labrador nor the cute face of a Chihuahua. The advantage of a "blue-blood" is that you know what kind of puppy you're dealing with. Every breed has its own traits, both physical and behavioral. Do you feel an affinity with as rambunctious a Briard as one could wish, or a Spaniel seeking a game? Lifestyle is not the same with an elegant, sporty Greyhound as with a peaceful bulldog who likes routine.

*A mongrel, but some female dog's son, an unpedigreed pup's a boon to someone who wants "a dog or nothing at all."*

## A Little Imp

In a litter, there's often one pup who's the ringleader. He's the liveliest, the most dynamic, the most playful, in a word the "alertest" one of the lot. He's a good choice: he has every chance of success in the socialization stage. A real blessing!

**Seven weeks for a working dog, ten weeks for a house-pet, those are the right dates for taking a puppy out of its original environment.**

*Whether he's running through the grass, playing at hiding and finding his stick, this young Coton de Tulear does not lack imagination. The older he gets, the more he will enjoy his games.*

The puppy becomes attached to his master more quickly if, before he arrives, a technique in widespread use with babies in childcare centers is utilized. All you have to do is send the breeder a handkerchief that has been tucked inside your sweater for a day. In the kennel, the pup associates the smell of his future master with that of his mother and with the place where he was born.

## Sad Little Animal

A puppy is a "sad little animal" when chosen out of pity, because of his tear-filled eyes, his trembling little body: be careful, he may be sick (he might have canine distemper, for instance) and there may be no hope that he will live. It is imperative to select a healthy puppy. He should have dry fur that feels slightly warm, resilient skin, an already muscular body, clean hindquarters, bright eyes, and a warm nose: that's a puppy in top form. How do you prove it? When you pick him up, he wriggles.

# A Real Dog's Life

*You don't encounter the same dogs on a city avenue and on a country road. Dressed for town—leash and rainjacket—groomed, perfumed, the town puppy trots alongside the gutter while his country cousin tears straight ahead, fur flying, through the woods. These extremes have nothing in common (gait, size, nor character) and yet both of them do lead a real dog's life.*

*Hear all, see all..Open air life is well worth the wait for these American Cockers!*

*A crowd is like a huge millipede. The whole trick, for a leash-trained city dog, is to avoid getting bumped into. This training needs to start early so that the young dog does not get frightened.*

## WHAT ABOUT LIFESTYLE?

### In Town

Comfort within the four walls of an apartment is an indoor dog's little corner of paradise. Hurrah for the basket's warmth when frost sticks to the windowpanes, for the soft sofa when storms toss the trees on the square! Early in the morning and at the end of the afternoon a walk is scheduled, for getting some air and making a trip to the gutter. Life is as peaceful as a long tranquil river, but still, the puppy needs to be a city-dweller at heart. He also needs to be of very small size in order not to "get in the way." A miniature dog in the city is like a fish in water, so long as he has the temperament for it: calm, not too exuberant, able to keep his voice down. But perfect adaptation depends mainly on the pup's education. It begins in the apartment and continues on the street. Walking on a leash alongside his master and showing respect for passersby are the first things the puppy learns, besides the "gutter." For letting off steam, the model pup fortunately has grassy areas designated for his use. Nobody is left out: the city is meant for dogs as well. But watch it: a creature so blessed has no excuse for breaking city regulations. If the cap fits, by all means wear it!

### In the Country

Trees along the river, hedges in bloom...such a lot of landmarks and play areas for a puppy! Nose to the ground, he stops, he barks, his tail quivering at each new thing he finds. In the school of nature, like the child who takes him there, he must keep in mind his lessons in prudence: not to eat anything unless his master gives it to him. A meatball may make his mouth water, but it's not there by pure chance: it could be bait for rodents. So he must be absolutely obedient! Walks through fields where he can rush down slopes at top speed do not mean that he can have total freedom. His leash, incidentally, should not be taken off him until he is safe, once he has learned to come when he's called. A country puppy deserves as rigorous an education as if he were going to stride along the city boulevards. True, the care he receives is less fussy than for his city counterpart: in the country the little jacket and the leather booties are as superfluous, out of place even, as perfumed baths, but careful surveillance is necessary just the same. Dangers are still present: the puppy may get a spikelet stuck in a foot or an ear, or fall victim to a snake!

## In the Suburbs

An urban setting, busy streets, suburban living…that's for the puppy who's escaped the big city; country views, the to-and-fro of lots of cyclists and walkers, such is the lot of the rural-city puppy, close to some small town, in a garden full of earthy smells. For both of them, territory, marked out by railings or fences, is of great importance. The puppy never leaves it except with his master. Wandering, here as elsewhere, is strictly forbidden, however tempting. But here the puppy is charged with a mission: he must guard the house, not bark too much—mustn't bother the neighbors—but bark anyway if intruders push the gate open…He has to acquire a sense of proportion. And as all work calls for reward, the puppy finds happiness in the garden where he can kick up his heels all he wants. However, a good guard dog must also find out about the street, get used to being in crowds, while being kept on a leash. That's where he learns to tone things down, and not to growl at the slightest thing. Once back in the house, he then knows when it's the right time to bark, and to stay on his guard and warn his master at the slightest departure from normal.

## What Will His Job Be?

House-pet dog, trackhound, setter: these jobs have nothing in common. From infancy, the dog is marked

*Sky, sun, and sea…weekends or on vacation, our show-off must not forget the training rules. Freedom does indeed require total obedience if it is to be free of danger.*

## Love of Home

When he has acquired a certain maturity, the puppy gradually gets used to being alone. But that doesn't mean he likes it. What he really likes is his master's return. His greatest wish? If only his master could work at home, or even not work at all!

by those characteristics. It is not a good idea to try to go against his nature. If he is not intended to stand guard or sniff out hares, he will never give satisfaction in those roles. As comfortable as a good sheepdog may feel when he's pushing ewes into line, put him down on a city square and he's like a bull in a china shop! Many groups of dogs make up the huge range of canine breeds (see page 25). So there's every opportunity to select the puppy best suited to the job you have in mind. Whether you're a mountaineer, a sailor, a housewife, or an airline pilot, you always have a good chance of finding the ideal companion. Shepherds and Bouviers, mountain-type Mastiffs, pet dogs, Setters, Retrievers, Nordics, Pinschers...you can hardly help finding the right one.

Are you looking for a real fire-eater of a dog? You can choose from the Siberian Husky, the Briard, the Appenzell Bouvier, and the Hovawart, all designed for a high-speed existence. Nice-natured? There's the Maltese Lapdog, the Bulldog, the Shetland, which like a fireside existence. Affection and sweetness above all? You encounter these qualities in the pet dog that can be taken to the office, to hotels, everywhere you go. Whatever the criterion, there are only too many to choose from (see the chapter "Which Breed to Choose?," starting on page 21, and "Dogs from A to Z," pages 221–235).

## SHARED LEISURE TIME
### Vacationing with Your Dog

Fresh air, relaxation, and fun: the vacation atmosphere suits this jolly fellow admirably. Playing games with a ball and plunging into the water's edge make him joyous. But watch out for sand castles because he also plays the bulldozer game! The budding demolition dog needs to be trained—on the beach and elsewhere.

Will he be able to tolerate the car? There is no reason to expect that he will be ill, badly behaved, or noisy. But you need to make an early start on getting him used to traveling by the rules: sitting in the backseat, or on the floor, at the feet of any passengers, or, alternatively, if he is going to grow a lot, in the luggage compartment, with or without a net separating him from the passengers.

## Sports and Outdoor Games

Jogging, dog agility, and bicycle riding are some of the sports that two can practice. For the puppy getting used to sporting activities for the first time, the partnership that develops between him and his master is of prime importance. He runs like crazy, catches things...keeps going until he's exhausted. So be careful! The first point is that he must be old enough to take part in sports, or in other words, that his bones have grown strong enough. But don't let him get involved in "exploits," for his abilities are still limited. Dauntless he may be, but he needs to use his strength carefully and not take unnecessary risks. For example, on the beach, there's no point in forcing him to jump into the water! Perhaps he'd prefer to borrow a boat to glide peacefully over the water.

Once he is over his boisterousness, a puppy is recommended for people suffering from cardio-vascular problems. An American psychiatrist, Dr. Aaron Katcher, prescribes such company as a therapy: just by being there, a little doggie lowers arterial pressure. He's the "anti-stress" puppy.

In summertime, a puppy may be bothered by heat, especially if he belongs to the **Bulldog** or **Boxer** breeds: the abbreviated shape of his nasal fossae makes it hard for him to breathe properly.

*Taking him far, far away, to the land of sand castles, is something you can do, provided you get advance information from transport companies and hotel officials. Relaxation and joyousness are for (young) dogs, too.*

**A puppy is always ready to jump aboard a sailboat or motorboat; with a lifejacket on (they come in three sizes, plus the one for miniatures) he's ready to take on the waves.**

## Doggy Traveler

Business trips or escape...if you have a vagabond soul you'd better have a practical spirit too, and choose a small breed of dog. A miniature or a toy, why not? Easy to tuck into a bag, this go-anywhere pup is admitted everywhere, including aircraft cabins. A privilege unknown to big dogs, which are subjected to forced separation and placed in the baggage hold. (See also page 213).

# Which Breed to Choose?

Chubby little bodies covered with silky hair. All puppies are cute and appealing. But be on your guard! A little dog may hide a future giant, a pretty little dear may turn into a cur. Before making his choice, the future master needs to find out what the adult dog will look like and what his characteristics will be, if he hopes to avoid surprises. But he is still sure to find the ideal pal, from a sportsman to an indoor pet, among the ten canine groups and 350 breeds listed.

Tiny though they are, tomorrow they'll be full-sized: giants or "miniatures," but with the sportiness of the Huskies, the sturdiness of the Briards, or the starlet stylishness of the West Highland White Terriers.

Every country has its favorites: the German Shepherd in Italy, the Yorkshire Terrier in Great Britain, the Labrador in France and in the United States.

Stroking is the drive belt between man and puppy. It's the means by which a man praises his pupil, conveys his satisfaction, and shows his affection.

The term "breed" can be used only if the dog has been registered with the American Kennel Club (AKC).

## Canine Directory

The American Kennel Club is in a way the dog's Social Register within the United States: only well-born puppies can be included in it. It is usually the breeder who takes care of the registration application, which will contain the puppy's breed, sex, color, date of birth, the AKC registered names of the puppy's sire and dam, and the name of the breeder. However, it is also a good idea for a new owner to request to see this information and to obtain copies of the sire and dam's AKC papers prior to assuming ownership of the puppy.

## LIKE MASTER, LIKE DOG
### A Customized Puppy

Among the 350 breeds listed by dog experts the ideal puppy is sure to exist. But there are hordes of question marks. Character is at least as determining a factor as looks. Who has the winning ticket? You're not just choosing a nice docile dog, you're choosing a future friend with whom you already feel some affinities. His canine body also needs to fit into your environment and your unconscious. In the home, he must not get in the way; in your heart, he must be perfectly settled in.

Whatever his age, the dog is an invitation to stroking: his fur, soft and floating or rough, now appears as a criterion for your choice. Do you want him to be soft to the touch, or smooth-haired with his muscles showing? To the matter of taste you must add practical considerations. While a short-hair makes no demands on us, thick heavy fur always requires care: brushing, untangling, shampooing. Color is a factor that cannot be overlooked: white fur, though dazzling and elegant, gets dirty so easily! Upon returning from a walk, when ticks and plant spikelets have to be tracked down, inspecting the dog's coat can be hard work. On rainy days, bathing and drying are requirements of the first order. If you dislike those tasks, they may have a negative effect on the way you feel about your little charge, and under no circumstances should anyone begrudge taking care of one's dog. Appearance, gait, and body-size are hard to imagine in a little ball of fluff. Yet in the great canine family you encounter David and Goliath, the two-pound Chihuahua and the two-hundred pound Mastiff. Characters and space needs are so different, from one breed to another! How could anyone suspect that an innocent, fragile puppy, left to his own devices a few months later, will be upsetting the established order, reversing the roles, and aiming for the master's place? The job of a good guard dog is the opposite of that of a bouncy creature having fun with the children, even though a dog may sometimes be able to fill both roles. Nice little rascal or Cerberus on his mission, the puppy does not always have the mind for the job. Over and above his measurements, his standard, and his classification in the dog world, his past, rooted in the world of human beings, speaks volumes. Dogs belonging to kings past and present, luxury dogs, strange dogs with no hair or no tails, no breed or no history, there are all sorts, as if made to measure to live with one specific human being rather than another. Friendly understanding depends exclusively on the human being, upon whom the choice devolves.

## An Education Adjusted to Breed and Work

Education molds the puppy, tempers him, shapes his behavior. It also prepares him for his future role. What is expected of a puppy? That he keep us company, keep guard, round up ewes, or flush out partridge? The objectives are not the same for a Yorkshire Terrier and for a Briard, and the gentle method used with a highly sensitive animal like the Afghan Hound is not suitable for a tough little character like the Dachshund. How can we have the last word without upsetting the puppy? The desire to please is unquestionably what actuates the house pet, whose task is to be pleasant to have around. It makes his upbringing so much the simpler, but it still depends on strictness: obey orders, be clean, don't climb on the beds or armchairs, don't destroy the apartment—these make up the basics of his lessons. To refine his manners, we require of him that he not bother the neighbors with untimely barking, not jump on visitors and not snarl. Lastly, on the street, the little companion of whom a few small services can be requested—minding the groceries—of whom a certain mannerliness may be required—giving a paw to greet friends—must primarily learn to walk on a leash without tugging. All these principles easily take root in his mind. There remains loneliness, his bête noire, which he does not learn to handle without some training. The guard dog can learn his job very early. For total efficiency, the master must take certain measures that concern not the little innocent, but guests. From the start they must avoid petting the

*The elegance of a Greyhound, the coat of a Spaniel, the eyes of a Labrador, and, obviously, a heart of pure gold...this mongrel is a success. Some masters find that he is "everything in one."*

*For these sled dogs, there is no happiness anywhere but in snow, open spaces, and racing, so it makes sense to reflect on the life that can be offered a newcomer to the home.*

## Canine Party

Every year, the American Kennel Club sanctions well over 8,000 events in which dog fanciers and their canine students can compete. These events include dog shows, obedience trials, field trials, junior showmanship contests, lure coursing, and herding competitions. Awards are given to the top canine in each event. So much color, so much style. What criterion makes these dogs leaders? That secret belongs to the judges, whose hair's-breadth evaluation is a reference.

puppy as soon as they arrive at the house: how else is the budding sentinel to learn the difference between his own and other people?

The puppy will very soon be invested with the panoply of the big boys—collar, and muzzle at six months—and follow his elders' example: walk on leash, come when he's called, get used to street sounds. Often, at five months, he is introduced to a dog trainer who analyzes his character and recommends a line to follow. The main thing is that he learn to see his place as being under the control of his master. The tone of voice is of prime importance, but certain principles are also important: he is the last one to be fed and he is given orders. His apprenticeship must be firm, but brutality is never appropriate, even for a future attack dog. The latter needs to be a perfectly well-balanced puppy, and his master needs to possess a highly developed sense of canine psychology. But specialized training, and even drills, are involved.

Discipline is also part of the program for the sporting dog that has to make special efforts. After short walks on an extending leash, interspersed with rest periods and ball-game sessions, the puppy is expected to go out for several hours twice a day. At six months, he will be old enough to accompany his master when he goes jogging, but will not dare run after a bicycle nor try to dive into a private swimming pool. Swimming, unless we're talking about a Newfoundland or a Labrador, is not always something he likes. There's no point in pushing him.

Whether it's a dip in the river, a long walk in the snow or agility training—with figure-eight courses and obstacle jumping—the activity imposed on a young dog must fit his capabilities. A game, rather than constraint, is what will enable the puppy to get started on his training, a very serious step for future champions. For that reason, action must always take breed into account, and also the abilities and particular traits of a young dog. It sometimes happens that a hunting dog shows fear, jumps at the sound of a shot, and at seven months does not always obey his master's orders: if that's the case, no point in persisting. On the other hand, if he instinctively tracks game, points, and retrieves, he should quickly be encouraged and trained, in the yard, to respond to calls, look for the ball, and bring it back to his master. It is only in the field that the training specific to hunting will take place, in which he will learn to obey the whistle.

## PUPPIES IN TEN GROUPS

Dog breeds are classified into ten groups by the Fédération cynologique internationale FCI (International Federation of Dog Experts). They are:

1. Shepherds and cattle dogs
2. Watchdogs, guard dogs, and working (police, guide, etc.) dogs: Pinschers, Schnauzers, Mastiffs
3. Terriers
4. Bassets
5. Nordics and spitzes
6. Coursers
7. Setters
8. Game flushers, retrievers, and water dogs
9. Lapdogs and pet dogs
10. Greyhounds

In addition, the American Kennel Club (AKC) classifies dog breeds into seven groups or classes of their own. These include:

Group I: Sporting Dogs
Group II: Hounds
Group III: Working Dogs
Group IV: Terriers
Group V: Toys
Group VI: Non-Sporting Dogs
Group VII: Herding Dogs

Finally, the AKC recognizes a Miscellaneous Class that includes those newer breeds being considered for inclusion into the official Stud Book of the AKC.

 **The Yorkshire Terrier is 20 times, the Cocker Spaniel 30 times, and the German Shepherd 70 times heavier at one year old than at birth.**

*The Labrador is No. 1 in the hearts of Americans. Multitalented, he makes an excellent guide dog for the blind.*

## Guide Dog for the Blind

The puppy destined to become a Seeing Eye dog undergoes his first campaign in a family. Before entering the School for Guide Dogs for the Blind where he will be trained for four months in the job of guiding, he needs to learn the basics of living in society. During this first stage, known as the "awakening," between two months and one year, he learns to be clean, to eat at regular times, to walk on a leash without tugging; he obeys orders: sit, lie down, come back when called. On the street he meets people: children, persons with disabilities, elderly people; he rides on buses and elevators. Soon he won't be the one following the guide.

## Dogs with All Kinds of Coats

*Wooly or rough, short or long, straight or curly,*
*fur is a matter of taste, but of upkeep as well.*

**The Belgian Shepherd**
*Long, short, or rough-haired*
*AKC Group VII*
24 in., 66 lbs.
(60 cm, 30 kg)

**Bearded Collie**
*Long, full coat*
*AKC Group VII*
22–26 in., 65 lbs
(51–56 cm, 20 kg)

**The Akita**
*Short dense coat*
*AKC Group III*
26 in., 85 lbs.
(70 cm, 38.5 kg)

**Pomeranian [German Spitz]**
*Heavy coat with ruff*
*AKC Group V*
12–14 in., (29–36 cm) for the
 standard (above)
Up to 9 in., (22 cm) for the miniature (below)

**Cairn Terrier**
*Thick rough coat*
*AKC Group IV*
10 in., 14 lbs.
(25 cm, 7.5 kg)

**German Wirehaired Pointer**
*He's a shaggy Bloodhound*
*AKC Group I*
12–24 in., 45–60 lbs.
(30–60 cm, 20–30 kg)

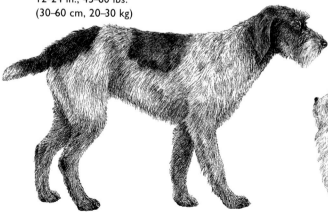

**Bichon Frise**
**[lapdog]**
*Long, soft coat*
*AKC Group VI*
9.5–11.5 in., 10 lbs.
(24–29.5 cm, 4 kg)

**Airedale**
*Short, wiry coat*
*AKC Group IV*
23 in., 45 lbs.
(60 cm, 20 kg)

**Briard**
*Long, coarse, bushy coat*
*AKC Group VII*
23–27 in., 60–85 lbs.
(58–68 cm, 30–40 kg)

**Pinscher**
*Short close coat*
*AKC Group V*
Miniature: 10–12.5 in., 4–9 lbs.
(25–30 cm, 2–4 kg)
Standard: 17.5–20 in., 26–35 lbs.
(45–50 cm, 12–16kg)

**Schapendoes**
*Bearded with mustache*
17–20 in., 33 lbs.
(43–50 cm, 15 kg)

**Schnauzer**
*Rough wiry coat*
*Giant (below, right)—AKC Group III*
24–27 in., 75–100 lbs. (60–70 cm, 35–45 kg)
*Standard (below, center)—AKC Group III*
18–19 in., 30 lbs. (45–50 cm, 15 kg) average
*Miniature (below, left)—AKC Group IV*
12–14 in., 9–15 lbs. (30–35 cm, 4–7 kg)

See Dogs A to Z, page 221

# Giants

*Hardly recognizable when fully grown, all muscle, sporting, or guard dogs*

**Anatolian Shepherd**
*Dominating*
25–28 in., 90–140 lbs.
(71–81 cm, 40–65 kg)

**Dogo Argentino [Argentine mastiff]**
*Puma hunter*
*AKC Group III*
23.5–25.5 in., 85–95 lbs.
(60–65 cm, 40–45 kg)

**Tatras Mountain Shepherd**
*Snow white*
24–27.5 in., 75 lbs.
(60–70 cm, 35 kg)

**Borzoi [Russian wolf hound]**
*Long narrow body and limbs*
*AKC Group III*
26–28 in., 75–95 lbs.
(65–80 cm, 35–45 kg)

**Kuvasz**
*Extremely strong*
*AKC Group III*
26–30 in., 90–115 lbs.
(66–75 cm, 30–50 kg)

**Great Dane [German Mastiff]**
*World's largest dog*
*AKC Group III*
28–32 in., 100–143 lbs.
(72–82 cm, 45–65 kg)

*Loving, funny, stubborn,
they have character.*

**Beauceron**
*Somewhat rough*
23–28 in., 75–95 lbs.
(61–70 cm, 35–45 kg)

**Tibetan Mastiff**
*Powerful and courageous*
AKC Group III
25–28.5 in., 110 lbs.
(65–70 cm, 50 kg)

**Rottweiler**
*A Mastiff*
AKC Group III
22–27 in., 85–110 lbs.
(55–68 cm, 40–50 kg)

**Shih Tzu**
*Little prince*
AKC Group V
8–10.5 in., 9–16 lbs.
(20.5–27 cm, 4–7.25 kg)

**King Charles Cavalier**
*King of hearts*
AKC Miscellaneous Class
12–14 in., 12–16 lbs.
(30–35 cm, 5.5–8.2 kg)

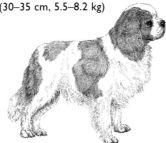

**Lhasa apso**
*Good luck charm*
AKC Group VI
10–11 in., 11–15 lbs.
(25–28 cm, 5–7 kg)

**Volpino**
*Blithe [little Roman dog]*
10–12 in., 9 lbs.
(25–30 cm, 4 kg)

**Yorkshire Terrier**
*Bold*
AKC Group V
8 in. maximum,
7 lbs. maximum
(20.5 cm maximum,
3.1 kg maximum)

**Japanese Chin**
*Formerly Japanese Spaniel*
AKC Group V
10 in., 7 lbs.
(25 cm, 3 kg)

**Tibetan Spaniels**
*Agile*
AKC Group VI
10 in., 9–15 lbs.
(25 cm, 4–6.8 kg)

**Chihuahua**
*Lilliputian*
AKC Group V
8 in., 4–6 lbs.
(20 cm, 1.3–1.8 kg)

**Pekingese**
*A lion's mane*
AKC Group V
10 in., 10–12 lbs.
(25 cm, 2–8 kg)

*In the mountains or in water, in polar or oily coats, their natural settings are like a second skin to them.*

## MOUNTAIN DOGS

**Pyrenean Shepherd**
*Knows his job*
16–20 in., 35 lbs.
(38–50 cm, 15 kg)

**Samoyed**
*Dreams about snow*
AKC Group III
19–23.5 in., 55–65 lbs.
(50–60 cm, 25–30 kg)

See Dogs A to Z, page 221

**Yugoslav Shepherd**
*Half-wolf, half-feline*
24 in., 110 lbs.
(60 cm, 50 kg)

**Great Pyrenees**
*The Great King*
AKC Group III
25–32 in., 100 lbs.
(70–80 cm, 45 kg)

**Saint Bernard**
*Famous*
AKC Group III
25.5–27.5 in., 135–170 lbs.
(65–70 cm, 60–80 kg)

**Barbet [a spaniel]**
*Has a little beard*
21.5–23.5 in., 45 lbs.
(55–60 cm, 20 kg)

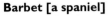

**Flat-coated Retriever**
*Adaptable*
*AKC Group I*
22–24.5 in., 55–65 lbs.
(56–61 cm, 25–30 kg)

**Glen of Imaal Terrier**
*Ancient breed*
14 in., 35 lbs.
(35 cm, 16 kg)

**Golden Retriever**
*Yellow coat*
*AKC Group I*
21.5–24 in., 55–75 lbs.
(51–61 cm, 25–34 kg)

**Newfoundland**
*A rescue dog*
*AKC Group III*
26–28 in., 100–150 lbs.
(66–71 cm, 45–68 kg)

**Cocker Spaniel**
*Popular*
*AKC Group I*
14–15 in., 25 lbs.
(38–40 cm, 12 kg)

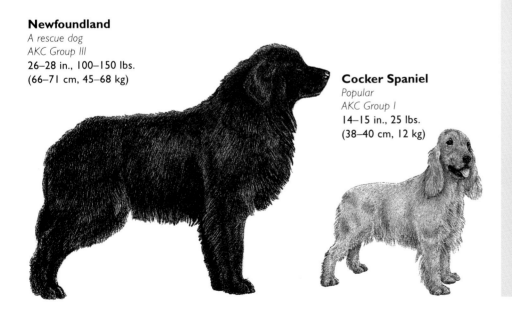

## New Wave Water Dogs

These oily, waterproof-coated dogs, always ready to leap into the water, have been banned by fishermen and wetland hunters. So the web-footed Cao de agua is no longer permitted to go out on fishing boats in Portugal. The Netherlands Spaniel, still called the Wetterhound, suddenly had to give up his traditional role as otter hunter, since these animals are now protected. The American Water Spaniel, so swift at flushing out hare, is on the road to reconversion. Some breeds, such as the "aggressive natured" Wetterhound, are now used as guard dogs, while others are so sociable that they become domestic pets.

31

## A Nose for Hunting

*Scent and energy,
game coursers' winning cards.*

### Hungarian Pointer
*Sandy in color*
*AKC Group I*
21–24 in., 50–65 lbs.
(52–61 cm, 22–30 kg)

### Beagle Harrier Hound
*Tri-tone*
*AKC Group II*
19–21 in., 45 lbs.
(43–48 cm, 20 kg)

See Dogs A to Z, page 221

### Jack Russell Terrier
*A digger*
14–15 in., 20–22 lbs.
(30–35 cm, 9–10 kg)

### Petit Basset Griffon Vendéen
*Hare-like coat*
*AKC Group II*
13–15 in., 35 lbs.
(34–38 cm, 15 kg)

### English Springer Spaniel
*Resembles the cocker spaniel*
*AKC Group I*
19–20 in., 50–55 lbs.
(49–51 cm, 23–25 kg)

### Bloodhound [Saint Hubert]
*A bass voice*
*AKC Group II*
24–26 in., 90–110 lbs.
(60–67 cm, 40–48 kg)

### Basset artésien normand
### [Normandy Artois Basset Hound]
*Two dogs in one*
10–14 in., 20–25 lbs.
(26–36 cm, 15–25 kg)

## Setters

*Impulsive*
*AKC Group I*
Irish setter (right): 25–27 in., 60–70 lbs. (52–62 cm, 20–25 kg)
English setter (left): 24–25 in., 55–65 lbs. (53–62 cm, 25–30 kg)
Gordon setter (center): 24–27 in., 50–80 lbs. (62–66 cm, 29 kg)

## Brittany Spaniel

*A champion*
*AKC Group I*
18–20 in., 35 lbs.
(46–51 cm, 15 kg)

## Dachshund

*Short-legged*
*Standard—AKC Group II*
8–10 in., 16–32 lbs.
(20–25 cm, 7.25–14.5 kg)
*Miniature—AKC Group II*
11 lbs. (5 kg) maximum

## German Pointer

*An athlete*
*AKC Group I*
21–25 in., 55–70 lbs.
(56–69 cm, 25–32 kg)

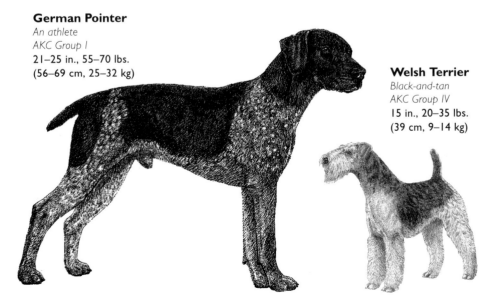

## Welsh Terrier

*Black-and-tan*
*AKC Group IV*
15 in., 20–35 lbs.
(39 cm, 9–14 kg)

## A Specific Role

Sporting dogs take on well-defined roles matching their natural dispositions. Thus, among track-hounds, responsible for finding game, there are the Pointer, the Setter (English, Gordon, Irish), the Spaniel (French, Brittany, Picardy, Pont-Audemer), the Picardy Blue, the Pointer (German, Hungarian, French, Bourbonnais, Saint-Germain, Auvergne, Weimaraner), and the Drachthaar (German Wire-haired Terrier). Among the Retrievers, which fetch game, the best are the Labrador, the Golden Retriever, the Chesapeake Bay, the Nova Scotia duck tolling dog. Lastly the brush-beaters, who look for game and flush it out in front of the master, are represented by the English Cocker Spaniel, the American Cocker Spaniel, the English Springer Spaniel, the Clumber Spaniel, the Welsh Springer, and the Sussex Spaniel.

## The Great Athletes

*Muscular and energetic, all dogs are athletic, but some, such as Greyhounds and sled dogs, are champion racers.*

**For the pleasure of being with his master, a dog enjoys starting some sporting activity. It also allows him to let off steam and develop his muscles, even if it's only by taking part in jogging or agility training.**

**Afghan Hound**
*Speedy*
*AKC Group II*
25–27 in., 50–60 lbs.
(62–74 cm, 20–25 kg)

**Hovawart**
*Multi-talented*
*AKC Group II*
22–28 in., 55–85 lbs.
(58–70 cm, 25–40 kg)

**A puppy starting a sport must be healthy, free of joint lesions and hip dysplasia, and show no risk of patellar luxation nor cardiac malfunction.**

## Athletes at All Levels

Sports are not the exclusive attributes of champions. The sheepdog hurtling, arrow-like, to round up lagging sheep, the gundog running until out of breath, and the rescue dog persevering to exhaustion are athletes too. Even the miniature poodle is very fast when he runs for fun. In his past history, the dog hardly had a chance to rest. On a daily basis, he constantly had to show endurance and energy. Turning mill wheels and butter churns and pulling the dairymen's little carts in the mountains were not the easiest activities in the world.

**Greyhound**
*King of the racing stadium*
*AKC Group II*
27–30 in., 65–70 lbs.
(68–76 cm, 25–35 kg)

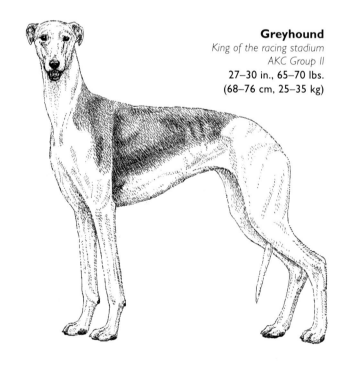

**Siberian Husky**
*A champion*
*AKC Group III*
20–23.5 in., 45–60 lbs.
(50–60 cm, 15–28 kg)

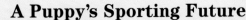

# A Puppy's Sporting Future

Depending on breed and predisposition, a puppy may, at the proper age (when his body is well developed and on condition that he is perfectly fit) take part in various sporting events,

## Snow

Natural capacities for smellling, endurance, and sharp-wittedness are required for the snow program. In difficult weather conditions, on uneven terrain, avalanche dogs save human lives; sled dogs and agility-trained dogs adapt to the most diverse conditions and display their talents alongside men.

Lengthy training is required for running a distance of 1,040 km in 2 weeks in a sled dog team, in the great European sled adventure called the Alpirod.

## Festival

At dog shows, a certain mastery is necessary to perform daily chores on stage. You can see Siberian Huskies, Alaskan Huskies, and Samoyeds, representing the sled dogs, German Pointers presenting the shi-pulka, Greyhounds and Whippets taking part in the hound races, Border Collies as sheepdogs, Malines as police dogs, and Briards, Collies, Belgian Shepherds, Dalmatians, Schnauzers, Cocker Spaniels, Fox Terriers, Whippets, and Poodles giving agility displays.

## Hunting Without Rifles

The dog must have hunter's blood in his veins for the field trials, reproducing a hunt scenario in which the target varies according to season (pheasant in winter, partridge and woodcock in the fall). As a finale, the trackhound is judged on his game setting and search, the retriever on how he brings back game, and the brushbeater on how he drives game from cover.

## Open Air

A taste for games and great agility are the requirement for fly ball, a new canine sport of British inspiration. It consists of catching and fetching back the ball after an obstacle competition in a team of four dogs accompanied by their masters. The speed required in the performance of jumps and pirouettes is the main quality for playing Frisbee. The point is to catch a polyamide disc, or simply a plastic lid, as it flies through the air. The best performers in this discipline (open to dogs of all sizes) are the Fox Terrier, the Collie, and the Malines Shepherd. Frisbee also suits the Pyrenean Shepherd—capable of jumping up to three or four times its own height to catch the desired object—medium-sized dogs such as the Hovawart, the Picardy Shepherd, the Doberman, the German Shepherd, and big dogs such as the Greyhound, the Great Dane (or German Mastiff, as it is known in France), and the giant Schnauzer.

**Whippet**
*A courser*
*AKC Group II*
18–22 in., 35 lbs.
(44–51 cm, 10 kg)

## Good Watchdogs

*To say nothing of Mastiffs, which bare their fangs when they are on guard, the smaller ones often have enough know-how to make themselves heard.*

**Doberman**
*A watchful guard dog*
*AKC Group III*
24–28 in., 55–85 lbs.
(61.5–72 cm, 25–40 kg)

**Appenzell Bouvier**
*Persevering*
19–23 in., 45–55 lbs.
(48–58 cm, 22–25 kg)

**Picardy Shepherd**
*Energetic*
22–25.5 in., 41–50 lbs.
(55–65 cm, 19–23 kg)

**Staffordshire Bull Terrier**
*On the attack*
*AKC Group IV*
14–16 in., 24–38 lbs.
(35–41 cm, 11–17 kg)

**American Staffordshire Terrier**
*Stubborn*
*AKC Group IV*
17–19 in., 40–45 lbs.
(43–48 cm, 17–20 kg)

**The Bullmastiff and Mastiff**
*Provide a sense of security*
*AKC Group III*
Bullmastiff: 25–27 in., 55–85 lbs.
(61–68 cm, 41–59 kg)
Mastiff: 27.5–30 in., 135–200 lbs.
(66–82 cm, 60–100 kg)

**Neapolitan Mastiff**
*Hard to deal with*
*AKC Group III*
25–30 in., 110–150 lbs.
(60–75 cm, 50–70 kg)

**Schipperke**
*Sharp-witted*
*AKC Group VI*
9–11 in., 10–18 lbs.
(23–30 cm, 3–8 kg)

*Bulky or of tiny stature, some play with children
and the rest are well-behaved with seniors.*

## FRIENDS TO CHILDREN

**Bernese Bouvier**
*A cart–puller*
*AKC Group III*
24.5–27.5 in., 85–110 lbs.
(58–70 cm, 40–50 kg)

**King Charles Spaniel**
*Friendly*
*AKC Miscellaneous Class*
10–13 in., 9–14 lbs.
(26–32 cm, 3.6–6.3 kg)

**Bouvier des Flandres**
*Protective*
*AKC Group VII*
23.5–27.5 in., 55–85 lbs.
(60–69 cm, 27–40 kg)

**Poodle**
*A merry creature*
*Toy—AKC Group V*
under 10 in. (25 cm)
*Miniature—AKC Group VI*
10–15 in. (25–38 cm)
*Standard—AKC Group VI*
over 15 in. (38 cm)

**Bichon Frise**
*Plays the clown*
*AKC Group IV*
9.5–11.5 in., 10 lbs.
(23–30 cm, 4 kg)

**Wirehaired Pointing Griffon**
*Like quick-silver*
*AKC Group V*
11 in., 8–10 lbs.
(28 cm, 3–6 kg)

**Scottish Terrier**
*Mischievous*
*AKC Group IV*
10 in., 19–22 lbs.
(25 cm, 9–10 kg)

**Leonberg**
*A mountain lion*
28–30 in., 110–160 lbs.
(65–80 cm, 50–75 kg)

**Shetland Sheepdog**
*Vigilant*
*AKC Group VII*
13–16 in., 20–25 lbs.
(35–39 cm, 7–8 kg)

**Norwich Terrier**
*Frisky*
*AKC Group IV*
10 in. maximum, 12 lbs.
(25 cm maximum, 4.5 kg)

## COMPANIONS FOR SENIORS

### Featherweights of Every Stripe

Small, gentle, and reassuring: this is how we think of an ideal dog for elderly persons, whether they live alone or in retirement homes. But not all featherweights are alike: some are too quiet for an isolated home, some over-inclined to bark. For instance, the miniature Spitz [Pomeranian] [12 in., 5–15 lbs.], both bodyguard and little "cuddly bear," places his courage and his voice at his master's service. Athletic when the fancy takes him, the miniature Schnauzer [12 in., 10–15 lbs.], always on the watch, is a delight, but you need the legs of a twenty-year-old to keep up with him. The Schipperke [9–11 in., 15 lbs.] is a jolly little chap with plenty of voice; the Pekingese, a born stay-at-home [9.5 in., 5–10 lbs.], or the Chihuahua [6 in., 2–5 lbs.], can gladden our hearts.

### A Ray of Sunshine in Retirement Homes

The importance of the human-companion animal bond is exemplified by the success of various pet therapy programs across the country.

While such programs have been implemented in a variety of facilities, many of these programs are geared towards retirement homes, exposing the residents therein to the unconditional love of a canine companion. The affection of a dog, a real ray of sunshine in people's hearts, can give the elderly a sense of usefulness that they may have otherwise lost.

**English Bulldog**
*A home-body*
*AKC Group V*
12–14 in., 14–18 lbs.
(30–40 cm, 22.7 kg)

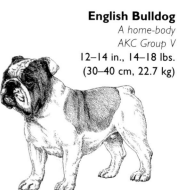

**Bichon Bolonais**
*Sedate*
*AKC Group V*
9–12 in., 6–10 lbs.
(25–30 cm, 2.5–4 kg)

**Pug**
*A mini-mastiff*
*AKC Group V*
12–14 in., 14–18 lbs.
(30–35 cm, 6.3–8 kg)

**French Bulldog**
*Mannerly*
*AKC Group VI*
12 in., 19–22 lbs.
(30 cm, 8–14 kg)

**Provided that he is neither mischievous nor a wanderer, a puppy is a good present idea for Grandparents' Day.**

*Unconventional mongrels, or thoroughbred puppies with no clubs, no hair and no tail; shaggy heads, six-toed paws; these are some unusual dogs!*

**EYE-CATCHERS**

**Kerry Blue Terrier**
*Greyish*
AKC Group IV
17.5–19.5 in., 33–40 lbs.
(44–49 cm, 15–18 kg)

**Bedlington Terrier**
*A lamb face*
AKC Group IV
16–17 in., 17–23 lbs.
(40 cm, 8–10.5 kg)

**Alaskan Malamute**
*A wolf face*
AKC Group III
23–25 in., 75–85 lbs.
(59–64 cm, 34–38.5 kg)

**Cesky Terrier**
*A bearded face*
10.5–13.5 in., 13–20 lbs.
(27–35 cm, 6–9 kg)

**Lundehund**
*Dozens of toes*
12–14 in., 14 lbs.
(30–36 cm, 6 kg)

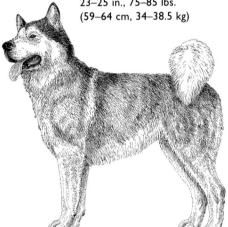

See Dogs A to Z, page 221

**Boxer**
*A hound face*
AKC Group III
21–25 in., 55–75 lbs.
(53–63 cm, 25–35 kg)

**Border Terrier**
*An otter face*
AKC Group IV
14 in., 12–15 lbs.
(36 cm, 5–7 kg)

## New Dogs

Of Australian origin, the Kelpie is an outstanding shepherd. A great achiever, this enthusiastic and tireless worker has great qualities: lively and intelligent, he is also docile, loyal, and devoted.

## THE "TAIL-LESS" ONES

**Old English Sheepdog [Bobtail]**
*Large head*
AKC Group VII
22 in., 75 lbs.
(61 cm, 35 kg)

**Polish Plains Shepherd**
*Gruff voiced*
16 –17 in., 40 lbs.
(40–42 cm, 18 kg)

## THE "HAIRLESS" ONES

**Crested Chinese Dog**
*In just his socks*
AKC Group V
11–13 in., 10 lbs.
(28–33 cm, 4.5 kg)

## THE "CLUBLESS" ONES

**Eurasier [Eurasian dog]**
*A certain ideal*
19–23 in., 45–65 lbs.
(48–60 cm, 20–30 kg)

## A SHEPHERD

**Australian Shepherd**
*His name says it all*
AKC Group VII
17–20 in., 48–60 lbs.
(45–58 cm,
22–29 kg)

## THE "VOICELESS" ONES

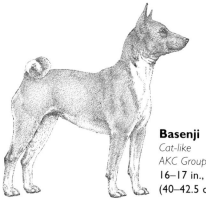

**Basenji**
*Cat-like*
AKC Group II
16–17 in., 22–24 lbs.
(40–42.5 cm, 10 kg)

**Shiba Inu**
*Restful*
14–16 in.,
13–18 lbs.
(35–41 cm,
6–8 kg)

## THE "NO BREED" ONES

**Mongrel**
*A bag of tricks*
Variable size and weight, no group

**Mastiff-hound cross**
*Lively*
Variable size and weight, no group.

**Bourbonnais Pointer**
*Keen-nosed*
20–22in., 35–55 lbs.
(51–57 cm, 18–25 kg)

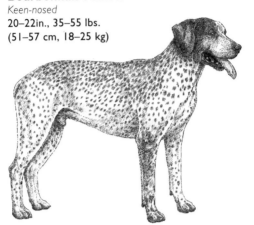

**Continental Miniature Spaniel**
*Papillon*
11 in., 6 lbs.
(28 cm, 2.5 kg)

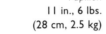

See Dogs A to Z, page 221

**Gascony Blue Griffon**
*A dog with a future*
17–20 in., 45 lbs.
(43–52 cm, 20 kg)

**Small Chinese Lion Dog**
*World's rarest dog*
8–9.5 in., 9–14 lbs.
(20–25 cm, 4–6 kg)

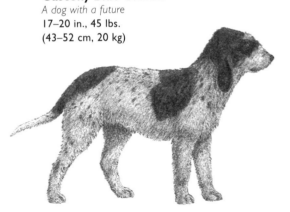

**Picardy Blue Spaniel**
*Just one color*
23.5 in., 45 lbs.
(60 cm, 20 kg)

41

# Dogs in the Public Eye

*Stage or advertising animals, these limelighters are star material and are worth their weight in gold.*

## ADS, ACTING, AND CARTOONS

**Collie**
*Faithful*
*AKC Group VII*
22–26 in., 45 lbs.
(51–61 cm, 20 kg)

**West Highland Terrier**
*Friendly*
*AKC Group IV*
10–11 in., 15 lbs.
(27–31 cm, 7 kg)

**Dalmatian**
*Likeable*
*AKC Group VI*
19–23 in., 45–55 lbs.
(56–61 cm, 20–25 kg)

**American Cocker Spaniel**
*A character*
*AKC Group I*
13.5–14.5 in., 22–30 lbs.
(37–47 cm, 10–13 kg)

**Basset Hound**
*Awkward*
*AKC Group II*
14–15 in., 65 lbs.
(33–38 cm, 30 kg)

**Skye Terrier**
*A flowing coat*
*AKC Group IV*
10 in., 12–15 lbs.
(25 cm, 5–7 kg)

**Bordeaux Hound**
*Big and strong*
22.5–26.5 in., 95 lbs.
(58–68 cm, 45 kg)

**Fox Terrier**
*Very popular*
*AKC Group IV*
15.5 in., 18 lbs.
(40 cm, 8 kg)

**German Shepherd**
*Brave heart*
*AKC Group VII*
22–26 in., 65–85 lbs.
(55–65 cm, 30–40 kg)

**Labrador**
*Dog about town*
*AKC Group I*
22.5–24.5 in., 60–75 lbs.
(51–59 cm, 30–35 kg)

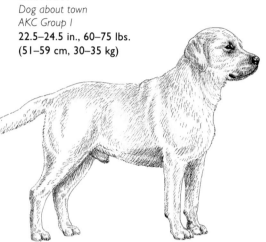

**Shar Pei**
*In a wrinkled coat*
*AKC Group VI*
15.5–19.5 in., 35 lbs.
(40–51 cm, 15 kg)

**Tibetan Terrier**
*In a long coat*
13.5–15.5 in., 18–30 lbs.
(35–40 cm, 8–13 kg)

**Maltese Lapdog**
*A toy dog for the parlor*
*AKC Group V*
8–10 in., 7–10 lbs.
(20–25 cm, 3–4 kg)

**Welsh Corgi**
*Royal*
*AKC Group VII*
10–12 in., 22–30 lbs.
(25–30 cm, 10–13 kg)

See Dogs A to Z, page 221

**Coton de Tulear**
*In his Sunday best*
12 in., 8–10 lbs.
(30 cm, 3.5–4 kg)

## AKC Statistics

Out of the 52 million dogs in the United States today, over 1.2 million of them are registered with the American Kennel Club (AKC). The three most popular breeds registered include first, the Labrador, followed by the Rottweiler, and finally, the German Shepherd.

# Puppy on the Way

*In his mother's belly, the future pup is tiny, and passes from embryo to fetus stage in two months. The mother, meantime, requires gentleness and care: the baby's life is at stake. But you can also set out to find a baby dog that already has his feet on the ground, at a friend's house, on the street, or at a breeding kennel. There are several possible paths and it's best to take your time.*

*After the 58th day of gestation, the event is imminent. Exhausted bitch and impatient master await the birth of two to ten babies!*

## EXPECTING THE PUPPY
### Intrauterine Life

It lasts between 58 and 62 days. Until the end of the second week, the embryo is no larger than 2 millimeters. After that stage, the growth curve differs according to breed. A medium weight measures 3 mm at 20 days and grows by 11 mm during the next 5 days. Then its growth is limited to 1mm per day. The embryo reaches 19 mm by the end of the first month of intrauterine life.

As of the 20th day, the outline of limbs appears: the contour of the mammae becomes visible at 25 days; the crest-like sketch of the ear appears as of the 26th day, at the same time as the pigmentation of the iris. On the 31st day the first hairs appear around the eyes.

This marks the end of the embryonic stage. At 33 days, the fetus' palate is formed so he'll be able to suck even before he's born. With well-formed toes, on both hind- and forelimbs, he's the spitting image of a future pup. Claws appear, then eyelids…From this time on, you can tell if it's a male or female.

Of the time spent in the maternal belly, the fortnight between the 40th and 50th days is the time of the fetus' most spectacular growth: during this time he puts on three-forths of his birth weight. The food assimilated by the mother has replaced the uterine secretions he first received. But he still needs carbohydrates, liquids, amino-acids, and minerals. On the 42nd day ossification begins: when the mother's belly is palpated, the little creature's movements can be felt. Does the mother lie down on her belly? Does she scratch it? Her offspring is fidgety and communication is fully established. None of the maternal emotions escapes the tiny pup: if she is well taken care of and protected from stress, the future puppy most likely feels good. He will feel the benefit of that not only in his first days of existence but also during the difficult socialization stages. At 45 days, hairs cover his body and hint at the color he will be: his coat will be completely grown in by the 53rd day. In his prenatal nest, the puppy straightens up, giving up his curled-up position. Five to nine days from now, he'll be pointing his muzzle.

### How Will He Look?

To know what the future puppy's little face will be like, you have to be familiar with his antecedents and have some idea of genetics. At the occurrence of meiosis—division of sex cells—certain characteristics were transmitted to the embryo. But among the millions of genes fixed to the 39 chromosomes of the canine species (compared to 23 in human being) the unexpected has its place. The ones that affect the expression of any given characteristic are in the hundreds of thousands. Disappearance of genes, redistributed genes…chance may intervene in strange ways. Telescoping of chromosomes, grouping errors, DNA mix-ups, appearance of new genes, all that may bring about mutations. The outcome is sometimes surprising: the white color of the Maremme Shepherd puppy, the short paws of the Dachshund, the long ears of courser dogs are examples of that. If chance abstains from shuffling the cards, you can expect to see a puppy that measures up to the standard of its breed.

### Getting Ready
#### Nutrition for the Mother

Exhausted by gestation, particularly during the final 20 days, the bitch is ravenously hungry. She needs high-energy food, suited to the physiological and neurological development of the fetus: zinc to prevent uterine inertia, selenium and vitamin E to make sure of muscle integrity, vitamin K to prevent neonatal hemorrhaging. It is imperative that her diet be enriched in the second month. The menu, normally consisting of 45% meat, 23% cooked cereals, 23% green vegetables, and also including edible oil (3%), dried yeast (3%), and vitamin-enriched mineral compound, is increased by between 20 and 25%.

A German Shepherd bitch weighing about 70 lbs. (34 kg) can no longer make do with a daily ration of 32 oz. (900 grams) when she's expecting babies. She consumes 3 lbs. (1,330 grams) of food at this time, that is, one and one-half times the usual amount. Frequent feedings (three to four times a day) are better than two

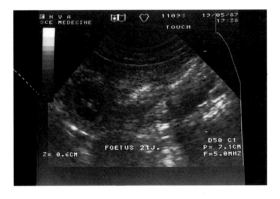

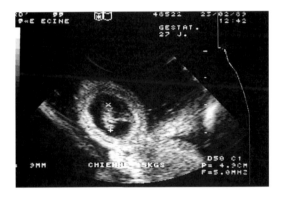

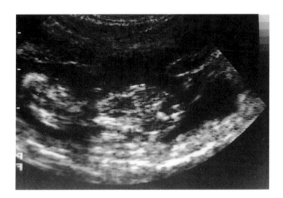

# Diagnosis During Gestation

## Echogram

Thanks to the echogram, (ultrasound) which permits the interior of the body to be viewed, diagnosis of gestation can be established from the 18th day onward, while the fetus is shaped like a hazelnut. As can be seen from the three slides from the French National Veterinary College at Alfort, development is very clear within a few days.

In the photograph at top left, which shows gestation at 21 days, the embryonic sac is easily identifiable because of the liquid it contains. It is round and even appears on the screen.

The photo at center left shows gestation at 27 days. The sac is growing longer. It is becoming oval. The fetus is clearly visible. At this stage, it measures only 10 mm. Cardiac activity can already be detected with the echogram.

The photo at the bottom left, presenting gestation at 40 days, shows very advanced fetal development. Numerous structures may become obvious: for instance the head, the neck, the thorax, the heart, the liver, or the umbilical cord.

## Radiogram of the Fetus

The veterinarian can evaluate the size of litter up to the 35th day. Past that limit, he can no longer distinguish one fetal shape from another. Then radiography has to be used—the examination is harmless to the unborn puppies—after the 42nd day, when the bones have become visible. However, that does not prevent surprises: the little family sometimes has far more members than expected.

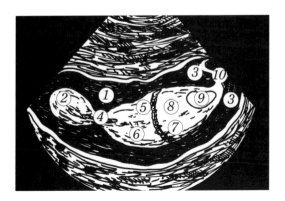

1. Fetal Liquids
2. Head
3. Uterus walls
4. Neck
5. Heart
6. Thorax
7. Abdomen
8. Liver
9. Bladder
10. Umbilical cord

*Is this Basset Hound bitch, walking "belly-to-ground," concealing a larger family than expected?*

large meals that overload her abdomen. Commercially obtainable "special purpose" foods make life easier and meet the future mom's needs.

The bitch does not get bigger until the 5th week, and the weight gain, prior to delivery, does not exceed 5–10%. Good feeding promotes lactation. The teats, which have already turned pink and then blue, are swollen and show secretion a few days before whelping occurs.

### Precautions Regarding the Mother

During gestation, the bitch's daily activity schedule does not change: walks, whether in the country or in town, are essential. But she needs some specific treatments. At the very beginning, the future mother is wormed at the same time as the household's other dogs and cats. This step enables her to get the best out of her food and prevents contamination of the puppies through the placenta.

The second preventive treatment: vaccination. Boosters, given 2 to 3 weeks before D-day, will have a beneficial effect on the litter: the colostrum ingested with the earliest feeding contains more antibodies and increases the puppies' immunity-related protection.

### The Nursery

The happy event occurs in the best conditions if the bitch is resting in a quiet atmosphere beforehand. A quiet corner is found for her away from hustle and bustle, or she is provided with a little room that can be used as both delivery room and nursery. The main thing is that her master stay nearby, because his presence is reassuring for the parturient.

A few days before the birth, the mother-to-be makes her nest in the delivery box, which she scratches just as a wild dog does. The box is made specially for her and her offspring, who will keep nice and warm in it throughout lactation. The cozy nest is made of wood or thick cardboard. Provided with an opening about 4 in. (10 cm) above the floor, it must be large enough for the bitch to turn around in it easily, and have room to stretch out and feed the puppies without being cramped at all. Along all four sides 2–4 in. (5–10 cm) above the bottom, safety rails are installed (stair carpet rods will do nicely). The rails are very useful: impeded when she turns over roughly, the mother dog is prevented from crushing the babies. For the delivery, clean rags make better bedding than newspaper, since printer's ink is sometimes toxic. The rags, which are easy to launder, protect a blanket that ensures comfort and provides warmth for the newborns. The temperature in the maternity ward is of vital importance: it must be between 79 and 86° F (26 and 30°C).

## LOOKING FOR A PUPPY
### Mongrel

There's no doubt about it: he's almost on your own doorstep. This sort of little dog, of no particular breed but not bad-looking, is everywhere to be found and waiting for a master. All you have to do is read the signs posted in stores, or ask your veterinarian, who is always aware of litters on the way. The building supervisor and neighbors may also be able to give you information. Lastly, newspaper ads can sometimes point you in the right direction. Surprising as it may seem, shelters managed by animal protection associations also receive puppies being offered for adoption.

### Purebred Puppy

To acquire a companion of this kind, you can of course proceed as for a little mongrel or go to your local pet store. But there is a standard procedure: contact the American Kennel Club (919-233-9767). Continuously informed of litters of available puppies, this organization also provides information on breeds and has the names and addresses of clubs and breeders. The option consisting of using professional canine breeders is more reliable than that of the animal shelters

The conditions under which the animals are kept are different, and in addition the young animal is somewhat prepared for living with human beings: his first steps are observed and he is already on the road to socialization. From the breeder a fair amount of information can be expected concerning the puppy's diet and vaccinations. He describes the personality and behaviors of the young doggy. He knows him as if he were his own child!

Finally, to find the dog of your dreams, you can also visit the dog shows or read newspaper ads and animal publications.

*Anything little is cute, they say. It's true as far as dogs are concerned. But be on your guard against losing your heart! In a cage, at an animal shelter, many times they have not, as at a breeder's, started becoming socialized. Let your choice fall on a healthy, lively puppy, who knows, moreover, that a human being is his friend.*

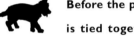 **Before the puppy is born, a bunch of rags is tied together to "prepare the field." Placed under the blanket, these humps encourage the chubby little fellow to get up on his paws.**

## Hereditary Diseases

Every canine breed is subject to a specific pathology and the dog belongs to one of the animal species most affected by hereditary diseases. In canine breeding, hip dysplasia, which causes limping in the German Shepherd, and cryptorchism—an anomaly in which testicles are located within the abdomen—are central concerns.

Patience and perseverance are the rule: in Great Britain it took ten years to eradicate a hereditary disease of the retina affecting the Setter.

# The Puppies Are Born

All damp in his fetus coat, the young puppy arrives in the world scarcely "complete," head forward, paws folded over the top of it. With rat-like face and squirming like a larva, he's not much to look at! But for his mother, he'd die. But how she looks after him! Industriously licking him, she pushes him toward her teats, and clumsily, he starts sucking right away. But his life hangs by a thread. How can we make ourselves useful?

*It only took three hours. Nice and clean, thoroughly licked by the bitch, the newborn Weimaraners are well protected.*

*Licking starts with the puppies' birth. The mother removes the fetal integuments, starts the breathing, and day after day, continues the big clean-up: head, brisket, belly, anus…The babies' lives depend on it.*

**A puppy that does not cry when he is born awakens the cannibal instinct of the mother, who will devour her infant in one gulp.**

**An amorphous, voiceless puppy is abandoned by his mother, who senses his feeble chances of survival.**

**A puppy isolated in the litter gets cold. At a body temperature below 95°F (35°C) he is incapable of sucking and his mother rejects him.**

## D-DAY
### Birthing

Over the past forty eight hours, the mother's temperature has dropped by one degree. Now abdominal contractions set in. The fetal integuments appear at the vulva. A few minutes more, and in sixty percent of cases, it's head first, limbs stretched out on either side of its head, that the newborn presents itself. He's scarcely free of the pelvic channel when the umbilical cord ruptures. An event-related incident? If the natural rupture does not occur, the bitch wastes no time in sectioning the cord herself, in a motion that seems to be inborn. In the same way, with no prior training, the parturient swallows the membranes enveloping the newborn and ingurgitates the placenta. Then in the most natural way she licks her baby, removing from him every last trace of fetal integument. The baby pup's entire body is minutely cleansed. As a result of this first moist, exploratory contact, the young canine, reassured by his dam, enters into life… .

From the psychological viewpoint, the mother's licking is indispensable: by licking the anal area she starts the baby's bowel movements; by moistening his muzzle, she helps him to breathe. Abdomen, back, and flanks, she turns her dear little puppy over and over, and shoves and pushes him until he reaches the maternal abdomen and finds the teats. Baby pup is well and truly adopted by his mother.

Thirty minutes later, on to the next one! Same scenario: the bitch, tirelessly, repeats the same moves for each of her babies. There are four or five of them, sometimes more. In two or three hours, the event is over.

### A Very Attentive Mother

The bonds between mother and pup are powerful. She coaxes him, ingests his excrement from which she draws the calcium needed for recycling milk; five or six times a day she will allow him to feed. She possesses this know-how even before giving birth. It's a question of hormones: a larger proportion of estrogens (female hormones) and the presence of prolactin, the lactation hormone, have an effect on maternal behavior. Finally, vaginal stimulation, as the newborn passes through the cervix, cements the bonds between mother and offspring.

They are further consolidated in the course of the next few hours after the birth. If her newborn were to be taken away from her the bitch would be far less capable of mothering. And in addition, if he is separated from his dam the tiny dog's chances of growing up are diminished. It becomes hard for him to gain a few ounces and to maintain his body heat. All bets are off! His paradoxical sleepiness increases instead of lessening.

## Assisted Birthing

In theory, the bitch gives birth without help. But the birth might be difficult (that's called dystocia) if the litter consists of a single puppy, or if the time between each newborn and the next exceeds one hour. It is necessary to intervene in such cases. A normal birth never takes longer than 6 hours.

You can try to deliver the puppies yourself, starting by energetically massaging the teats so as to start the contractions again and bring on expulsion. If that does not work, you have to pull the newborns from the uterus after putting on sterile surgical gloves. Next you release the little pups from their integuments, and then the nostrils, the mouth, and the back of the throat are cleared in order to get their breathing started.

What do you do next? Placing a finger between the newborn's two back legs, you raise him, with his head hanging down, to let the fluids drain away. If the puppy still isn't breathing, you blow into his mouth and nostrils. Still nothing happening? There's still hope if you can hear a heartbeat. In that case, you plunge his head and the nape of his neck into cold water. Baby pup then takes his first breath. Using clean cloths, you rub his chest to speed up the breathing movements.

There's sometimes a long wait between one pup and the next. When the proper amount of time has been exceeded, the veterinarian performs a cesarean section, especially when dealing with small breeds

## Young Mama and Bad Mother

It sometimes happens that the bitch having her first litter, because she is inexperienced, is not interested in her pups. She leaves them whining with hunger, refuses to feed them, forgets them in a corner of the nest. Helpless, the pups are left to their sad fate.

This "unfit" mother herself has probably been a victim of low blows in the family pack. Poorly integrated, a bitch is unable to assume her own motherhood. She may also be having pain—mammitis or a genital infection—which diverts her from her offspring.

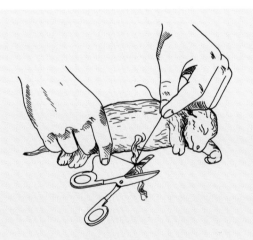

## Cutting the Cord

Not all mothers prove effective at breaking off the cord. Some breeds are still awkward. Being used to living symbiotically with human beings, bitches lose the instinct for finding solutions. Some are prognathous in their lower jaws and cannot free the newborn from his fetal envelopes. Then you have to intervene to allow the pup to breathe. Before making the cut, tie the umbilical cord with clean string at ½ in. (1 cm) from the puppy's abdomen. Then just above that, section the prenatal link with sterilized scissors. Leave as much cord attached to the puppy as possible; too long is better than too short. Lastly, clean this ultrasensitive area with an antiseptic such as tincture of iodine, which is applied with a compress.

## Colostrum Above All

For his first feeding, the puppy takes in a thick, protein-rich liquid, indispensable for any newborn: the colostrum. This secretion (which is also called "first milk") flows for twenty-four hours, which is long enough to bring essential immunoglobins to defend against infection. If deprived of this vital substance, the puppy needs to receive a polyvalent serum in conjunction with antibiotics and large doses of vitamins A and B.

 **The puppy often enters this world in the middle of the night. It's a good idea to know the telephone number of the veterinarian on emergency duty.**

**The puppy falls victim to dehydration or hypoglycemia if he does not get colostrum in the first two hours after he is born.**

**A puppy neglected by his mother must be cleaned up and dried by her master: any scrap of dried, stuck-on fetal integument may cause dermatitis on his neck by the fourth day.**

## Vagrant Puppies

Canine vagrancy should not be tolerated in American society. On public roads, it is mandatory that a dog be kept on a leash and muzzled, or else he is captured and then taken to the pound. With no owner and no permanent home, any dog that has not been vaccinated for rabies or lacks a rabies vaccination tag is usually euthanized.

whose abdomens do not expand, or with brachycephalous breeds, which have large heads. As soon as you have recovered all the pups, you have to position them very close to the bitch, so as to avoid any rejection on her part. This danger cannot be overlooked, because maternal behavior has not been strengthened by vaginal stimulation.

### Removing Puppies

When the birth is unplanned and there is no place for the puppies in the household, a decision must be made as promptly as possible. Do they have any chance of being adopted by a neighbor or a friend? Can a home be found for them through the want ads? If so, the litter has a life to look forward to. Unfortunately, puppies are not always adopted right away, and the bigger they get, the more problematical their fate becomes. It would be unthinkable to leave them out in the wild in hopes of their finding a home. That would be a cowardly, cruel act, and is punishable by law. With no family and reduced to vagrancy, these little ones are doomed to suffering and death. One must therefore be resigned to taking a very disagreeable step, but one that at least is less overwhelming for one's conscience: remove them quickly from their tragic existence.

Even before the mother has had a chance to lick them, the newborn pups can be taken to the veterinarian. But it is no light-hearted matter for the animal doctor, or his assistant, to end a life.

## PORTRAIT OF A PUPPY
### An Incomplete Creature

Short, sticky hair, the body of a rat or even a fieldmouse [1 lb. (500 g) for a German Shepherd, 3 oz.(80 g) for a Chihuahua], the looks of a newborn puppy would not win any beauty prizes. It's hard to imagine this pinkish scrap of a dog one day having the sumptuous coat of an Afghan Hound, the bearing of a Polish Shepherd, or the cute face of a Yorkshire Terrier! The puppy is one of those creatures that come into the world still unfinished.

Deaf and blind, he starts out in life with few skills. His autonomic nervous system is in the process of being developed, and the cerebral cortex is nonexistent. Aside from those of touch and smell, he has no functional senses. And the visceral motoric system is in neutral: so he is incapable of defecating or urinating. He moves with difficulty, because his barely innervated muscles hardly favor motion.

On the other hand, as to reaching the teat, everything goes swimmingly. The fact is that he possesses the "burrowing reflex," which lets him burrow under the maternal fur to make his way to the nipples. The awkward little thing actually pulls off an exploit or two: he is said to be capable of crawling for over 44 yards (40 meters) without showing the slightest sign of weariness! Certainly, his suction technique is not yet perfect. You can hear chomping sounds until he can get his tongue around the nipple. After which he gulps down a mouthful of tasty milk every second.

When he's feeding, you'd never take him for a fool! If anyone has the peculiar idea of putting a finger into his mouth, he breathes in and sucks, but soon finds out that there's no milk. Clumsy though he is, and with no one to depend on but his mother, with whom he communicates mainly by touch, the newborn pup is not the type to stay silent. After his birth cry, he has four basic sounds in his repertoire, and passes, according to his state of mind, from whimper to shrill cry, from mewing to growling. From hour to hour, distress cries become more and more intense. The work of the mother dog, constantly listening to her offspring, is only just starting.

**The weakest puppy in the litter must be placed on the rear teats: they are easier to suck and have more milk.**

*To move her infant to another nest, the bitch has only one system: carrying it in her mouth.*

## Sterilization (Spaying)

There are a number of contraceptive methods for avoiding unwanted pregnancies.

One such method is temporary sterilization, practiced by oral means or by injection, using synthetic steroids derived from progesterone. However, due to the dangers and risk factors involved with administering sterilizing hormones to dogs, temporary sterilization is strongly discouraged among the veterinary community.

The recommended solution is *definitive sterilization,* or ovario-hysterectomy (ablation of ovaries and uterus), which relieves the bitch of heats and bleeding.

There is also sterilization for males. This is *castration,* or removal of the testicles.

*It's so cozy sleeping cuddled up together! Body heat exchange thus helps these Kuvasz babies not to get cold.*

**Ambient temperature must be at least 86°F (30°C) on the day of the birth.**

**Thirty percent of orphaned puppies are victims of hypothermic cardiorespiratory syndrome, caused by getting a chill.**

**The puppy must be weighed three times the first day of his life: at birth, 12 hours later, and 24 hours later.**

**The puppy must be handled from the very first day. His being gently turned over on his bedding promotes the development of neurons and vestibular nerves, and stimulates his sense of balance.**

**A puppy who loses more than 10% of his birth weight must ingest water with glucose in it to avoid hypothermia.**

## OUTFITTING THE NEWBORN
### Warm Towels and Special Feeding Bottle

The clumsy newborn does not necessarily know how to feed properly. He chews the nipple rather than getting milk down. His tongue pops in and out and does not stay wound around the nipple, and the feeding is inadequate. So it has to be supplemented by bottle-feeding.

Provision must be made for a "special puppy feeding bottle," which can be bought at a pet supply store or from the veterinarian. More suitable than a doll's feeding bottle, which may be too small when the puppy starts to make headway, it is equipped with a nipple and a brush. You may also want to get a bottle-warmer, which can come in handy: the newborn needs his drink to be warm. Warmth is indispensable to the baby pup's health: for each feeding, warm towels are needed to wrap around his little body, which must be protected from the slightest chill.

### A Nice Clean Nest

When the litter is complete and the mother dog has finished her cleaning task, the soiled fabrics, blood-spotted and damp, must be removed. Soft dry cloths or old cotton material, carefully laundered, are both comfortable and hygienic. The nest will remain spotless until the babies are weaned: the bitch will clean up any waste from her little ones.

## WHAT FUTURE IS THERE FOR AN ORPHAN?
### An Adoptive Mother

Every effort must be made to save a puppy whose mother has died after giving birth. The key to success consists of imitating the mother's attitude: she licks her baby, moistens his fur and certain body areas; so the puppy will have to be cleaned up, and rubbed in those exact places. These maternal actions are not dispensed haphazardly. Their function is a vital one, ensuring urination or accelerating the maturing of the brain…. But the best solution is still to find an adoptive mother of the canine species: a bitch who has just had a litter or is having a false pregnancy. Adoption by this "pretend mama" requires a certain amount of diplomacy on the part of the master. Rejection of the orphan must be avoided. To put the pup into the nest, take advantage of some occasion when she leaves it. The pup will rub against his nest-mates and absorb their smell. The bitch should be hoodwinked! However, she is not always fooled. If she growls, the bottle-feeding solution will have to be considered.

## Bottle-feeding

It's a long drawn-out, repetitious occupation that ties one down, but the point is to save the life of an orphaned puppy. For the first two weeks, during which bottle-feeding is essential, you have to be very available in order to make sure that the feeding bottles are sterilized and prepared. Over a 24-hour period, eight feedings are scheduled. Patience is absolutely necessary, for the feeding puppy takes his time and his sucking rhythm must be observed. Haste would cause swallowing the wrong way and the milk might come back down his nostrils or get into his lungs. Very severe pneumonia could result.

Such incidents can be avoided if the puppy does not swallow any air. To that end, he must be held like a human baby, with his head supported on the forearm and his muzzle pointing upward. He must ingest his nice drink effortlessly. The nipple lets the milk seep out very gently. During this time, the feeding, being given at a temperature of 102°F (39°C), must not get cold, just as if it were milk from the teat of the bitch. So the water for diluting the milk powder must be heated to 122–131°F (50–55°C). When the skin on his abdomen is stretched, the puppy has had enough food. The well-filled abdomen is the only sign of repletion. Before he falls asleep, his anal area is moistened with a damp compress so as to activate defecation and urination.

Hunger prevails over everything else: three hours later, our little glutton wakes up and cries. He's hungry. Time for the next feeding already!

*When the puppy is an orphan, there is sometimes no alternative to bottle-feeding. Warm towels and suitable feeding bottle are indispensable then, and much patience is needed as well.*

**An undernourished puppy has a flat abdomen, and dry, wrinkled skin.**

## Substitute Mother's Milk

There is no existing milk that can be directly consumed by a puppy. Goat's milk approximately meets his needs, but it is too low in fat and minerals, contains too much lactose, and causes diarrhea. Cow's milk must necessarily be modified, that is to say, made more like mother's milk. For use in the event of an emergency, the recipe consists of mixing a can of unsweetened condensed milk, the yolk of an egg, a tablespoon of whipping cream, half a tea-spoon of honey. But this is only a stop-gap milk. Nothing is as good as the replacement milk: it is available from veterinarians, pet stores, and dog food distributors. It is sold with a feeding bottle and a nipple suitable for the stature of an average puppy. It contains skim milk powder, a mixture of fats, minerals, and vitamins, and reproduces the composition of female dog's milk. It's the best thing for a puppy.

# The First Stage

The neonatal period is still fraught with dangers for the little puppy. Blind and deaf, he nevertheless does not lack a sense of smell. He grows visibly: at eight days, he is twice as big as at birth. But he is far from sturdy and illnesses lie in wait for him. After the first three days, during which he is at risk of catching a chill and/or starving to death, he still has to escape the syndromes affecting newborns. Finally, at ten days old, he barks for the first time.

*Before achieving adult body temperature, the puppy is very fragile. To survive, he sleeps closely cuddled up to his brothers and sisters, like these young Cocker Spaniels.*

## FIRST STAGE OF LIFE
### Physiological Development

The pup, being very fragile, can hang on to life only if he successfully maintains his body temperature. It rises from 96 to 98.6°F (35.5 to 37°C) the first week, and from 96.8 to 100.4°F (36 to 38°C) the second week. Still about a week to struggle on! When he has reached adult temperature, the newborn has made it to the light at the end of the tunnel, and his continued existence becomes less questionable. But long before that time, the newborn has found a way to keep from getting cold: he snuggles up to his mother, with his body squeezed up against those of his brothers and sisters. The little group is as warm as a hot-water bottle, and that's the best way to escape the dangers of hypothermia.

In the neonatal period, the young dog's skeleton is almost entirely composed of cartilage. His bone structure is built up gradually as he absorbs the minerals present in his mother's milk. But this construction, known as osteogenesis, is by no means assured: osteolysis, the pathological destruction of bony tissue, may occur. The critical spot is in the connective cartilages, where long bone growth takes place, and which are the influx points for large amounts of calcium contained in the blood. Accurate regulation occurs simultaneously in the digestive tract, the kidneys, and the bones. The slightest irregularity in this operation is harmful to metabolism. How many people are aware, for instance, that the vitamin D indispensable to bone maturation also causes destruction of bony tissue?

Young as he is, the little pup already has room enough on his canine jawbone for all his teeth! They

**The puppy takes 8 or 9 days to double his birth weight. A feat that takes a human baby 5.5 months, a colt 50 days, a calf 35 days, a baby goat 22 days, a piglet 13 days...**

are present in their budding stages in the maxillary bones. But only the milk teeth, harmless to the nourishing teat, will come through within a few days. There are 28 of them (but in the adult there will be 42 teeth).

At this age, the puppy, who moves around only in response to reflexes, has a nervous system that is still in the process of maturation. But his suction reflex operates perfectly: the little glutton lifts his head up, brushes back his mother's fur to seek out the nipple, and kneads the mammary gland. How good his know-how is! He is fully in control of his tactile senses, and his well-developed sense of smell reveals his species: within twenty-four hours of being born, he can tell the difference between a feeding bottle nipple and his mother's.

Well nourished, he springs up like a mushroom, but his size is misleading: there is no certainty that a long-bodied puppy will be a large dog, or that a broad-backed newborn foreshadows a stocky adult. He wastes no time, however. In 8 days, the baby pup doubles his birth weight. An exploit otherwise achieved only by kittens, whose performance is equally good, and baby rabbits, beating all records in only 6 days.

It's at the end of the neonatal period, on the 14th day, that the young dog's eyelids open. However, that does not mean that the puppy can actually see the surrounding world. He does begin to register his very first sounds, and finds out that he too makes a noise when he yaps!

### Behavioral Development

Discretion is not his strong point: the little puppy whines as soon as something is not right. There are any number of pretexts: he's cold, he's hungry, he hurts, he's all alone, or else he needs to defecate. He bawls for his mother, who must hurry up and lick the anal area, for his visceral motor system is still not working. Whining to get attention: that's his latest find. A "stunt" so effective—mama dog is always right there—that he'll continue using it later to seek his master's attention.

*Mother's milk is good for this little Dachshund, who will double his birth weight in 8 days! Dog's milk actually contains four times as much fat as cow's milk and almost twice as much protein.*

As you can see, the young dog does not lose his head: he takes advantage of the situation, gives distress cries, constantly calls out to his mother for help. To vary his repertoire, he mews, which is another way of begging. If he really does hurt a lot, or if he is afraid of getting hurt, he alerts everyone around him with shrill cries.

Then when everything is all right again, he gives a growl of satisfaction. Loudmouthed, he does not wait until he's a week old to start yapping. To communicate with his brothers and sisters, he uses all his singing talent: vocalization, plaintive tones, sniveling. He complains, he's content, it all depends. Pups pass the word around, then have a decibel competition. At nine days, the noises are at their maximum: what a cacophony! Finally, at ten days, Baby Pup is in tune with his peers: he barks for the first time. With his snail's body and lizard's feet, the young dog is sort of remote-controlled when he moves about. Guided by the sensory-motor system of his species, he turns around and around in the cozy nest, never taking the slightest initiative. For a fortnight he constantly nuzzles his mother's fur, forever in search of the teat, which he reaches by crawling, while his head bobs back and forth. Once he gets hold of the nipple, far be it from him to want to squabble with his brothers and sisters—that's kitten behavior! He's fine where he is. No one is going to push him out of there, his mother can relax: he has no desire or even thought, nor yet the strength, to venture outside.

| TABLE COMPARING VARIOUS MILKS | | | |
|---|---|---|---|
| Ingredients | COW | EWE | DOG |
| Fats | 3.7 | 7.4 | 12.9 |
| Proteins | 3.4 | 5.5 | 7.9 |
| Casein | 2.8 | 4.6 | 5.8 |
| Lactose | 4.8 | 4.8 | 3.1 |
| Ash | 0.7 | 1.0 | 1.2 (g/liter) |

## Sleeping Like a Dormouse

Like all newborns, the puppy spends the better part of his life in the arms of Morpheus. It amounts to about ninety percent of the biological day or nycthemera. The rest of the time is devoted to feeding. For the first week, he sleeps in a heap with his brothers and sisters. Then he changes position, and stretches out to his full length beside the other puppies. The shivery little creature thus avoids caloric loss and maintains his body temperature. Now dozing, now overtaken by a light sleep, then cradled in an intermediate state before plunging into a deep sleep, he goes through the cycle of slow sleep, to which is added paradoxical or REM [rapid eyelid movement] sleep. During the latter, he breathes rapidly, his heart beats fast, he whimpers in his sleep, and his body twitches violently (this is sometimes called "seismic sleep"): now our friend is in dreamland. But the journey in the clouds will not last long. From the first days onward, the period of REM sleep dwindles, gradually decreasing up to the age of 2 months. There are endless naps for the little pup, by day as well as by night.

## FEEDINGS
### Good Dog's Milk

More voracious with every passing day, the infant has plenty to satiate his hunger: his mother feeds him on demand. Assuming that she weighs about 44 lbs. (20 kg), she can produce 25 oz. (700 g) of milk a day, sometimes more. Lacteal secretion amounts to 3% of her weight, with peaks as high as 8%. Richer than either cow's milk or sheep's milk, particularly in fats and proteins, dog's milk is extremely nutritious for the young puppy. In half an hour his abdomen is blown up like a balloon. Every ounce he gains shows that he has absorbed 2.6 oz. (2.7 g) of milk. But though the nursling may be as round as a barrel, he has no reserves of fat. After his long nap, if there is no nipple for him, he shouts. That's his way of sounding the alarm: if he has to wait too long between meals, he may fall victim to an illness that's often fatal: hypoglycemia.

## Feeding the Bitch

She has a Gargantuan appetite: three times her usual ration! So a 26-lb. (12-kilogram) Cocker Spaniel bitch usually satisfied with 16 oz. (450 g) of home-prepared food a day has not really had enough to eat until she has gobbled up 2.5 lbs. (1,350 grams). Her menu consists of 22 oz. (620 g) of meat, 11 oz. (300 g) of green vegetables, 11 oz. (310 g) of cooked rice, and 4 oz. (120 g) of food supplements: one-third oil, one-third dried brewer's yeast, one-third vitamin-enriched mineral compound.

The daily ration of over 1800 Kcal per pound (4,000 Kcal per kilogram) of dry food has been given a high fat content, like the foods specially designed for lactating bitches. Thus the mother who has to feed her offspring can be certain of not losing more than 5% of her initial weight. If she is fed three or four times a day, she can make it through the third week of feeding, when milk production is at its highest.

At that time she needs to receive plenty of calcium and phosphorus supplements to withstand maternity-related demineralization and acute hypocalcemia. She needs magnesium, which moderates irritability, and even vitamin C, which makes her less nervous as regards human beings.

## THE HAND OF A MASTER
### Indispensable Assistance

In his nest, the nursling enjoys the closeness of his family. In the presence of his mother and his brothers and sisters, he will discover the beginnings of language and the keys of canine behavior. But a domestic dog simply cannot do without contact with human beings. It is the master's job to stimulate him, to touch him, and to stroke him, from infancy onward, to initiate him into his future life as a pet or as a working dog. The touch of a hand serves as a trigger to socializing him: with his very sensitive muzzle, he catches its scent, sniffs at it, tastes it, and remembers the flavor as well as the smell.

Each day, the repeated sense experiences help him progress along the road to living together. One additional advantage: the training of his brain is more

*Feeding a five-member club is a lot to ask of this Pyrenean Shepherd bitch. She eats three or four times a day, and her ration is tripled.*

 **An only pup does not suffer from the lack of company. In his earliest infancy, it's heat he seeks, not contact.**

## Milk Fever

Worried and jumpy, the bitch is not herself. She's panting, whimpering, salivating, pacing, and her heart is pounding: she is in obvious distress. She cannot possibly suckle her offspring: and in any case she is showing obvious indifference as regards her baby pup. This is happening at the end of the first fortnight of suckling. Suddenly she has cramps, she limps, and ends up falling over, victim of an attack of eclampsia, which is also known as lactation tetany, and more commonly as milk fever. In under twelve hours, her temperature rises to 108°F (42°C). The bitch falls into violent convulsions. This affliction is more common in young mothers, small breeds, and bitches suckling more than three pups. Milk fever also affects bitches who are underfed during lactation or gestation. For at least twenty-four hours, the nursing mother must be relieved of her task. The ideal is to offer the infant mixed feedings, consisting half of bottle feeding and half of breast feeding...if the mother tolerates him!

63

*Picking the puppy up hastens socialization. This simple gesture, repeated daily, teaches him that human beings are an allied breed.*

Twelve percent of pups do not live beyond two weeks. The most sensitive are the orphans: thirty percent are victims of hypothermic cardiorespiratory syndrome caused by getting a chill.

## Light and Sound

To promote integration of the puppy into our environment, we need to familiarize him with the ambiance of daily life. Music, voices on the radio, telephones ringing, the vacuum cleaner's humming...the sound background is quite useful even before the full development of the hearing centers.

Likewise, mirrors, lamps, and spotlights softly illuminate the puppy's world, even while he is still blind.

quickly completed, and in his subconscious, he recognizes, as he did in the pack, one leader: a human being. These subtle ideas are perceived as a result of a few pats and gently spoken words, when it is time for weighing, during the first fortnight of his life.

### Care During the First 3 Days

The baby pup's start in life is difficult, particularly during the first 3 days. At risk of all sorts of evils, from dehydration to chills, to say nothing of hypoglycemia, he's in a tight corner. If his mother is tired, he's in great danger. His master must take over immediately to provide indispensable support, that is, provide a series of services without which the little dog is condemned to die.

Waking the newborn before each feeding, warming him on hot-water bottles or towels are things that need to be done to keep him alive. Often affected by the hypothermia syndrome—getting cold, stopping feeding, being rejected by the mother—the pup must be gently rubbed down with a damp cloth, and then brought back to his wet-nurse 2 or 3 hours later. Bottle-feeding becomes a necessity when the bitch has insufficient milk. It requires a schedule of eight feedings over a 24-hour period for the first 2 days, six on the 3rd and 4th days, five from the 8th to 16th days. But this is not the only task that falls to the master: the puppy's digestion must also be supervised. He needs to get the best advantage out of the milk he ingests. His weight, which changes between 5% and 10% every 24 hours, will be checked daily, recorded, and compared to previous findings.

### BOTTLE-FEEDING SCHEDULE

These 36 hours are not without anxiety. The slightest diarrhea, sign of a digestive disturbance, calls for the puppy to be put on a low diet. If the puppy starts drinking more than usual—a common event when the mother is feeding only one or two babies—the milk feeding is replaced with rice-water or carrot-water for a day or two, until the colic has subsided. The perineum must be massaged with cotton soaked in lukewarm

| AGE | BIRTH WEIGHT | | | NUMBER OF BOTTLE-FEEDINGS |
|---|---|---|---|---|
| | 8–12 oz. (250–350 g) | 12–18 oz. (350–500 g) | over 18 oz. (500 g) | |
| Days 1 and 2 | 12 ml | 12 ml | 12 ml | 8 |
| Days 3 and 4 | 20 ml | 30 ml | 40 ml | 6 |
| Days 8 to 16 | 35 ml | 50 ml | 70 ml | 5 |

*Starving when his mother lacks milk, the baby pup must be fed patiently. After the bottle-feeding, keep an eye on digestion. His weight is recorded every day and compared.*

water after the feeding. Without this action, the puppy remains incapable of evacuating urine and excrement. Are his kidneys functioning normally? If not, the puppy becomes dehydrated. His skin is flaccid and dry, and retains fingerprints when pressed. If he becomes both hypothermic and hypoglycemic at the same time, the nursling will not recover unless he receives serum glucose injections.

## DISEASES OF THE NEWBORN
### Syndromes of the Newborn

Besides the viral and microbial illnesses affecting baby puppies, there are four major syndromes of the newborn that could be fatal to them.

The *hemorraghic syndrome* appears between the first and fourth days. It may be caused by sectioning the umbilical cord too short. The puppy is limp and hardly moves. Blood is observed in the urine, and that indicates a blood platelet deficiency. That is why, from the onset of gestation, there is emphasis on the usefulness of vitamin K, necessary in the production and coagulation of blood.

*Toxic milk syndrome* results from a genital infection in the mother, who may have been underfed during her pregnancy. The pup bawls, his abdomen is distended, and his anus is red. He is suffering from malnutrition, diarrhea, and dehydration. He must be bottle-fed with reconstituted milk substitute.

*Swimming pup syndrome,* which occurs around the second or even the third week, is revealed by a

 **Ambient temperature needs to be between 86 and 91°F (33 and 30°C) the first week, then 80°F (27°C) the second week.**

**A puppy that's not growing absolutely must be bottle-fed by his master.**

## Licks

The mama dog has plenty to do to help her puppies grow. After the interminable feedings, which keep her busy six times a day, she has to clean all her little charges. Anal licking to stimulate fecal discharge and urination in the babies, licking their chests to regulate their respiratory rhythm, their heads to start brain function...It's more than just a clean-up.

*This Yugoslav Shepherd can sleep the sleep of the just. He will be spared most illnesses if his mother has been vaccinated.*

## Esthetic or Barbaric

Tail docking, which takes place on the fourth day in order to bring the puppy into conformity with the standards of his breed, is a common practice in the U.S. However, at the Council of Europe a number of countries voted against this esthetic surgery: Sweden, Norway, Denmark, Switzerland, Germany, the Anglo-Saxon countries, and France. The reasons given: the barbaric nature and non-necessity of the amputation.

The dog's tail, provided with 22 coccygeal vertebrae, does indeed serve as a rudder for swimming, a balancing device for jumping and changing direction, and lastly as a means of expressing states of mind. Certainly, not all breeds of dog are so favored: anurans are born without tails—the Bobtail [Old English Sheepdog], Brittany Spaniel, Catalan Shepherd—and brachyurans are born with an unusually short tail.

flattened rib cage and the pup's inability to get up on his paws. This illness affects mainly young "heavyweights" reared on tiled or parquet floors. Surfaces with no bumps or obstacles do not promote the puppy's motor capabilities.

*Wasting syndrome,* or fading puppy syndrome, brings together a whole series of syndromes connected with infectious diseases. Malnutrition aggravates matters.

### Bacterial Diseases

*Omphalitis* is a very frequent umbilical infection that affects newborns between the first and fourth days. The navel is edematous, the area around it is hot, reddish to purplish in color, and very swollen. The puppy's abdomen increases in volume. Strict hygiene of the cord area, particularly in the earliest days, is the best preventive procedure.

*Impetigo of the neck* affects the puppy between the fourth and tenth days. It is shown by little scabs and abscesses. The mother, as a result of so much licking, has blisters in her mouth. This poor state of health and hygiene arises when fragments of fetal membrane have dried on the puppy's skin and have become infected. The newborn must then be cleaned with Betadine.

*Juvenile pyoderma* is another skin disease. This illness of neonates takes the form of an inflammation of the eyelids. They become thickened, ulcerated and scabby, and the puppy's head is swollen. It is a sign of an extremely low immune state.

*Neonatal ophthalmia* is probably the most frequently encountered illness. The eyelids are still closed and underneath them there is a large amount of pus which considerably enlarges the contour of the eyes.

*Septicemia,* which leaves the newborn hardly any chance, occurs between 2 and 40 days.

### Viral Diseases

*Viral Herpes* affects puppies under a week old. This disease, for which there is no vaccine, may be transmitted either by the mother at the moment of giving birth, or else by contact with infected animals of the same type. The baby pup has a runny nose, and marks may appear on his skin. He has abdominal pain and diarrhea, the latter detail being hard to observe because the bitch absorbs the excrement and cleans her baby. He weeps, and dies within 18 hours. But there is one very easy way to combat this disease: all you have to do is increase the heat in the room to 101.3°F (38.5°C) to prevent the virus from propagating. The herpes virus evolves only at temperatures below 98.6°F (37°C). In addition to the warming-up solution, a treatment must be administered by the veterinarian. Once a period of a fortnight has elapsed, and if the temperature is high, the pup is protected.

## Congenital Defects

In addition to hereditary illnesses, transmitted by the parents, and which may appear several months or years after birth, congenital defects have developed during intrauterine life. These diseases are due to anomalies in genetic heritage. Thus some races are predisposed to particular types of diseases. Tumors of the hypophysis [pituitary gland], stenosis (narrowing) of the nostrils, elongation of the velum [soft palate] are more likely to affect the brachycephalous breeds with flattened noses. Cataract problems are encountered in the Afghan Hound, the Airedale Terrier, the Alaskan Malamute, the Labrador Retriever, the Bobtail [Old English Sheepdog], and the Poodle; the Basset Hound and the Boxer, for their part, are more likely to have glaucoma problems. Problems of behavior with the Cocker Spaniel, of hearing with the Dalmatian, malformation of lips and palate in the Dachshund, the English Bulldog, and the Shih Tzu. The German Shepherd and the Labrador Retriever, for their part, have inherited hip dysplasia, the Yorkshire Terrier dysplasia of the retina. No breed seems to have been spared.

## Frog Belly

Pustules on the inner thighs, slow growth...the puppy is surely being bothered by the presence of ascarids [roundworms], which are often responsible for nervous and digestive disorders and rachitis [rickets]. The unfortunate pup will have a very distended abdomen that is sometimes called "frog belly." These incidents can be avoided by administering as early as the first week a worm preventive treatment. Worming is all the easier for a nursling, because the medication may be presented in the form of a paste placed in his mouth by means of a syringe.

The canine species is prey to 300 hereditary diseases, and the number is growing annually by about a dozen, given the importance of purebred dogs.

Parvovirosis, canine distemper, and adenovirosis spare the newborn if the mother has previously been vaccinated.

## The Unwanted Dewclaw

The dewclaw, or first digit, is a useless appendage. Declaw amputation therefore takes place as early as the fourth day for some puppies, is intended to preserve hunting dogs or hounds from the paw damage sustained on uneven ground. In addition, this surgery, said not to be painful if done when the animal is very young, makes grooming easier in dogs with heavy coats. So the dewclaw is cut off in puppies of the miniature breeds, Alaskan Malamutes, Belgian Shepherds, Bernese, Boxers, Dalmatians, Rottweilers, and Saint Bernards. It is customary for a Briard to have a double dewclaw on his hind feet, like the Great Pyrenees, who also wears a single dewclaw on his forefeet.

# The Second Stage

Everything's changing from one day to the next in this transition period. The baby pup has his eyes wide open and an excellent nose. He's discovering the world, all ears, surprised at hearing his own barking. This little scrap of a dog, still a bit tottery when he moves around, already has conditioned reflexes. He licks, nibbles necks. Meddling with everything by the time he's three weeks old, he is starting to get scolded by his mother. But the boisterous little creature's health is still very fragile.

*Rascals in the making they may be, like these two Highland White Terriers, but when they're discovering the world, things can be tough.*

# A TIME FOR EXPLOITS
## Physical and Behavioral Changes

Such a metamorphosis! During this period, the changes experienced by the puppy are spectacular. Physically, he's like a tadpole trying to turn into a beautiful frog. The stuck-down eyelids open like a flower. Unfortunately, it sometimes happens that the young canine remains cut off from the world: his eyelids stay closed, he is afflicted with tied eyelid. He has to be taken to the veterinarian for an operation.

Even though his eyes are wide open, the nursling still doesn't have much expression in his gaze. Why not? Because he's still blind. He won't be able to take in his surroundings until he's about 17 days old.

At 21 days, the pup perceives sounds very well. He hears his brothers and sisters yapping and his mother barking, and realizes that he makes some funny noises himself. It's a big event in a puppy's life to express himself with "woofs"! He can even let it be known that he's hurting, having become very sensitive to pain.

Here he is then, endowed with sight, hearing, and an increasingly acute sense of smell. He's fumbling his way around his world. He can walk and stand upright: his sense of balance is becoming more acute, and his muscle tone is getting adjusted. And that's not all: he's discovered yet another locating tool: his mouth. Everything he finds gets sucked and licked. A dab with his tongue and he gets to know substances. The result is all the more exciting in that between 14 and 20 days he cuts his milk teeth: two canines on each jaw, and six incisors dominating the upper jaw.

From the behavioral point of view, the pup's development is phenomenal. Whereas he once had an immature nervous system, which kept him in a larval sort of life, he gradually acquires conditioned reflexes. Such progress will start him communicating, first with his own kind, then with human beings.

So he is very attracted by his mother's mouth, and he licks and nibbles the corners of her lips. That is a sure sign of his species: all young canines of that age show this behavior in the wild state; it's their way of asking their parents to regurgitate predigested food.

This happens at a time when the babies need to get used to food other than their mother's milk.

## Acting Like the Big Boys

Still hanging on his mother's lips, the nursling will tend to retain this infantile behavior, known as neoteny. It is a ritual that is the canine equivalent of a sign of friendship. So it's not surprising if later on he licks his master's mouth, thus showing his submission and his desire for appeasement.

With his mouth, the young dog sketches the rules of canine relations. His head turned toward his own kind, his tail between his legs, in a crouching position, he shows his friendly intentions. Later on, as an adolescent, he will use the same behaviors to appease dominant animals who have broken certain rules. Some baby habits persist, but attitudes become ritualized. Often, during his lifetime as a dog, he will roll over on his back, tail between his legs, ears flattened, belly up…This position represents the puppy's submission to his mother.

The fact is that at this age, the rambunctious creature has to learn to obey. Watch out for blunders! The mother doesn't beat about the bush: she administers his first punishments. And if the baby, led on by his brothers and sisters, shows any sign of insolence, she loses patience and puts a stop to it.

Within the family, friendly understanding is the keynote. At twenty days, the puppy is capable of seeking out his nursing neighbors. That solves any body temperature problems and at the same time develops a sense of investigation. An explorer is born: becoming as inquisitive as a cat, the young pup wants to know everything and it's in contact with his brothers and sisters that he'll satisfy his appetite for knowledge. By the motions that he uses on the other pups' bodies as he brushes against them, touches and pushes them, he heightens his senses of touch, of hearing, and of smell. He climbs up on his neighbor's back, he licks him from his chops to his ears. He starts to use his mouth for attacking, nibbling his adversary's neck, for the outlines of combat are

*They can see at 17 days, hear at 21 days, but they walk hesitantly still. The litter gets bolder bit by bit: like these Bearded Collies, the puppies wander farther from the nest, climb on their relatives' backs, lick and nibble each other, and start to play. The bitch is never far away to restore order promptly and gain obedience.*

The puppy of 15 to 21 days old has no notion of fear. For him the hand of a stranger is absolutely identical to the body of a puppy.

"Anyone who acquires a puppy becomes his substitute mother and father" (Dr. Patrick Pageat)

## He Cries When Anything Separates Him from His Mother

Despite his spectacular progress, the barely three-week-old pup still isn't very smart. He is walking, yes indeed, but he's still very wobbly on his legs. And he still needs his mother to keep him out of traps. How can he get to her when he has to get around some obstacle? He whines, he snivels. Fortunately the mother dog gets him out of the maze.

starting to appear; he squeaks and shakes his head when he picks up an object. All these gestures, becoming more specific from one day to the next, are advance indications of the behaviors current in the lifestyle of the group.

## VARIABLE GEOMETRIC GROWTH

The puppy grows fast, in size and in weight, but at a rate that varies from one breed to another. The smaller the stature of the clan to which he belongs, the faster he grows. A miniature dog has already reached five-sixths of his height, but he's still a featherweight. He'll be fully grown at three months, or much later if the subject is a heavyweight.

If a human baby were to follow the growth curve of the Yorkshire Terrier, he'd weigh 154 lbs. (70 kg) by the time he was a year old. Imagine his taking the German Shepherd's route, and he'd weigh 440 lbs. (200 kg). Among the canines, genetic factors as well as feeding are the keys to this feat. But success is not guaranteed: unsuitable food, unfavorable external factors (worms, parasites) may hamper development. So in the short period of time taken up by growth, it is essential that the puppy lack for nothing.

## FOODSTUFFS

The second stage is a decisive phase in the puppy's growth. This transitional period is marked by less frequency in maternal contacts and feedings. Food is a matter requiring precision. Feeding a well-balanced commercial or homemade growth ration is essential. It must be energy-giving, but not too abundant. There is no point in hastening the growth of puppies belonging to giant breeds! It is excesses of this sort that cause bone disorders, which are frequent in puppies. "Overdosing" on vitamins and minerals often leads to hypertrophic osteodystrophy. High fever, painful swelling of the limbs—the dog is on the verge of paralysis.

In veterinary circles, osteochondrosis is the name given to the whole range of diseases and handicaps such as limping, elbow and hip dysplasia, observed in particular in large-breed dogs, especially in the males, as early as four to eight months of age. Vitamin D, which promotes the fixing of calcium in growth areas, must be dispensed in a measured way, otherwise it causes osteofibrosis, destroys bony tissue, and sets off demineralization. The bones, which are fragile, become as soft as rags. They bend and break spontaneously. These breaks are known as "greenstick" fractures.

The fact is that the puppy needs calcium more than vitamin D. One pint of dog's milk, which is unquestionably the richest food, contains 1.9 g of calcium (compared to 1.2 g in cow's milk) and also contains 2.1 g of phosphorus (compared to 0.9 g in the ruminant's). Every day a growing puppy needs 200 mg of phosphorus for every pound he weighs, 9 IU of vitamin D per pound, and 250 mg of calcium for every pound.

### Food Supplements

The nutritionist Roger Wolter recommends, for a two- to three-week-old puppy, an appetizing, digestible, and balanced food supplement. Gradually brought in to replace milk consumption, it allows avoidance of a "weaning crisis" and sudden diet changes. To this end, a liquid food is prepared, with a special reconstituted milk or cow's milk as its basis. It is concentrated to 20% unsweetened dry matter, to which are gradually added meat juices, liver, chopped meat, cooked eggs, and cereal flakes. Baby food in little jars can also be used, with the addition of foodstuffs that will be consumed in adulthood. The simplest and most economical method consists of mixing with the additional milk an increasingly larger proportion of the complete food. That's the way to go about weaning.

### Good Hygiene

For the orphan as for the puppy whose mother is exhausted, the number of bottle feedings is reduced from five to four.

The scenario is always the same, based on spotless hygiene: sterilization of the bottles, use of a bottle heater, the necessary preparations made for bottle-feeding

*This young Labrador who wants for nothing has all the luck on his side. The second stage is a decisive phase in the puppy's growth, in which milk consumption is gradually replaced with appropriate foods.*

*Grabbed, nibbled, turned over in all directions, toys accelerate this little Dachshund's tactile and olfactory development. They are strongly recommended at the time when the puppy begins to engage in exploratory activity, which will lead to games.*

## An Orphan's Problems

When the animal no longer has a mother, it is the responsibility of the breeder or owner to develop the young pup's faculties. Feeding time is ideal for getting the little canine used to human beings, whose smell and taste he will perceive by licking. As any human baby, the young puppy must not be cut off from the world but must be familiarized with sounds on television and voices on the radio. Noisy, brightly colored toys will contribute to his awakening. To promote his tactile sense and his motor activity, an anti-bedsore pad should be used, placed over a bladder filled with water or with little expanded polystyrene balls. That feels something like the movements of his mother's body and stimulates the puppy.

(moistening of the anal area). It is a good idea, at the moment of defecation, to place the pup on some newspapers at a distance from the nest, so that he does not soil the basket.

## CANINE PEDIATRICS

Until he is weaned, the puppy is very vulnerable. Vaccines alone are no guarantee against diseases. Hygiene and environmental conditions are of capital importance. Canine pediatrics makes every effort to eradicate a fair number of diseases, but some problems still remain insoluble. This newer discipline is becoming subject to specialization, much like cardiology, dermatology, surgery, ophthalmology, neurology, and dentistry.

### Sophisticated Techniques

Canine pediatrics does benefit from the contributions of modern technology. Often used as a complementary examination, radiography permits more thorough diagnoses thanks to the use of x-rays. Depending on their radiopacity, the constituents of the puppy's body absorb the rays: radiopaque bones show up white, liquids and soft tissues, which are less radiopaque, show as gray, air shows as black. If a bone becomes gray, if a lung fills up with liquid instead of containing air, some deficient state is detected. Ideal for revealing bone and lung problems, radiography does nevertheless have one major lack: it does not permit distinction between liquids and solids.

To palliate this lack, recourse must be had to ultrasonography.

This modern medical imaging method gives useful indications as to the treatment to be used. Some practitioners, at the peak of progress, have at their disposal an electrocardiograph (EKG), which locates problems in the cardiac system by means of electrodes (clamps or needles) applied to the skin. Variations in the electrical activity of the heart in relation to time are transmitted to a graph. If the latter shows discrepancies with what is normal, there is some anomaly in the way the heart cells are functioning.

*At two weeks, these baby Hungarian Pointers get a food supplement: a mixture of milk and dry matter, with the gradual addition of meat juice, liver, cooked eggs, and cereals. It gives the mother a rest, and gradually replaces milk.*

## Feeding the Mother

During the first three weeks of lactation, the female's ration must be gradually increased up to three times the usual amount. For that, high-energy, high-protein foods are used that are also rich in fats. The bitch must not lose more than ten percent of her weight. Food is therefore provided on demand, with fresh water always available. Minerals and vitamins are also given as food supplements.

*The smaller the puppy's breed, the faster he grows. And when it comes to acting silly, is there a growth curve? The saucy look on this Bichon Bolonais' face hints there may be.*

**The twenty-one-day-old pup will start exploring the premises. This is the time for removing packets of insecticide and insect traps from inside the home.**

**Weaning can start at the age of fifteen days for an orphaned puppy.**

Other state-of-the-art equipment: electroencephalography (EEG), which examines the electrical activity of the brain and can show brain lesions; electroretinography (ERG), which examines the retina and shows functional possibilities. This examination is very useful before an operation for cataracts, an abnormality that can be discovered as soon as the eyelids open.

To conclude, surgery offers spectacular results, whether phako-emulsification (cataract surgery) or osteosyntheses, very complicated bone repairs, are concerned.

## Diseases of Puppies
### Canine Distemper
This highly contagious disease, frequent in puppies that have not ingested colostrum or are born of unvaccinated mothers, emerges around the third week. The virus incubation period is 3 to 7 days.

The young dog has a cough, and his eyes and nose are runny. He usually has digestive problems (vomiting, diarrhea, loss of appetite). Signs of nervousness are observed—trembling, convulsions.

In the advanced stage of the disease, the puppy develops encephalitis or meningitis: he is restless and keeps turning around and around.

Recovery is possible, but it is often accompanied by sequelae: hepatic weakness, blindness, epilepsy... Death is often waiting.

### Infectious Canine Hepatitis
Loss of appetite, high temperature, thirst, anorexia, prostration, vomiting and bloody diarrhea, abdominal pain, convulsions, jaundice: the symptoms of this highly contagious disease are variable.

Sometimes the animal dies without showing the slightest sign. If he manages to recover, he may be left with a blue-tinged cornea (in about 20% of cases), the sequela of keratitis. Lastly, during the convalescence period, his urine presents risks for his unvaccinated litter-mates.

## Parvovirosis

It affects puppies over five weeks old. The critical period is between the sixth and eighth weeks, for a dilemma has to be faced. This is actually the time at which the proportion of antibodies of maternal origin is both inadequate to protect the pup from the parvovirus and too high for vaccination to be effective. Vomiting, and in particular diarrhea, often hemorrhagic, are the clinical signs of this very contagious, mortal disease. The digestive tract is literally scoured by the virus. The nursling very quickly becomes dehydrated. Intensive perfusion-based treatments are often necessary. The tenacious virus may remain present in given area for over eight months, despite the use of disinfectants.

*Is this young Mastiff incubating some illness or other? Until he is weaned, a puppy is very vulnerable and vaccines are not an absolute guarantee against illness; so it is important to be careful about environmental conditions and hygiene.*

 **In the third week, the puppy's body temperature is 100.4°F (38°C)**

**A puppy exhibiting the startle reflex has completed his transition period.**

# Primary Social Adaptation

The puppy is now of an age to learn to live with his own kind and around human beings. The social adaptation period is starting: he will pass through a number of stages, like any young creature, from attraction to aversion. During this phase, he begins to identify with his own species and to become interested in other living beings, and he can perceive the differences. His neurological maturing is fully accomplished.

*These young Abruzzi Shepherds, like all canines, are unaware of the species to which they belong. They will find out between the third and seventh week, during what is called "impregnation."*

*This affectionate Chow Chow is very demonstrative: at five weeks, the puppy recognizes his mother by sight.*

## A Matter of Time

In the animal world, nidifugous creatures are characterized by their ability to follow their parents from the time they are born and by very advanced brain maturing: they complete their social adaptation right away (that is the case with birds such as geese, chickens and ducks, and some herbivores, such as colts). Social adaptation takes longer in nidicolous animals, born deaf and blind, with a poorly developed sense of smell, and no motor capabilities: such is the case with dogs.

## SOCIAL ADAPTATION

Social adaptation is not exclusive to the canine species. Every individual becomes aware of social relations and assimilates the way they work. Social adaptation of the young canine occurs in two phases: the period of *primary social adaptation,* or training, which lasts from three to seven weeks, and the period of *secondary or true social adaptation,* which extends from the tenth to the twelfth week (see page 103). These two periods are separated by a period of uncertainty (see page 99). The limits of the period of social adaptation are genetically set: so they are the same for all breeds of puppies.

The time devoted to learning is dominated in the first place by the *attraction phase,* which starts when the puppy enters his fourth week of existence, and the *aversion phase,* which starts at five weeks. The sixth week corresponds to the *critical phase.* But at seven weeks, the puppy who is now aware of every aspect of the codes of relationships among his own kind—mother, brothers, and sisters—may be separated from his dam. Things have to be done fast: a week more, and he would suffer from the stress of this separation.

What happens in primary social adaptation? Imprinting, life in the pack, and education by the mother are its three principles.

## IMPRINTING
### (from 3 to 7 weeks)

It's because of his neurological maturity that the puppy will be able to enter the imprinting phase that will allow him to recognize his own species.

Between the 20th and 25th days, the puppy's sense, auditory, and visual organs function perfectly as a whole. From day to day, his motor and sensory capabilities grow more marked: he can move, react, interact. To motor capabilities is added acquisition of "remote" senses: smelling, seeing, hearing. The puppy watches objects in motion, and if he pricks up his ears he can hear sounds wonderfully well. It is these ultra-sharp faculties that will bring him, between the fourth and sixth weeks, to grasp the language of his brothers and sisters. In his brain, still developing but already receptive to information, things will gradually become organized. Up to five weeks, neurological maturing will continue: retaining facts, memorizing...his central nervous system is well developed now.

How precocious he is! From the time he is 1 month old, the reactivity of his nerves is similar to that of an adult dog. Human beings do not reach this level of maturation until they are 2 years old, hence the custom of comparing a child of that age to a young dog of 4 to 6 weeks.

## Imprinting

He uses his nose, his eyes, his entire body to record life's messages. At this age, everything is indelibly recorded in his memory, making up a veritable imprint. This extraordinary, indeed unique, phenomenon occurs only once in a puppy's existence. So he mustn't miss his mark. In this the young dog is no more eccentric than any other animal: the gray goose bonds in an exclusive way with the first creature that takes care of her, as was recorded by Konrad Lorenz, father of the theory of imprinting, in 1935. The famous ethologist had already done this experiment on the Colvert duck: that animal was similarly attracted to the first person who bent over him at the time when he was hatching. Thus, whatever the species, the young creature is fascinated by his first contact: his mother, his brothers and sisters, and even a human being. The puppy raised without his mother prefers a human being. The problem is that then he rejects his own species.

## Species Recognition

This phenomenon is not inscribed in his genetic inheritance: the puppy does not know to which species he belongs; he has to find that out. Put a 3-week-old Chihuahua in with a litter of kittens, and he could hardly care less about his own brothers and sisters. Next, the puppy will be interested in the specific or supra-individual characteristics of one species in an overall, generalistic way, without, however, identifying one individual in particular. He has to wait until he is

*Separation occurs as early as the 7th week between a Weimaraner bitch and her baby, destined to be a working dog, whereas it will take place toward the 12th week among pet dogs.*

five weeks old to recognize his mother by sight. But through his sensory perceptions, he does distinguish one species from another, and recognizes his own. That's great progress already! It is a very considerable advantage, which will enable him to spot the enemy, learn to get away from any danger, take refuge with friendly species to seek protection. In the natural world, it's a matter of survival; at home, the issue is how to live in peace with other dogs (these are intraspecies relations), and also with the cat and the Guinea pig (interspecies relations).

## Social Adaptation to Human Beings

It's through the olfactory, auditory, and visual signals specific to each species that the puppy, endowed in particular with an ultrasensitive sense of smell, spots the differences between his own kind and human beings.

To avoid his becoming fixated on a human being as regards sex or age, it is preferable to bring him simultaneously into contact with women, men, and children, whose odors are not the same. Any excesses are harmful in contacts begun with the

*Between 6 and 12 weeks, every young dog, like this Yorkshire Terrier, goes through a critical period: he is distrustful. It's a touchy time when relationships with the human environment must be particularly controlled so that the puppy can achieve his psychic balance.*

young dog: if handled to excess, he will be too submissive; left too much alone, he will be weak, inactive, and unsociable. The puppy cannot get by with food alone: he needs to sniff, to lick the hand that serves him, to hear a voice talking to him. After six weeks, the bonds must become even closer so that fear of human beings does not set in. A puppy that has had little contact with human beings during the primary socializing period does actually run the risk of being fearful. He just cannot look his master in the eye, and he seeks refuge between his protector's legs. His gaze is shifty, he is always on the defensive, and he cannot stand being touched. At six months, he will hide in corners, jump at the slightest noise, stop playing. On the street he will always be on the alert, and his sexual life will be a failure. If, in spite of everything, a bitch of this type is ever successfully inseminated, she will be indifferent to her puppies.

Of course, one can still count on the secondary socialization period to associate the puppy with human beings, but in that case we're talking about taming with food. That's a far cry from the domesticated, cooperative puppy.

### The Critical Period

This period occurs after the aversion phase, during which the puppy stops being fascinated by new species. Between 6 and 12 weeks, the young dog becomes distrustful. The change in attitude is very obvious: a 25-day-old puppy already reacts defensively or by drawing back if someone he doesn't know puts a hand into his basket.

During this touchy period, the time devoted, on the one hand, to relations between the puppy and his own kind and, on the other hand, to relations with human beings needs to be properly apportioned. At the age at which directions are beginning to be shaped, the dog's psychic and sexual balance depends on it.

Raised solely in the company of human beings, the young animal tends to take the latter for dogs, unless he considers himself a human being. Lastly, if he remains in an exclusively canine setting, he is afraid of

### Compulsory Passage

Some observations made in children are also pertinent in the animal environment. At the beginning of this century, Maria Montessori, the Italian schoolteacher who founded the famous Montessori schools, thus indicated the connection between neurological maturation and imprinting. Now, the latter takes on all its meaning in canine psychology. It is important, at that very time, to develop imprinting opportunities. Deprived of these opportunities, the puppy cannot bloom.

members of his own species. If he is still unaware of their code of expression, he runs the risk of being aggressed at any time.

## LIFE IN THE PACK
### (from 4 to 6 weeks)

The puppy is making progress in his group living. Imitation gives him the key to approaching his foster-brothers. Perfect locomotion enables him to discover the first signs of pack life and learn the communications code. Now he has all his faculties, he is constantly exploring places, finding his proper space. Using a variety of postures, he will be initiated into combat games. Apprenticeship in the hierarchy begins as the first signs of sexuality appear.

### First Approaches

At 5 weeks, the puppy has all the morphological characteristics of the adult dog. He has amazing facial expressiveness, contrasting with the rigid 3-week-old mask. In control of his facial muscles now, he snarls, moves his ears, and expresses himself to his brothers and sisters at last!

### Approach Technique

Contacts with his siblings are very brief: they last only a few seconds. At four weeks, curiosity is the young puppy's only motive as concerns his own kind. Though the approach ritual may not yet exist, the "exercise over" one is soon set up: the puppy presents his hindquarters or else licks the other one's face, a gesture he will make later, and which, as a result of the sitting position, takes on an appeasement value. The approach technique takes shape as days go by: head to head or head to tail, that's the way it's done. As he did with his mother, the puppy then displays his inguinal area. This attitude will last, absolutely unchanging, his whole life long.

### With the Gang

The puppy has perfect locomotion: he walks, runs, can already negotiate obstacles. His movements become

*Men, women, children... Just like this Bearded Collie, a puppy at the age of social adaptation needs to be in contact with people of all ages. That's how he practices his sense of smell, and how his curiosity and self-confidence are developed; left all alone, he might become unsociable.*

 **The 6-week-old puppy no longer sleeps in a group, but on his own.**

**The puppy that goes out on the street accelerates his social adaptation, but it is imperative that he be vaccinated.**

*Off on our adventures! These Hungarian Pointers have made up a gang and are following each other in single file. Group living really has started.*

daily a little more diversified up to the 30th and 40th days. Running, jumping, using undulations in the terrain, diving into a hole, burrowing into a tree-trunk, bouncing onto a plank, rushing down a mound of earth...what he wants to do is move. The puppy, born clumsy, is changing his gait. Now he's agile.

One fine day, he's taking a walk, following his brothers and sisters. Each one, all in a single line, is carrying a little something in his or her mouth: now we recognize the first signs of group activity. Next the steps become better and better coordinated: the pups are starting to follow each other: group living is well and truly launched.

## Communication

All it takes is one movement within the litter, and we have general mobilization! It reminds you of a herd of sheep: everything that enchants one excites the others, anything that sparks the curiosity of one attracts the gang. That's how the idea of signal-behavior, so important in animal communication, gets started. Tail, paws, ears, the whole message system starts up. A noise occurs in the house: action stations! The whole litter sets sail, in one and the same rush of unity.

## Discoveries

Now that the puppy is picking up his pace, hurling himself at cushions, climbing over the basket, he will be observed changing posture frequently. Sitting or standing still on his four legs, with his front muscles stretched, he is ready to touch the ball, or push it. Every discovery has its concert of growls, cries, or howls. Exploratory behavior is at its height: the field of investigation is growing larger. Space is no longer restricted to the area around the basket. Inside the house, the nosy little creature locates the places that will become his playground.

## Combat Games

As he plays, the puppy will learn quite a few things. He soon realizes that by lying down on his back to invite others to play, he gets a sudden reaction: the whole troop rushes up, always ready for all sorts of tricks. The rambunctious little things are hardly through their first 4 or 5 weeks of existence and they're into war games: nibbling each other's ears, catching each other by the nape of the neck. The mouth becomes a weapon, a muzzle can be stuffed into it, or the tip of a paw, and then the jaw is closed. That really hurts: the victim cries, groans, and withdraws. That's how winners are distinguished from losers.

## Hierarchy

Playing is not merely for relaxation: it enables the puppy to test his dominance and submission attitudes. Is he giving his paw, lying down on his back, spreading his hind legs? He's defeated. Seated, to show he wants peace, he accepts his position as underling. That's how hierarchy is established among young dogs. This is a magic attitude: to make himself understood, the dog will turn to it over and over again during his lifetime. At the end of the social adaptation period, the puppy's social position is still not entirely stable in the hierarchy, but at very least he knows what he has to do to rank himself in one category or the other. So now he has completed one great stride in his life in the pack.

## Sexuality

Play is also a lot of sensations: the first signs of sexual activity are already appearing, perceptible in particular in the male. Through play arousal occurs. Between the fourth and seventh week, pelvic area movement becomes increasingly frequent.

## EDUCATION BY THE MOTHER
### (as of 4 weeks)

The puppy's physiological maturing causes events to occur. Thus cutting the milk teeth is followed by biting.

### Cleanliness

Until the puppy is four weeks old, the mother continues cleaning his anal-genital area. The baby lifts his rear leg, slaps his tail, licks his dam's lips and still begs for food regurgitated by the mother. But this habit is going to cease: the bitch, little by little, stops stimulating her baby's anus before defecation and urination, considering him big enough to manage on his own. Actually the puppy does now have the advantage of better sphincter control. It's up to him to become clean. So he leaves his nest, all alone, and heads for the chosen place for depositing his soil, at a sufficient distance from the basket.

### Biting Inhibited

The bitch has not yet stopped intervening: if she did not keep order, debauchery would reign. The pup goes too far: he keeps on tugging at her nipples even when they are empty. To stop him, his mother shoves him roughly with her jaw. If he cries, she puts a stop to his shrill whining by licking him. But if he does it again, she gets angry. By this time the milk teeth have all been cut: they are very pointed and can tear flesh. Now the little carnivore is trying to nibble on his siblings. There's sniveling and whining in the litter. The mother dog reacts at once, grabs the culprit by the scruff of the neck and forces him to let go. End of incident.

**A puppy who wears a ribbon around his neck from the time he is 4 weeks old will get used to a leash more easily.**

*Opening of "war games" for these two Old English Sheepdogs, who start by having a roll on the grass. Playing is not mere relaxation: it permits development of the senses and physical faculties, but also teaches how to communicate.*

**The 5-week-old pup no longer soils his nest and can be cleanliness-trained.**

 **The 25-day-old puppy needs an ambient temperature of 64 to 68°F (18 to 20°C) as soon as preweaning begins.**

**The 3- to 4-week-old puppy must be in contact with his own kind to avoid strictly human imprinting.**

## Milk Teeth

During the third and fourth weeks, six incisors appear, as well as the third and fourth premolars on each jawbone. The second premolar comes through between the 28th and 33rd day. From the 52nd, sometimes as late as the 100th day, the puppy has a full set of milk teeth. And, boy, can he bite!

# Weaning Time

The time of endless feedings is drawing to a close. At night, the young dog still has the reflex for drinking from the nipple, but now he has to learn to eat like a grown-up. This transitory phase is uncomfortable and tricky for everybody: for the mother, for her offspring, and even for the master. All goes well if the puppy has already developed a taste for little pieces of meat. At seven weeks, he finally abandons the maternal nipple and goes to his feeding dish five times a day.

*Between the fifth and seventh week, puppies discover meals in a feeding dish. The master must then be careful to suit rations and foodstuffs to breed. These Old English Sheepdogs certainly do not have the same needs as a Bichon.*

*Staying with his mother is no solution for this English Bulldog. In any case, after the fifth week, the milk is no longer enough to feed the litter.*

## DIFFICULT BEGINNINGS...
### For the Mother

This time, the infant has exceeded the limits. He is sucking on udders containing no milk, pulling on the empty nipples, being stubborn. Between the third and fifth week, milk flowed in abundance, but after this time, the lacteal supply system weakened. The exhausted mother gets annoyed. She is out of patience with her greedy pup. She pushes him away, gets up in the middle of a feeding session. Isn't her baby old enough now to lap from his dish?

To keep on nursing would be unwise in any case. Milk is no longer nutritious enough for the nursling, whose growth would be delayed, and the mother dog, too much weakened, would be in danger of falling ill. It is therefore necessary to hasten the drying-up process and reduce the female dog's food ration. The way to start is by making her fast for a day. Before she resumes her usual maintenance diet, her food will be distributed as follows: one-fourth the amount the first day, half the next, one-third on the third and fourth days, one whole portion the fifth day. Resumption thus proceeds gently and this process increases the chances of avoiding the risks of contagion, mammary congestion, and mammitis. Six weeks after the birth of the babies, the nursing mother is almost free again. She takes care of night service only. When her offspring reaches the age of seven weeks, she has all her time to devote to her life as a dog.

### For the Puppy

The noise he makes yapping isn't over yet! This din will last until he has forgotten the taste of the nipple. Frustrated because he cannot suck any more, cannot enjoy the delicious magic potion, so soft and sweet, the nursling is under stress. This is also the age at which the spirit of competition takes hold in the litter: the stronger ones crush and push away those less vigorous. Expelled from the clan, the unlucky ones may not be able to master the situation. Weaning is indeed the period at which mortality is greatest. However, the situation can be reversed to the young dog's advantage: if he has been made familiar with preweaning since 2 or 3 weeks of age, it will be easier for him to switch from milky gruels to small-grained dry foods or ground meat.

### For the Master

Whose side do you take? That of the puppy clinging to his mother, or that of the exhausted bitch who no longer wants to feed her litter? You are still unable to decide, but separation between the nurse and the starvelings must be promoted. It is necessary: the health of both mother and babies is at stake. Also at stake is the physical and mental development of the young dog, whose destiny is to grow up like any other baby animal.

### What's to Be Done?

The puppy must be encouraged to eat solid foods, even if his appetite is very small. For that, you pull him gently towards you, and level with his muzzle, you hold up your index finger which has been dipped into his feeding dish. Licking the master's finger is reassuring. After thickened milk, the little dog that has had three weeks of complementary feeding discovers other tastes: that of meat cut into small pieces, dry foods in small granules. Moreover, this method allows

*With encouragement from his young mistress, this little 7-week-old German Shepherd has made a brilliant transition from the nipple to the food dish. He must gradually be incited to discover new tastes so that soon he will be having five meals of this type every day.*

the puppy to "taste" the human hand. Thus he will be confirmed in his idea that man is a friend and his social adaptation will be all the better for it.

Gradually everything does get done: after one single meal of this type, scheduled in between traditional suckling sessions, the puppy goes on to two, three, four, and then five meals of this type every day. It can then be said that the mission has been accomplished. Baby pup no longer needs mother's milk. He even needs to give it up completely, because he is losing his ability to digest lactose. On his menu, a mixture of lean meat (veal or beef), green vegetables, carrots; and cereals can be

**Right in the middle of the weaning period, the puppy runs the risk of getting parvovirosis. Vomiting and especially diarrhea, often hemorrhagic, are the clinical signs of this very contagious and fatal disease.**

**Vaccinations against canine distemper and parvovirus should be initiated in a puppy at 6–8 weeks of age.**

*An indoor bed or basket, it doesn't matter which, so long as the place is soft and comfortable: the puppy will soon adopt it. A bowl for his meals, another one with fresh water always available for him. The only other things that need to be found are a few toys to complete the gear of a young puppy just leaving his mother and his brothers and sisters.*

planned, mixed together with two drops of vitaminized calcium and some bone meal.

At five weeks, the nursling's appetite increases. The ration needs to be larger and more consistent. The distribution of meals is done according to the type of foods chosen: four meals a day, served every 6 hours if they consist of gruels or reconstituted milk; three meals a day if the puppy is being offered solid foods; finally, night and day, he must have dry foods constantly available.

Acquiring a taste for good things, the puppy shows he's a good trencherman. Watch out for overdoing it! He can turn into a ball of fat. His diet is sometimes prescribed down to the last fraction of an once by the veterinarian, at the time of the purchase examination. Feeding is indeed a matter of precision: it differs in proportions according to breeds of puppy. They do not all grow at the same rate, nor show the same avidity, the same precocity. A Husky, for instance, is much handier at swallowing biscuits than a Shih Tzu is. To take care of

such difficulties, there is a choice of various weaning foods commercially available: gruels, granules, biscuits. These products, developed for a specific period in puppy feeding, have a dual advantage: they are practical and appropriate for his body and needs.

At 6 weeks, the puppy is big enough to eat by himself and has a meal every 4 hours. "Self-service" may help him regulate his appetite all by himself, but he must be supervised, because at that age the intrepid little creature will ingest anything he finds (this craving is known as pica): buttons, bits of string, pebbles. He is capable of eating twice as many of them if he has the slightest alimentary deficiency; sometimes, affected by coprophagia, he will eat his own excrement the way a rabbit will. Don't let him get into any bad habits! By the seventh week, the young dog is eating four times a day. His menus can be composed of 25% cooked rice or oat flakes, 25% cooked vegetables, and 50% finely chopped raw meat or, as most veterinarians would recommend, a high-quality commercial puppy ration. He can also be offered boneless fish, or, occasionally, a little cheese.

## His Gear

As soon as he is no longer attached to the nipple, the puppy must have his own dish. It doesn't matter whether it's made of metal or plastic, with or without decorations. The main thing is that he get to recognize it as his property. Even while he is still tiny, he absolutely must learn not to eat outside his dish. Since the poisoning caused by rodent bait, particularly, is fatal, this precaution will avoid many a terrible event.

His bowl should preferably be very heavy or set into a frame, because the little scatterbrain will soon have everything overturned if his container is too light.

Lastly, the puppy must have his indoor nest, placed in a corner of the house where he will not be in anyone's way and where he will not be bothered by household traffic. At the beginning, he will be content to explore his little home, soft and round like a maternal abdomen, made comfortable with cushions and rags. Then he will make it his own.

*What can this just-weaned Pinscher still need? Bowl and food dish, nest and basket, everything is there, except a toy. But his young master's plush monkey, stolen away on the sly, will do very nicely. Beware of dangerous substances, however.*

# Toward Autonomy

*The puppy is eating as if there were two of him now. His ogre-sized appetite gives him Herculean strength: he is on the right road. Germs? He is strong enough to fight them off now, and he is just the right age to be vaccinated. For him, everything is going to happen fast, especially if his destiny is to be a working dog. He's ready to leave his mother now.*

*A real dog's life! Raised under the same roof, these two Border Collies may be heading for different horizons.*

## THE END OF WEANING

The young pup has adopted a new rhythm: four times a day he dashes to his food dish. His appetite still hasn't settled down completely, but he knows the pattern: when someone goes toward the kitchen and fills his dish, it's no mystery, it's time to eat. Though he's still tiny, he seems insatiable. Until he has reached 40% of his adult weight, the puppy devours food. His energy needs are twice those of an adult dog. So a little Fox Terrier, both of whose parents weigh about 16.5 lbs. (7.5 kg), displays a voracious appetite until his weight reaches 6.5 lbs. (3 kg), eating twice as much as his parents. His energy needs are 1,240 Kcal per day!

### The First Vaccines

Now that he's grown much less sensitive to bacterial and viral diseases, the puppy is no longer subjected to intense, constant surveillance. This is a good time for vaccination, which will give him long-term protection against diseases. Before this date, vaccines should not, in principle, be administered to the young dog: on the one hand, his low temperature weakens the cellular immunity component; on the other hand, the antibodies distributed by the colostrum ingested on the first day obstruct vaccine-related immunity. This phenomenon concerns all vaccines. It raises the problem of parvovirosis, which affects canines as of the fifth week. What can be done? There is no way to do anything before the pup has reached his seventh week because of the danger of destroying his immune defenses. The first session is thus scheduled for that date, or even sometimes as soon as the sixth week— it all depends on the vaccines. But for all that, will the young dog escape canine distemper, infectious hepatitis, parvovirosis, and rabies? He will not be really immunized until after administration of a booster, planned for 3–4 weeks after the initial immunization (see page 148).

## READY TO SEEK A MASTER

When the puppy is destined to perform a heavy task such as hunting, sledding, tracking, or guiding the blind, the merry creature has no time to waste: at 7 weeks, he is cut out for work, stronger than a pet puppy (who needs 5 more weeks before fleeing the home of his birth), perfectly weaned, able to leave his mother, brothers, and sisters. He's a speedy fellow, with a fine future ahead of him.

But the master still needs to pick the lucky number! To be certain of acquiring a puppy endowed with the right qualities, starting with sociable behavior, his attitude toward human beings, he can be given the Campbell test, named for a well-known American ethologist. Five short examinations (the last three take no longer than 30 seconds) allow the puppy to be evaluated successively for his social attractiveness, for his ability to follow a human being, for restraint, for social dominance in two different positions. A veritable radiographic record of canine qualities.

| BREED | Energy needs Kcal/day | Weight to reach in lbs. (kg) | Adult weight in lbs. (kg) |
|---|---|---|---|
| Chihuahua | 200 | 0.9 (0.4) | 2 (1) |
| Yorkshire | 525 | 2.6 (1.2) | 6 (3) |
| Dachshund | 825 | 4.4 (2) | 11 (5) |
| Pug | 1,110 | 6.2 (2.8) | 15 (7) |
| Bulldog | 1,650 | 9.7 (4.4) | 24 (11) |
| Cocker | 1,780 | 10.5 (4.8) | 26 (12) |
| Britanny Spaniel | 2,170 | 13 (6) | 33 (15) |
| Standard Schnauzer | 2,545 | 16 (7.2) | 40 (18) |
| Collie | 3,400 | 22 (10) | 55 (25) |
| Beauce Shepherd | 4,000 | 26 (12) | 65 (30) |
| Boxer | 4,570 | 30 (14) | 75 (35) |
| Greyhound | 5,140 | 35 (16) | 90 (40) |
| German Mastiff | 6,800 | 48 (22) | 120 (55) |
| Saint Bernard | 7,880 | 57 (26) | 145 (65) |

**DAILY POST-WEANING MAINTENANCE RATION FOR PUPPIES ***

* Until they have reached **40%** of their adult weight.

*This Barbet [a spaniel] seems to have no defects or faults. But on the merest diagnosis of suspicion of any redhibitory disease or defect, a suit for annulment of sale may be brought.*

## The Purchase Examination

Acquisition of a puppy must be immediately followed by the purchase examination at the vet's. Treatments against worms and parasites are prescribed there. Auscultation is all the more important in that the practitioner, as he checks the state of his patient's health, confirms that the young dog is not suffering from any diseases. As soon as a diagnosis of suspicion is established, if it concerns a redhibitory illness, the sale can be annulled with the vendor. But the animal doctor is not a seer: he is not in a position to give a diagnosis when the patient is incubating parvovirosis or distemper. So long as the illness has not been revealed, so long as the animal is not showing any symptoms, nothing can be said!

## Redhibitory Defects

Discovered and observed by a veterinarian, redhibitory defects may permit the master, to demand his rights. But action needs to be taken very quickly. The redhibitory period being 30 days, time is short if the incubation period of these diseases is taken into account: 8 days for distemper, 6 days for infectious hepatitus, 5 days for parvovirosis. Only retinal atrophy may be detected earlier. As for coxofemoral dysplasia, or deformation of the hip, it is visible only at 6 months, as is testicular ectopy. But though reimbursement of the puppy's purchase cost may be secured from the vendor, there is still the emotional experience of losing a little friend.

## Hidden Defects

Hidden defects are defects, which are definitely present in the puppy, that escape the buyer's eye. Just like the redhibitory defects, the hidden defect may allow action for annulment of sale. After the vet's expert examination, there is a choice between two solutions: request for annulment of the sale, giving reimbursement of costs and return of the young animal to the breeder, or partial reimbursement of acquisition costs, in exchange for which the buyer keeps his little companion. The latter option is a joy to children, certainly, but it's a bitter pill when the little dog is not what you expected he would be.

*Thanks to the Campbell test, the young dog's character can be evaluated. This Dalmation ready to follow his new master is sure to make an obedient companion.*

**The "puppy, has had shots" as the ads often read. This includes the two necessary injections against the most widespread diseases: canine distemper, infectious hepatitis, lepospirosis, rabies, and parvovirosis.**

## Looking-glass Game

Looking at a mirror, the puppy reveals his own inner portrait. He's the nicest creature imaginable if he backs off and if he comes forward with his ears pricked up; still and tense, there's a well-balanced, confident, bold puppy; if he growls, with his head turned aside, he's unstable and unsociable.

## First-day Mishaps

His first journey completed, punctuated by whining and weeping, the little companion arrives home with misgivings. He makes a puddle? Too bad. He throws up? Not a word! Any reproach would be traumatizing, grumbling would turn him into a sniveler. The first night, if he keeps on weeping, you just have to harden your heart. He's not in such bad shape, outside the bedroom door in his basket! The next day, order is restored. Baby pup feels at home and sleeps the sleep of the just.

## THE CAMPBELL TEST

Reactions to the Campbell test reveal the young dog's future behavior. The exercise must be done in a quiet place. Four or five different attitudes are expected for each of the five examinations. The results considered as a whole give an accurate idea of the young animal's personality.

The first effort is to find out what degree of social sense, trust, and independence he has. To do so, you kneel down, clapping your hands. What does the young puppy do?

(A) He comes jumping toward you with his tail held high, and nibbles your hands.

(B) He arrives with his tail high, prancing, watching your hands.

(C) He comes to you, but keeps his tail down.

(D) He comes hesitantly.

(E) He stays where he is.

Next you try to find out whether the puppy is capable of following you. To do so, you stand close to him and then move away a few steps. What does he do?

(A) He follows you spontaneously, tail up, and tries to nibble your feet.

(B) He follows you easily, tail high, and keeps up.

(C) He follows you easily, but keeps his tail down.

(D) He does not move, or else if he does come toward you, he keeps his distance.

The third test consists of evaluating possibilities of restraint in the puppy. You make him lie down on his back and you place one hand on his chest. How does he react?

*Two of them going to the same master:*
*these Pyrenean Mountain dogs have no*
*idea how lucky they are! It's a fact that*
*it's not always easy to take two dogs into*
*the home, but still, it is an ideal solution.*

(A) He struggles vigorously, flounders about and bites.

(B) He struggles hard, fights like a fiend, but refrains from biting.

(C) He struggles for a while, then gives up.

(D) He doesn't move a hair and tolerates the pressure of the hand.

The puppy's level of social dominance remains to be tested. You lay him flat on his abdomen, and stroke his head, neck, and back. What effect does that have on him?

(A) He jumps up, prances or scratches, bites, growls.

(B) He jumps up and prances, but does not growl at all.

(C) He moves so he can lick your hands.

(D) He turns around to lick your hands.

(E) He doesn't budge.

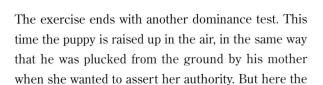

The exercise ends with another dominance test. This time the puppy is raised up in the air, in the same way that he was plucked from the ground by his mother when she wanted to assert her authority. But here the future master lifts the animal, placing his hands under the puppy's abdomen. How will he react?

(A) He struggles like a fiend, bites, growls.

(B) He spins around like a top.

(C) He struggles, then calms down and licks you.

(D) He doesn't budge.

The results are extremely useful: if A's and B's are in the majority, the puppy is a brawler. The profile of an independent emerges behind a puppy who has a lot of B's: you can already imagine him in the fields, in the countryside, but absolutely not in town. A charming, obedient puppy is the one who collects C's! In a studio apartment or in the country, he's the cream of the canine crop. And what of the little one who collects D's? The pup is a sweet little friend—that's the whole picture. But have a care: the company of human beings is indispensable for him. Lastly, the puppy with a majority of E's is timorous. His master needs to be very good at psychology. In any case, whatever the side the puppy ends up on, you must pet the little dog and compliment him at the end of the test, and take him back to his mother.

# The Critical Age

*Backsliding: the puppy seemed to have made a good start, and now everything seems to scare him. This is the moment if ever to take him by the paw and guide him. Then, much more sure of himself, the young dog has acquired one certainty: human beings are his friends. Soon left to his own devices, distanced forever from his mother, he has to learn some paradoxical things: to plunge into the crowd to become sociable, while learning about solitude through necessity.*

*In midcourse, every young puppy goes through a touchy period. He quickly becomes frightened if his master is not there to reassure and encourage him.*

*Fear, which sets in during the eighth week, may be poorly handled by the puppy. Every event takes on an exaggerated importance, so the example of his mother and the presence of his master are particularly important at that time.*

## APPEARANCE OF FEAR
### (eighth week)

This is not the first anxiety the little dog has encountered, but until now it used to slide off like water from a duck's back, thanks to his mother's reassurance. At eight weeks, a change occurs in the puppy's mind: he is afraid. This is a normal feeling: in a natural setting it produces the survival instinct and enables the dog to escape from danger through a series of reflexes. This fear may be badly handled by the puppy: each event then takes on a disproportionate importance and becomes a veritable nightmare. As it happens, the young animal is very vulnerable at this time. Everything becomes imprinted in his psyche, and the imprint left behind by fear may diminish his attachment to human beings. Between him and his master, barriers may arise, especially if the puppy is affected by some hereditary fear. At this precise moment, every young canine needs to be helped to get through the tunnel.

### Getting Around the Obstacle
#### The Mother's Example

The way you need to go is difficult, but to avoid deviations, the puppy has a fair number of sources of protection, starting with his dam. She faces the unknown without flinching, hears thunderclaps without whimpering. The Mother Courage image is ideal for the young dog: he frames his attitude on that model and will have no trouble overcoming the most unexpected events with bravura. Conversely, however, if our born imitator has before his eyes the sight of a traumatized mother, he will be stressed, anguished, terrorized, and the road to perfect sociability will be strewn with obstacles.

## Benefit of the Setting

There's strength in unity, and solidarity emboldens cowards. It is in company with his brothers and sisters that the puppy gains self-confidence. The setting and the environment are also guarantees of success. Is the young dog growing up among sounds, smells, sensations, and motions that develop the senses? This subtle blend constitutes a firm basis from which he will draw his strength and his autonomy. A varied existence, which is entertaining to him and draws him out of his fear, constitutes the best protection. But the company of living beings, both animal and human, remains an essential component. Alone the young puppy is subjected full blast to fear, which takes hold of him like an obsession. During this period of discomfort, it is also best to avoid sudden changes: do people realize that the arrival of a baby in the house, at the time when the puppy reaches his eighth week, will turn him into a scared puppy? It is easy to see why placement in a kennel or bringing in another dog are definitely not recommended at this time.

## The Miracle of Education

Taken in hand by the breeder, the puppy will not take long to get rid of his panicky fear. The use of psychology is absolutely necessary. Raising the voice is to be avoided: it would be ill-advised to chide the little scrap of a dog still all at sea in our world. Any violent gestures—noises, hitting with a strap, shaking by the scruff of the neck—are more than ever to be banished. No sending into isolation either, as a way of punishing misbehavior. Indulgence is a necessity: how would the young dog, feeling ill at ease, deal with a lack of understanding in a friendly species?

## Serenity Above All

As fragile as he is, the puppy will soon be himself again provided that he has the benefit of a peaceful life. There are scores of incidents to avoid: the noise of dishes breaking, motorcycles backfiring, fireworks crackling which may haunt him for the rest of his life. If he is hurt in an accident, he will forever be pursued

*Beware of reprimands! At 8 and 9 weeks, this little Akita Inu could not deal with threatening gestures.*

by a fear of cars. Behavioral disturbances, a timorous attitude, the eight-week-old puppy's unfortunate experiences have some vicious results, as if, even this early, his life as a dog were something of a failure.

## COMMUNICATION IN DANGER

The state of torpor into which the puppy is plunged imprisons him in a sealed world. Petrified, tetanized, he is shut off from the outside world. At the slightest call, he is on the defensive and little by little his profound obsession is transformed into aggressiveness toward human beings. He should go toward his master, but he recoils, frightened, and gets into attack position. He seems to have lost the socialization code. The human universe is inaccessible to him and communication has broken down.

### Mistakes to Avoid

There is a way, however, to save the puppy from the abyss, if both vigilance and tolerance are used. Let's avoid clumsy mistakes! Our gestures have a meaning in canine language. Shame on anyone who overcome by anger grabs the guilty party by the scruff of the neck and shakes him like a nut tree by way of reprimand. In

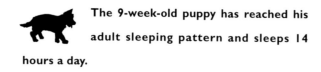 The 9-week-old puppy has reached his adult sleeping pattern and sleeps 14 hours a day.

# The Language of Stroking

Fondness, affection, happiness, . . . strokes need no words, but they do have their own language. Great understanding can be built up between master and puppy, because the latter is capable of interpreting every one of the strokes according to the place chosen for it on his body. On the lower body there is no more boss. But if he is stroked on the upper body, the puppy knows, on the contrary, that he had better behave himself. A stroke on the head: it's the master giving orders. That's how it's done among dogs: the dominant pack-member places his paw on the head of his vassal to emphasize his hierarchical position. Is the dog of a submissive temperament? In that case, he considers this gesture as a mark of benevolence. But the stroke is not always evaluated in that way: if the puppy is independent, it will cause him extreme annoyance. With such a sting to his pride, a rebel sets sail: it is hard to be relegated to the bottom of the ladder when you think you are doing the steering. The dog does not take the huff in the same way if he is stroked on his back. Of course, this is a sign of domination, but an invitation to play as well, and as such accepted without a fuss by our little joker. A caress on the flank is unambiguous. It's a sign of kindness, that's all. Don't dogs rub up against each other when they meet? Stroked on the neck and chin, the puppy stretches his neck out and asks for more caresses. For him, this caress is worth all the money in the world: it's a sign of friendship that is more important to him than anything else there is. This is where his mother administers licks and pushes with her head, and the blissful pup adores being loved like one's own child.

On his chest, and the puppy is happy! Motionless, like a statue, all he wants is one thing: that it continue for ever. It's in this position that he will later on be found in romantic company... . Lastly, to reward your dog, there's nothing like a rub on the abdomen. This is proof of deep attachment, and also a very effective way of reassuring him when he's afraid.

the little dog's mind, the punishment is received not as a warning but as a death threat. A frequently committed mistake is looking the little scoundrel right in the eyes to instill confidence and frankness, as happens among human beings. But the puppy very well knows that people are displeased with his behavior, and once again, he feels threatened. This is how errors pile up and the puppy, far from meeting our expectations, ends up showing some very strange behaviors. There are plenty of reasons for him to feel disorientated: what does he make of it when, to invite him to come and play, we grab him by the front paws and place them on our shoulders? We have just given him the idea that he is the boss, and there he is, delighted at getting his stripes. Except that a few seconds later we stroke him to remind him that all he needs to do is obey, and everything gets foggy. All these inconsistent attitudes confuse him.

## Stroking with Understanding

Showing affection is not limited to rubbing a hand over the puppy's body. Stroking carries a message with it. In the mind of the little dog, we are not giving the same message when we stroke his head as when we stroke his flanks. By watching dogs using this channel of communication among themselves, which consists of rubs and light touches, you can understand perfectly the subtle differences in their "talk." They do not have the same intentions when they rub against a chest and when they lightly brush the top of a head. So we need to be understanding and place ourselves within the young canine's scope. When he comes looking for strokes and lies down on his back, it is appropriate to approve his attitude. By performing this act of allegiance to his master, he is meeting the image we expect of him. Isn't he becoming a model little dog?

## Listening to the Young Dog

As of right now, an attentive ear should be given to the puppy's language. Certainly, at an early age, the vocalization patterns—there are eight to twelve of them—do not have any precise meaning. But they are varied if dialogue with the master exists. A puppy barking into a void, with no response, with no echo, reduces his repertoire. The young dog also has his own body language. His ears can tell you a lot. Just by their shape and the way they are held, which differ from one breed to another, though you can't make head or tail of that. Like rose petals in the Whippet, heart-shaped in the Pekingese, spoon-shaped in the Netherlands Shepherd, like filberts in the Bedlington...Standing straight up like those of the wolf, the coyote, or the jackal, half-drooping or low. What a panoply! In some puppies, they even are just plain non-existent due to ear cropping. In that case, language is reduced to its simplest expression.

## INDEPENDENCE
### (tenth week)

He's a big boy now. He exudes self-confidence and determination. But the young dog is aware of one thing: it is the human being, his "master-dog" that he must obey. As in the pack, he gives his respect to a single member, the dominant one, and is ready to take orders. What is his pleasure? To please his master and obey him, for he trusts the human being blindly. But it doesn't take much to upset him: if he is given an unclear order everything gets confused in his little doggy mind. He becomes unstable and loses his bearings. However genuine it may be, the puppy's social adaptation is not really stable. And from now on, it depends solely on the human being.

### Getting Used to Being Alone

Now he has to prepare for the vicissitudes of living with us, starting with his master's absence. Perhaps he will have to wait long hours at home, on workdays. Let's face it, that's nothing like joyous life in the pack, where the dog communicates by signs and runs in a group. How can the stress of solitude be imposed on him without making him suffer? By accustoming him from an early age, even before he is finally separated from his brothers and sisters, to the absence of his little family. That is the job of a good breeder: he chooses a time when the puppy is tired with his day's activities, almost falling asleep, and he puts him in a

*Genuine social adaptation for this Cairn Terrier: at 10 weeks, a young dog knows that it owes obedience to a human being.*

**Solitude does not exist for the puppy lucky enough to be in the company either of an adult dog who acts as a model for him, or of a cat who adapts to his situation and makes him feel secure. In their absence, he can be helped to tolerate this condition by being given a chewing toy on which he can sharpen his fangs. Another distraction: play him a recording of "his master's voice."**

*Stairway treads, elevators, street noises: learning about life involves new experiences for this Hungarian Hound, as for any young dog.*

room all by himself. No need to prolong the trial! One minute is enough. The total silence brings anguish; then, in a perfectly ordinary way, the breeder goes to meet the forsaken creature, without getting sad about what happened to him, and strokes him. The next day he repeats the operation without increasing the amount of time in isolation, for apprehension is still just as intense in the young dog. The point is not to turn the trial into torture: a puppy that hates the darkness must always have a little light in the room.

As the days pass, solitude is more strictly imposed on him: the breeder dresses to go out, closes the door behind him, leaving the young animal alone for about ten minutes. Without a single compassionate word, he goes back to the puppy to say that it's time for a walk. Little by little, the puppy accepts these absences.

Success is related to certain principles: no tears and no affectionate outpourings on leaving, no festivities upon returning. Stroking and caressing are scheduled for a few minutes later, and don't forget the morning and evening outings.

### Knowing About the Environment

Conversely, the puppy has to adapt to our noisy, busy world. He absolutely must mix with others, hear unfamiliar voices, ride in the car, go for walks outside the yard. Engine noises, auto horns, all this racket makes him feel like joining in. Later, it will all seem ordinary to him. The sooner he is plunged into the uproar that makes up his environment, the better he gets used to his new lifestyle. You no longer see him changing into a statue of salt at the sight of a Mastiff, nor seizing some mongrel by the throat. In town as in the country, he feels at ease, and he can live anywhere.

### Halfway Through Growth

Things move very fast: the puppy, if he belongs to a small-statured breed, is already half-grown. At 3 months, a miniature Spitz [Pomeranian] weighs 4 lbs. (1.8 kg) and will soon reach the 5.5 lbs. (2.5 kg) adult weight, a Pekingese is at 5.5 lbs. (2.5 kg), exactly half the adult weight, a Dachshund weighs 8 lbs. (3.7 kg) compared to the 15–18 ultimate pounds (7–8 ultimate kilos), a Scottish Terrier, whose adult weight is 20 lbs. (9 kg), weighs 9 lbs. (4 kg). Small-statured puppies have a very short growth phase compared to the large breeds. The German Shepherd or the Labrador will not reach this stage until they are at least 5 months old. After this growth period comes the slow phase. No question of being ravenously hungry: more than ever, food is rationed.

*Days are less gloomy, the absence of the master is less hard to take, when cat and dog share their solitude. Some very sociable breeds turn out to be cat lovers, like this Shar Pei with this Chartreux in their matching coats.*

# A Puppy to Bring Up

*The puppy has left the maternal nest for a new home. For him, nothing is the way it used to be: he still seeks the smell and warmth of his mother, he can't hear his brothers' and sisters' shrill barking any more... Here, the noises are strange and scary. But if he is warmly welcomed, things will all be better tomorrow. It will be time to start teaching him good manners.*

*Don't be taken in by this English Bulldog's redoubtable appearance. Behind this descendent of fighting dogs there hides a rather good-natured couch-lover. He makes a patient and obedient companion.*

*It's best to put a washable cushion in the basket, until these King Charles Cavaliers learn to be clean.*

To instill confidence in the puppy as soon as he arrives, a wind-up clock and a hot-water bottle are placed in his basket: the ticking and the warmth suggest a heart beating and his mother's presence.

## The Hurricane

After a day of adjustment, the timid little creature recovers his spirits. You find out that he's both boisterous and as clumsy as a bull in a china shop. Nothing in the house is spared. Before the hurricane passes through, it's best to clear sideboards, remove statuettes and figurines, and put crystal dishes and glasses away in the cupboard. With one leap or a swipe of his tail, the clumsy animal could knock everything flying.

## A WARM WELCOME

Lost on this new planet, our pup is overwhelmed. He doesn't move, he looks sad. With gentleness and patience, he has to be gradually accustomed to his environment. How should that be approached?

Nice and calm in our arms, he observes the world around him. To help him find out about the premises, he is then taken into each room in the house and familiarizes himself with its odors. He is already being shown the boundaries of his territory: he needs to learn that some places are off-limits to him. For that, his habitat must be clearly defined: a corner for sleeping, a corner for relieving himself, a corner for playing.

The first few days, he will be best off in the kitchen: the good smells and the activity taking place there appeal to his senses and capture his attention. In addition, the kitchen floor, easier to clean than hardwood floors or wall-to-wall carpeting, is perfectly suitable for our dirty little friend. It is best to avoid his getting into the bedrooms: if he sleeps near his master, he'll soon be taking himself for a top dog. The ideal is to place his basket in the hallway, near the door, so that he knows he's not all alone; a bit later in the day, his bed can be moved nearer to his master's office or workshop. Thus, in his mind, his "bed corner" will be associated with a comfortable refuge.

## HIS GEAR

It consists of the puppy's personal effects, the things that will belong to him and will be indispensable for each activity.

### For Eating

His food dish is the only container from which he dines. It is a principle of training which will avoid problems for him (including poisoning). Deep and stable enough, the dog dish is equipped on the reverse with a nonslip rubber ring which allows perfect adherence to the floor. Nothing is more annoying for a starving young dog than a plate that jiggles! The bowl, in plastic or metal, is heavy enough that he cannot push it right or left or overturn it. In the best examples, it has a wide opening in the middle of the lid; the anti-splash bowl, set on a plastic-coated mat, is very practical: a wipe with a sponge is all it takes to clean up spills.

## For Sleeping

Made of wicker and padded fabric, printed or otherwise, the basket insures that the little dog will be comfortable. It is best to protect it with a washable cushion until the puppy has been house-trained. This "nest" should also be large enough so that its occupant can still use it as an adult.

## For Relieving Nature

Specially designed puppy mats are commercially available. Made of cellulose fiber, they are capable of very great absorbency. The plastic-coated underside makes it possible to protect floors. But this is a temporary solution only: it is best to teach the little dog very early to relieve himself outside the house.

## For Grooming

Brush and comb will soon become familiar tools to our appearance-conscious friend, just like the toothbrush and the nail clipper.

## For Playing

He needs toys he can bite. These hard or soft objects not only save your table legs, they also help develop his fangs. Tennis balls, bones treated with fluorine or made of hide, furry monsters or ones that make noises...there are lots to choose from.

## For Growing Up Happy

A doghouse is a haven of peace for the puppy: two houses make his happiness complete.

The indoor house is his home, his cabin, his ivory tower, where he makes his little world. This is what the experts call his "isolation area." Reminiscent of the maternal abdomen, this cozy retreat must be the same length as the adult dog in his lying down position, but

*At first, the doghouse seems huge, but the little spaniel will grow up and will be very glad to be sheltered from the rain and the wind.*

no longer, so that it envelops the little canine when he's missing his mother, and avoids heat loss. A comfortable material, sufficiently soft, is much more suitable than a fabric that matches the living room drapes. In the shops you can find charming folding houses strengthened with foam, with a roof attached by press-studs. Inside, a cushion with flaps invites the young dog into *la dolce vita*.

But if you are a good do-it-yourselfer, you can make this little house at home. A cardboard box with cotton batting or an old quilt will do and allows for a little luxury: we can give our pet a nest on each floor of the house. With a daytime retreat and a nighttime dormitory, the puppy has everything he can possibly need, and has no desire to invade the master's bedroom.

An outside doghouse, located in a corner of the yard, near the gate or along the side of the house, is indispensable for a future guard dog. He needs to have an all-season shelter, to protect him from drafts, windstorms, thunderstorms, and heatwaves. The perfectly watertight doghouse must be raised 4 in. (10 cm) above the ground. It is covered with a roof that overhangs its sides to let rainwater drain off. Built of wood (fir, pine, or cedar) it is insulated with fiberglass.

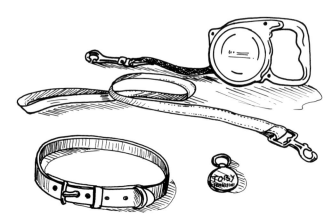

*Collar, ID tag, and leash—the perfect gear for a civilized young dog.*

The floor is covered with straw, which is replaced as needed in the interests of hygiene. Turned away from the direction of the dominant winds and drafts, the doghouse is protected by a thick curtain secured over the doorway.

### For Enjoying the Fresh Air

Thanks to the collar and leash set, the little lout is going to become a civilized dog. This linkage enables the master to communicate what he wants. So it is best to delay using the retractable leash, which does not transmit impulses. Select instead a 6-foot (2-meter) leather leash secured to the collar. When fitting a collar, be sure it is not too tight; you should be able to slip 2 fingers between it and pup's neck with ease. It's not a bad idea to add a disc engraved with the puppy's name and his master's address, in addition to having a tattoo: two precautions are better than one if a day should come when the puppy gets lost.

### For Going Visiting

Collars decorated with a bow tie, black velvet for evening and tartan for town, or washable braided polyamide for every day...there are endless possibilities for smart doggy dressing. But the essential thing is a woolen garment, if your puppy is fragile or of small breed. A sweater, a raincoat, a jacket, booties—there is a whole range of clothing for dogs.

### For Traveling

A pet carrying bag is essential for the purchase inspection trip to the vet's. It allows the scared pup to retreat into his shell. Indispensable for any journeys by bus, train, or car, it is made of plastic or leather, with or without a peephole.

## THE EDUCATION PROGRAM

Learning is the puppy's prime task. It begins very early, under the authority of his mother, who teaches him to be clean, orders him to be silent when he raises his voice, and forces him to obey. Whether he is 7 weeks old or 12 when he enters his master's house, the puppy is able to receive the basics of education. Value does not wait upon years for a model little dog.

At the human being's school, the program will become more stringent and more substantial. In it the young dog will learn the principles of cohabitation with human beings and prepare for the exam for entry into social life. Firmness and seriousness are essential for the person who succeeds the mother dog and assumes the schoolteacher job. Uncompromising, he never gives in: in order to avoid upsetting the little student, he maintains a consistently logical attitude.

### Giving Him a Name

Even before starting the program, the master begins by teaching the puppy to respond to his name. It is best to choose a short, monosyllabic name that cracks like a flag in the wind: the puppy will be able to respond to it right away.

The dog can also be named for something about his looks, size, and personality. This pretty name needs to fit him like a glove, because he will have it and hear it throughout his life, every time he has to come and eat, obey, and respond to our calls.

### A Few Principles of Education

A good master must be able to "think like a dog" and put himself in the animal's situation. It must be remembered that dogs reason by association of ideas.

That is an infallible method for making oneself clear to a puppy. For every utterance, word, or intonation there is a corresponding precise gesture that makes sense in one specific situation.

The important thing is to provide a landmark for the young dog and therefore choose a code that will never change.

It matters little whether you speak to him in Hebrew, French, or English! He is not yet receptive to the meanings of words (later on, he'll understand about 40 words), but to sounds. To obey, as also to show his argumentative side, he relies above all on his master's voice, judging for himself whether that voice is firm or too gentle…What he is interested in is the boundaries of the seizure of power.

The only barrier is an order issued with authority, which has nothing to do with the kindly words proffered during a walk. The words "sit," "lie down," and "keep still," accompanied with appropriate gestures, are the keystone of training: immediately, the puppy submits to the master's will and that is how perfect understanding comes to exist between the two friends. Through obedience, the puppy will succeed in blending into the world of human beings.

Another rule to remember: long hours of training cannot be inflicted upon him. The little scrap of a dog does not have great powers of concentration. Rest periods must be frequent, and rehearsals, which promote assimilation, are compulsory.

## Rewards

You also have to know how to give the little dog "good grades." Rewards, also known as positive conditioning, are of the highest importance in his training. Every

*With this rascally little Cocker, there's plenty of work to be done. Don't wait until he's shredded the ladies' skirts to teach him the rules for living in the home. Seriousness and firmness are necessary, otherwise he might try to be master.*

*Scared, this little Collie has lost control. It's best to "call it a wipe" the first time, but deal reasonably severely with any future incidents.*

## Trainer's Minivocabulary

*Conditioning:* also known as Pavlov's reflex. A stimulus sets off a precise response in the puppy. For instance, if he has been struck at the very instant the telephone rings, he will tremble every time he hears it ringing.

*Systematic desensitization:* this procedure, first used in 1958 by Wolpe, is inspired by the method practiced by an allergy specialist: to free his patient of his handicap, the latter is gradually accustomed to the allergens. In the same way,

the puppy is gently brought into contact with the element that sets off the undesirable reactions and the tolerance threshold is pushed farther.

*Immersion:* this technique, also known as implosion or flooding, consists of bringing the puppy unrestrictedly into the phobia-provoking setting. For instance, a puppy that is frightened on the street is supposed to get over his fear by being plunged into a crowd.

time the puppy obeys, brings the ball back, stays quietly beside his master, or refuses the biscuit a stranger tries to give him, he deserves a reward, which will encourage him to repeat his "good behavior."

But what rewards should be given? Should we opt for the pleasures of the stomach? Lumps of sugar lead to dental caries, and cookies, loaded with glucids (and how many little sweeties in a day?) send the puppy along the road to obesity.

Pleasures relating to feelings are better. The puppy expects kind words, and monotonous speeches leave him cold. The reward that goes straight to his heart is disarmingly simple: a flattering expression ("What a good dog!" for instance) and he's in heaven!

The best demonstration of affection is unquestionably a caress, which is the best affirmation of the bonds of friendship. That is what dogs do among themselves, making skin contacts important in strengthening bonds. Just like a kind word spoken in a pleasant tone, a caress must be given with gentleness and sincerity. An automatic, tense gesture does not make the puppy happy: it stresses him.

### Punishments

There is another side to the coin: you also have to know how to reprimand the disobedient friend. Punishment is certainly no picnic, but it is as necessary as the mother dog's reprimands of her offspring were at an early age. She promptly punished her baby, without waiting: that was the secret of her effectiveness. The puppy is a creature of the moment. Thirty seconds after his offense, it is already too late to grumble at him: he's forgotten his misdeeds and cannot make any connection between the act and the reprimand. So it is senseless to admonish him in the evening when much earlier, during the morning, he has torn a velvet cushion apart or broken a crystal vase. Moreover, he will think that the reprimand is connected with his master's return, and that's regrettable.

You don't need to yell: a loud voice, a glare, a finger pointed at him, and "No" spoken with severity are all it takes. This sort of stance is clearly no encouragement to a little wheedler, and the puppy is perfectly capable of perceiving the different shades of meaning. Punishment stops there. There can be no question of smacking your dog. The hand is intended for caressing, isn't it?

One gesture is permitted, however. You pick the little devil up by the scruff of the neck and you hold him up in the air for a few seconds. This is exactly what his mother used to do when he broke the laws of the canine tribe. Being lifted up makes him lose his sense of direction and distances him from the landmarks he has made on the floor. So he begs for pardon and, in more scientific terms, has reached the "homeostatic threshold."

## FAMILY LIFE

The circle grows wider: the young dog is now an integral part of the family. The harmony reigning in the household is an essential condition for the puppy's behavior to be normal. Everyone must use the same method, the same messages. No disagreements, please, on the teaching to be dispensed to him!

### At Home

Once he's settled in his home, the puppy will receive a number of obedience lessons.

### He Is Clean

It only takes 48 hours for the young dog to relieve himself where he is told to do so. Arm yourself with patience for a whole weekend, during which the main subject of concern will be the urgent needs of the little newcomer. There is nothing superhuman about the trial, because being clean is merely a revision for the puppy. His mother has already taught him not to "sign" where he has been by leaving pheromones, substances present in stools and urine, as visiting cards. The site of the "offense" is therefore never his basket: in the wild, a nest so soiled would be too easy for a predator to find. But the pup needs to learn that the entire house must be kept free of his odors. Isn't

*The puppy is gradually accustomed to wearing a collar and walking on a leash. You must stop him pulling and be able to show him who is boss. For his first walk, this King Charles Cavalier seems to be balking. He may just be tired, so it's not a good idea to insist for more than twenty minutes.*

**The cleanup required after each of his "accidents" must not take place with the puppy watching: he would interpret the scene as an invitation to play.**

**The age of puppy cleanliness varies, depending on individuals, from 5 weeks to 4 months.**

## Pee-Pee Stop

To control the puppy's urges, use can be made of an aromatic compound based on essential oils and fatty acids, a reproduction of natural pheromones. These products create an olfactory stimulus that attracts the puppy to the same place every time and speeds his house training.

this the den where he is sheltered from danger? The first day, he will go out many times: as soon as he gets ready to soil the carpet, quick, out he goes. An area is picked out to serve as his "toilet": in town, it will be the gutter, in the country, a field near the house. You encourage him in a quiet voice, saying "Do pee-pee." In a few days' time regularity can be required: early in the morning and late in the evening. Just give him his food and drink at regular times.

But you can't expect him to give you the moon. What can you do when you are gone all day, knowing that he cannot wait for more than 6 consecutive hours? You have to leave him a special mat, line a place with floor cleaning pads, or give him a wooden box lined with newspaper. There is one inconvenience to this method, however: the puppy may permanently associate newspapers with urination, and not hesitate to sprinkle any magazine that may be lying about on the floor. The ideal? Dog toilets, but they are limited to small models.

The house-training lesson needs to be learned quickly. If it isn't, you need to raise your voice and bring the puppy right back to the place he soiled. There's no need to turn to barbaric methods—rubbing his nose in it, for instance. It's better to be crafty and throw a newspaper at his head just when he's soiling the floor. This punishment from the sky will be more effective.

### He "Sits"

This lesson is not too hard because the "sit" position, which is a waiting and observing attitude, is natural to carnivorous animals. To teach the puppy to hold this

position, you say "sit" while pressing lightly on his lower back and lifting his head up. He must keep still, resting on his hind quarters, his body straight, the front feet parallel. He must at all costs be prevented from lying down. Later, the order can be backed up by raising your hand above his head, palm and fingers quite flat, as the order is given. This lesson will teach him to be patient while his meal is being prepared, while waiting on a train station platform, or while you are waiting in line at an ATM.

### He "Stays"

The order is as follows: "Stay!" No motion must be detected in the puppy's position. Once learned, this lesson is very valuable on the street, when traffic signals have to be obeyed and cars avoided. The teaching method is the same as for the "sit" position. You don't take your eyes off your student until he is perfectly still, frozen like a statue. To get perfect results, you have to be categorical.

### He Goes to His Basket

You teach him the words "basket" or "mat," it doesn't matter which, so long as he knows he needs to get back to his place. So when dangerous work is being done, he leaves us alone and is not at risk of having a hammer fall on his head. Another advantage: he is not underfoot when we have visitors. Lastly, this restraint prevents the puppy from demonstrating territorial aggressiveness.

### He Comes When Called

Like being clean and the "sit" function, returning on call is an innate behavior. The puppy returns

*Small as he tries to make himself, this nice little beggar has well and truly done a bad thing. You have to know the right way to reprimand your little friend. Striking him is out of the question: the puppy is quite capable of understanding nuances, and "no!" in a firm tone is sufficient.*

## Nasty Faults

The little newcomer cannot be perfect. If all he did was please himself, he would readily go around breaking things, smashing in the sofa, reducing everything to bits. So he has to be brought under control very quickly, and if in the weeks and months to come, he repeatedly commits acts of vandalism, he'll have to wear a muzzle, just for so long as it takes to correct his nasty fault, like a child wearing a dental prosthesis.

Another bad habit: stealing. Not just dolls, gloves, and dish towels, but the ham out of the kitchen as well. You can't leave a steak on a plate. The sneak thief, when he's caught in the act, is carrying everything off in his ravaging jaws! By having him eat at regular times, a quarter of an hour before everyone else (he must not see us at the table if he eats first) he will be satisfied and be rid of this bad habit. If he persists anyway—nobody achieves perfection overnight—there is still one very effective trick: give him bones and toys made of hide on which he can exercise his teeth.

The puppy may also become a professional barker. He barks when anyone goes out in the yard and as soon as we leave for half an hour. We must not let this troublemaker give tongue in just any situation. He endangers our relations with the neighbors. It's better to provide your howling dog with an antibark collar. The smell of citronella that emanates from it as soon as he abuses his fine voice is so unpleasant to him that it shuts his mouth right up.

Does he bite children, does he chew things? That may happen when he is 3 or 4 months old and his milk teeth are being replaced. To end this sort of misdeed, you need only take inspiration from the bitch, who stops such activity by threatening. Clapping your hands, remembering the basic commands, and putting the naughty dog in the submission position are enough to get him back on the right path. There's no need to punish him: his mother harbored no resentment toward him, but she knew how to make him respect her dominance. It's up to the master to show understanding: around 4 months, aggressiveness increases in the little canine, at a time when the hierarchy between him and his master should be well established.

*The puppy should get used to his future town gear in the yard. Before his first expeditions to the outside world, a light collar is put on him. Then, when he is playing, a length of string is allowed to hang around the collar. Finally he is equipped with a leash that he drags after him, which you pick up from time to time while you run with him. Thus he learns to take direction when running and playing chase games.*

## Dangers in the Home

It is particularly when he is very young and crazy about exploring that the puppy is subject to poisoning. He licks and gnaws anything he finds within reach.

House plants are not exempt. Wisteria blossoms, daffodil, narcissus, iris and tulip bulbs, yew leaves, philodendron stems, ivy, hydrangeas, and lily of the valley cause severe abdominal pain.

The puppy may also have nervous disorders: if he has chewed sweetpeas, rose laurel, rhododendrons, mistletoe, or ivy, he trembles and has convulsions. Beware, too, of sleeping pills that may be left lying about, and household products! Laundry soap, mothballs, and chlorine bleach should be kept in a locked cupboard.

spontaneously to his mother or his brothers and sisters, instinctively obeying the "laws of social attraction." So this training can be given at the very beginning of the educational program.

He is given his first lesson at home: when his meal is ready, you go to meet him, carrying his dish, then you call him by his name, saying it once or twice, followed by the command: "Here!" When he arrives, he is given his meal and rewarded. The same session will take place several days running. Then the time is changed—outside mealtimes—and so is the place, and his attention is attracted if need be with a treat. A guaranteed success. On the other hand, there's no point in calling him if he's concentrating on some activity, because he's deaf to anything around him. If he does hear us and refuses to obey, we use an indirect method as we call his name in a playful voice. We hide, he looks for us, and the trick is played. Total effectiveness is required for this lesson: immediate obedience may save him from a car accident.

### He Has Good Table Manners

However sweetly he looks at you when you are at the table, you must not give in: the puppy must not beg. It's better to spare him temptation by having him eat quietly before we do. Does he have his meals in the same room as the rest of the family? If so, there must of necessity be a break between his supper and the family dinner... because the little thing has a good memory. It probably reminds him of the manners in force within the pack: the dominant dog is served first, while the others wait until he has finished to feed themselves. The young dog would soon get the idea that he's a top dog!

### He Wears a Collar and Leash

It would be tactless to put a rope around his neck as soon as he arrives in the home. It's best to wait until he's become familiar with his new environment, has set up some landmarks, and feels quite at home in the new setting. After 4 or 5 days of adapting, while the bonds of trust between him and his master are growing firm, he is ready to slip on his neckwear.

Any choke collar with sharp points is to be prohibited! This equipment is used only by trainers who have decided to correct a bad student. Just choose a collar that can be adjusted for his size.

## He Is Good with Children

A big fuss is made of the puppy when he arrives at a house. That makes him feel like laying down the law. When he plays with the children, who remind him of the puppies in his litter, he tries to gain ground. One day he nibbles, and maybe will even go so far as to bite and threaten…You have to react very quickly and stop him from behaving like that.

But the children must make an effort too. Their shouts and arguments ring in the puppy's young ears, and his nerves are sorely tried. Like the children, the puppy hasn't finished growing yet, and his bones are still fragile. He must not be bounced around right and left, hauled up, meddled with, and excited to the point that he needs to defend himself.

## In the Yard
### He "Fetches"

This is very practical training if you want the puppy to bring the newspaper, his leash, or any other object. To teach him to fetch, you choose the moment when he is carrying his toy from one place to another in the yard. When he moves away, his treasure held tightly in his jaws, you follow him, and then you grab one end of the toy and say "fetch," while leading him back to the place chosen. He will associate his booty with the movement and with the order given. The cunning little creature may only pretend to hand over his toy. If, to tease him, you blow in his ear, he will end up letting go of it!

Granted, fetching does have a slight drawback. Being very much a creature of habit, the puppy tends to take everything, pick up everything, and give everything away. It's not long before he's built us Ali Baba's cave with his finds. But if, on the other hand, the only thing he knows how to fetch is his ball, we are up against another problem. On the beach, he can't stop himself sneaking someone else's ball to please his master!

*This cute little Dandie Dinmont Terrier is a regular plush toy in the arms of this little boy. You have to keep an eye on things because though communication is easily established between pup and child, there are dangers for both of them. The puppy may try to dominate and be aggressive, the child may handle the animal too roughly.*

**The recall lesson is also scheduled for outdoors. This positive reinforcement session avoids puppy escapades if he's playing truant.**

*Ball games are the games of choice for puppies. Sometimes, however, they are completely transformed into pirates, like this Soft-Coated Wheaten Terrier who has seized a brush. Will he bury it deep in the garden with the bones?*

### He Stays in His Own Territory

Of course he wants to see the countryside, but he must not take off on his own. The yard where butterflies hover, where branches sway, and birds hop around must suffice for the puppy's entertainment. If he tries to escape, a harmless but sufficiently deterrent fence can be installed.

### He Spares the Lawns

This lesson is a hard one for a young Terrier or other hunting dog, who loves to dig. A Jack Russell Terrier, a Fox Terrier, a wirehaired Dachshund, or a German Jagd Terrier will destroy everything and build regular trenches. Damage is inevitable: if the puppies are digging after a fieldmouse, they cut through roots.

Every puppy has a weakness for a freshly dug flowerbed. To his eyes, it is the sign of the recent passage of some animal. Besides installing a little fence around bushes, the only way to stop him doing damage is through trickery. The "prepared hole" is one filled with puppy excrement. When he finds himself facing this heap of horrors, he swears he'll never go there again! The hollow can also be filled with seeds or grasses. After the seeds have been covered with earth, a 3-foot (1-meter) galvanized grating is placed over them. When the flowers grow over the top, the puppy will not walk there more than once: the feel of the grating is very unpleasant!

You can also invent a few booby traps. For instance, the master hides behind a bush, and while the little imp is preparing all sorts of mischief, he turns on the garden hose close to the pup. Like a scalded cat, the puppy fears *cold* water! Other scenarios are also effective, in particular the "natural disaster" one, also known as aversion conditioning. When he is just about to do some silly thing, you violently shake a metal can filled with coins: that'll be the last time the astonished puppy will dare go into that accursed place!

One last detail: the stage manager must remain invisible. The puppy must not find out that the crafty trick has been played by his master. So far as he knows, all calamities fall out of the sky!

### He Does Not Harm the Flowers

They move in the wind and are of many colors. What lovely toys for the puppy! He amuses himself pulling the heads off the daisies and knocking the marigolds flat...A string stretched between two pegs in the middle of the flowerbed, at the height of his chest, will stop his ravages. If he chews on the bark of a shrub, the trunk can be dabbed with tar. But his ball, which distracts his attention, is still the best solution for avoiding damage.

## LIFE IN SOCIETY

A good upbringing is not limited to the rules in force in the family. The right way to live in society is something that must also be learned. That is how a puppy brings honor to his breed and increases the number of his friends among human beings.

### On the Street

When he has become well adapted to his new setting, the puppy takes deportment lessons for when he goes out.

### He Walks on a Leash

Walking on a leash is part of the puppy's educational system. By preventing him from pulling in all directions, we keep him in his place as underling and remind him that the master alone holds authority. The puppy must keep up and adapt to our pace. But that is not so easy: he keeps pulling at the leash to get us to run. The first session lasts 20 to 30 minutes: we set the distance within which the puppy must keep close to us: a meter or two, more if we're taking a country walk:

*In the yard as in the house, the puppy may not urinate where he chooses. He can be taught to prefer graveled and pebbled places. But flowers and shrubs attract many dogs, like this Gordon Setter who seems to appreciate his owner's tulips.*

## Dangers in the Yard

He chews on aconite, columbine, and hemlock. By tasting the lovely plants the puppy is risking his life.

But other products used in the yard are toxic: they cause two-thirds of all poisoning in domestic carnivores. Feasting on rat poison, the young canine is struck down by these anticoagulants, of which a scant 5 g is enough to kill a 7-lb. (3-kg) puppy. The strychnine used as rat poison, metaldehyde, and the crimidineú used by some people to fight crows add to the list of very dangerous poisons. Chloral-based herbicides and insecticides containing carbamates will kill a puppy in less than an hour. Beware of carelessness, and of clutter in the garage! Antifreeze, whose aromatic smell attracts the puppy, must also be well out of the reach of the inquisitive little creature; the ethylene glycol that it contains is a fearsome poison. A mere one-teaspoon dose will kill a 9-lb. (4-kg) puppy.

*Placed in the rear, separated from the driver by a protective net, these two Collies are safe in the car.*

**In pet supply shops a whole range of bags and shovels are available, the use of which makes it possible to leave sidewalks clean and avoid fines.**

## Fear of Firecrackers

At every firecracker noise, the puppy runs in all directions, desperately seeking a place to hide. He breathes in rapid gasps, his pupils are dilated. He urinates where he is, and has vomiting and diarrhea attacks. Sometimes he sinks into such a state of anxiety that he mutilates himself and becomes aggressive. To help him get over his fear, you have to get him out of his torpor by having him play as if everything were all right. It is up to the master to keep his head: but perhaps he ought to call in the vet, who can administer antianxiety drugs to the terrified puppy. Fear of firecrackers may be hereditary, or else reflect a failure in the puppy's earliest training. If he has not been familiarized with a varied environment his ability to adapt to new events will have remained very low.

you place the dog on your left if you are righthanded, and you never change sides again; holding the handle in your right hand, you grab the middle of the leash in your left hand and you give the order: "Walk on." If the puppy decides to balk, you give the leash a tug to relax it, then drop the strap on the ground.

### He Goes in the Gutter

To get the puppy used to the gutter, you merely need to have him walk along the sidewalk. During the walk, you tug the leash to bring him along in the right direction, that is, into the gutter, where he will relieve himself. Until he has done so, he must not return to the house.

### He Is Good in the Car

Very young, the puppy must get used to the car. The adventure begins with very short trips that he will preferably make on an empty stomach to avoid nausea. If he hesitates to get into the vehicle, put a collar on him, and stay calm. Take your time opening windows, put a treat on the seat, then settle him in his place.

He should travel in the rear, on the backseat or at the feet of any passengers, or else in the back of a station wagon, separated from the passengers by a net, or otherwise. In no case does he remain near the driver. It is best if someone stays with him and gives him one of his toys to reassure him. Stop regularly to let him stretch his legs. Trips are then gradually lengthened until everything goes off well. For safety's sake, it is a good idea to protect your puppy with a harness. This very practical device is provided with a clip that automatically closes over the safety belt buckles and adjusts to the puppy's abdominal measurements.

### In the Country

During the discovery lessons, the puppy gets lessons in behavior.

### He Obeys the Come-back Call

The come-back lesson must be regular and short. The equipment used during this session comprises a long leash with a winder or a 40-foot (12-meter) rope. You walk your puppy as if he were not tied up: suddenly you apply tension and you call him back. If he comes back, you congratulate him. If he turns a deaf ear, you give a sharp tug to bring him back to the house. Disappearing from his sight is the only way to get him to come when he dawdles.

His pleasure is finding his master, hiding behind a bush, or among leafy growth...The little game avoids our getting cross. It's not reasonable to scold him when he does come toward us: if we do, he will connect returning with reprimands. If he remains deaf to all calls, you have to attract his attention with an unexpected noise: a shrill whistle, gravel being thrown...In a panic, the puppy takes to his heels to get to safety near his master.

## He Walks to Heel

This is no beginner's lesson. The puppy has to learn to walk at his master's heel, without changing sides. On a short rein, his head is almost level with our knee, except if he is very small. The order is repeated: "Heel!" If he tends to lag behind, you pull lightly on the leash. If he pulls us forward, he gets a little tap on the nose with the loose end of the leash. If he tries to pull away, you pull him with your left hand then let go. Then he thinks it's fun to walk in front of our legs: instantly the leash is gathered up again, and the order "heel!" is given in an authoritarian tone of voice. As soon as the puppy has started getting it right again, his reward is pats and kind words.

## He's Respectful to the Mailcarrier

It's not the uniform but the busy mailcarrier's hasty retreat after depositing the mail that may upset the puppy. The speedy motion arouses the puppy's hunting instinct, by which any speeding object is potential prey. When the mailcarrier approaches and then withdraws within the dog's view, the latter becomes aggressive and attacks.

One's first reflex, which is to restrain the dog by his collar, is to be prohibited. Whereas you want to make

## City Pup

Any well-brought-up puppy uses the "doggy-sites" and green areas organized for his use:

In addition, every master should be armed with "pooper-scooper" equipment when taking a city pup for a walk in order to comply with local ordinances. Indeed, "urbanimal-ization" has come a long way.

## What Does He Put on to Go Out?

Outdoors, the young dog must always wear the signs of a civilized dog, or else he will be considered suspect. It's his dog collar that symbolizes his entry "into society" and promotes his integration into it. Blue or red, made of flowered cotton or rhinestones, matching his mistress' skirt or made of leather like his master's coat, the collar is complemented by the leash.

During the winter, should he be covered up to go out? There are plenty of clothes for dogs and they are useful for the puppy used to the warmth of a comfortable, cozy house, for those who have smooth hair like the Dachshund, the Pinscher, the Braque, and the Boxer. For unless he is ill, nothing in the world must deprive the puppy of going out. Like all mammals, he is in any case capable of homeothermia (he regulates his body temperature according to the exterior) and has protective tissue as a result of his fat reserves (6% of his weight).

Lastly, his coat is a valuable asset: the Collie and the Briard's "underfur" amounts to veritable padding.

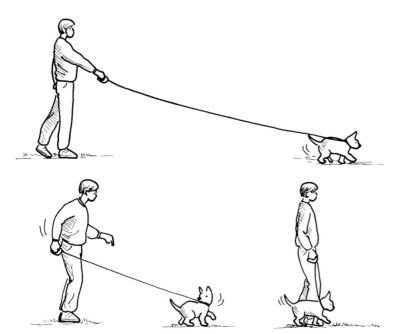

*To teach the puppy to walk close to his master, he is given the order "heel" with a light tug on the leash.*

## No Admission

Not being allowed to enter grocery stores, the puppy must be tied up outside while he waits for his master to finish his shopping. But beware: the dog does not always like being petted or teased by passersby... .

## A Budding Ruffian

The puppy that jumps all over people is only funny for a while. If he happens to have dirty paws, he becomes undesirable. In any case, his attitude is impolite and becomes dangerous as he gains weight: a child or an elderly person may be knocked down by a Labrador or a Great Dane. To restrain the young dog in his outbursts of affection, we must not punish him, but discourage him instead. We also need to train him by putting ourselves at his level: we crouch down to stroke him, we don't raise the ball above his head. To correct his bad manners, the "come when called" sessions are resumed at mealtimes.

him pull back, the little devil plunges forward as if being encouraged to bite! If he really does have some grudge against the unfortunate mailcarrier, he should be shut up in one room as soon as the mailcarrier is seen arriving. A firm, authoritarian attitude is essential.

Repeating "No!" as often as necessary will make him clearly understand that he must not break the rules.

## HIS LIFE AS A DOG

To be happy and live in peace among his peers without causing scraps at every street corner, the puppy needs to learn to control his wild instincts. The son of the canines domesticated by human beings 6,000 years ago must not regress by showing his fangs! So here are a few useful lessons in good citizenship.

### He's Friendly to Old Dogs

The older dog will want just one thing: to protect the little one. But great diplomacy is required. It's the old dog that needs pampering, not the baby. That procedure will bring the two doggies closer together instead of dividing them.

### He Gets Along with the Cat

The puppy must have an open mind and tolerate other animal species. But the master can contribute to friendly understanding between brothers who are enemies. No jealous animals! If you stroke one, you have to pet the other and show no preference for the newcomer over the "old" one. Neither of them can stand the slightest unfairness: cat and dog are both highly sensitive. To avoid setting them against each other, strategic points must be observed; that is, their feeding stations—each has his own dish, his ration (his specific food), and their sleeping quarters—each has his own basket. And this way you will find pup and cat curled up in each other's paws, fur still damp from mutual grooming, worn out from furious romping. For once they are used to each other, they are as thick as thieves. Slippers in shreds, vases in pieces, youthful blunders are inevitable, and for doing silly things, unity is perfect. The best duos are often related to the breed of puppy. Very sociable, the Poodle and the German Shepherd turn out to be charming cat lovers. It is the same with the stay at home Bulldog and Pug, independent animals like the Whippet and the Greyhound, protectors like the Shepherds and the Newfoundland, and "cat-dogs" like the smart-looking Afghan Hound.

## He Doesn't Chase the Guinea Pig

How can you expect him to be a good boy when he's a ratter? All he wants is to chase after the little rodent and catch it! However, if you take precautions, strictly forbid going near the cage, and maintain total vigilance, you can hope for relative tranquillity, especially if you are dealing with peaceful breeds such as the Bichon Frisé, the Coton de Tulear, the miniature Schnauzer, and the miniature Poodle.

## He Makes Peace with the Chickens

The sight of feathers may well make him think of absolute orgies, especially if he's a hunting dog, but the farm dog still mustn't attack the chickens. If the puppy dashes after them at the first move they make, he must be stopped in his tracks and the disaster plan must be activated.

*Absolute trust, total submission: that's what this Poodle is expressing by lying on his back. He learned the meaning of body language in his earliest infancy in the litter, and thus accepts the master's dominance.*

## Poison

Learning to refuse bait is a lesson of capital importance for the puppy. It can avert death by poisoning. If he ingests a rodent bait, containing anticoagulants or predator bait containing strychnine, the disaster is irreparable.

The danger is all the greater in that dogs love to forage in the countryside, on the lookout for anything that's lying around and anything edible. So he needs to learn never to accept any food offered him unless it's in his own dish. To achieve this, get a friend to offer the puppy a treat. If the greedy little thing takes it, the friend must grip the puppy's snout.

The animal growls, but he will understand in the end. The same scenario is repeated, but with another friend helping. Then, one day, you trick your companion yourself by putting a treat under the salad basket, in the yard.

Have a care! He tends to try to have prohibitions lifted. You must never give in: poison is still poison.

# Someone to Play With

*The baby's solitary exploratory games are replaced by games for two, between master and dog. Endless games take place indoors as well as in the open air, for pleasure, for relaxation, for the sheer joy of being together. Up to six months the baby pup enjoys games more and more, and his pleasure—a canine's privilege—will not decrease with the passing years. With playing to look forward to, our friend the dog has a happy life. But what sort of games does he invite us to play?*

*For playing, this Doberman is developing an iron constitution, strong muscles, and unshakable good spirits.*

## GAMES FOR TWO

Joy of living, overflowing energy, instincts revealed—the puppy has a thousand reasons for playing. But unlike the kitten, who when deprived of games learns nothing about living, hunting, or the rules of survival, a puppy that doesn't play is still safe and sound. All the same, if he throws himself unstintingly into playing, he develops an iron constitution, strong muscles, and unshakable good spirits. The happy hours he spends with his favorite partner—his master—help him grow up harmoniously. His infectious joyousness is synonymous with relaxation, and with cooperation as well. Thanks to play, the puppy's aggressive tendencies disappear: he becomes a model of obedience. The game is definitely worth the candle.

### Come and Play

Human beings and dogs were meant to live together. The puppy is a charmer who knows the art of inviting his master to come and play in order to lead him into his own simple and invigorating little world. Hindquarters in the air, chest to the ground, he makes a bow, his eyes riveted on ours. He wiggles in an ephemeral belly dance, wobbling back and forth, with graceful little movements. The silent invitation is clear and unmistakable: "Will you come and play?"

You are unmoved by his call: a good sport as well as obstinate, the young dog is not so easily discouraged. To convince you, he'll deploy all the secrets of seduction. Lips stretched horizontally, jaws slightly parted, he smiles from ear to ear, irresistibly. It's a laugh in mime. The puppy uses it over and over again, sure of his own charm. The glow lighting up his funny little face escapes nobody: the puppy enchants us. "Are we going to play?" he insists.

Wasted effort: your mind elsewhere, you are unmoved as a marble statue. But the mulish creature knows what he's doing. Imperturbable, sitting quietly, he waves a forepaw in the void. You'd think he was signaling to you. No reaction? Really, you are the limit. In his untiring perseverance, the puppy uses another tactic, less well-mannered but effective, ideal for waking up lazy and indecisive people: the "nose-push." It's a habit he's had since his earliest infancy, when he used to shove his nose into his mother's teat, impelled by a wild desire to be suckled. Will he have to turn to major solutions? Rudely, the nervy little thing pushes you with his paw: "Move yourself, we really are going to play," he seems to say.

His master is definitely not listening. A touch of craftiness is displayed in his next invention: a gift—a pebble, a ball—which is supposed to melt his interlocutor's heart and finally get a reaction from him. He holds his present between his forepaws, then deposits it before his beloved master: "I'll give you this if you come and play with me." Good try, but the master has a stony heart. The puppy hasn't given up yet, however! There's still the fatal weapon, the stratagem nobody can resist. Even ducks, in the past, targeted by hunters in North America, fell into this trap set by poodles. The invitation to play, a regular ballet featuring a puppy prancing, running, jumping, leaping, and zigzagging, fascinates human beings as well as wild ducks. You'd have to be blindfolded not to succumb to temptation. Let the party begin!

### What Games Does He Play?

The puppy's scenario is rarely as complex as that. Most often, people let themselves be charmed and lured into the game at the first convivial sign shown by the little scamp. You dash out along the track: but you've hardly got into your stride when a wild race, part chase, begins. The puppy flies. You keep up as best you can…The game changes: the last one goes ahead, the hunter becomes the hunted. Sprint and change places…You are panting, he speeds up, runs rings around you the better to encircle his prey. He runs until he's almost out of breath, yaps, sets off again, sure of winning.

The most common game is "Catch me if you can." He also likes "Anyone who goes hunting loses his position." Lastly, he seems to be offering you his ball, but it's just another trick. He doesn't let go of it when

*If by chance this young West Highland White Terrier is concealing any aggressive tendencies, play is an excellent remedy. This way he learns obedience, and cooperation with his master or the children is thus strengthened. Hindquarters in the air, chest to the ground, he makes his invitation irresistible.*

## Games Dogs Play

Along with adults, the puppy does not hurl himself recklessly into games the way a kitten does. He hesitates, shyly. Besides the age issue, a size problem may also restrain the puppy's spontaneity. Yet this experience will be useful to him in his relations with his peers for avoiding violent fights involving biting. So it is the biggest one who induces the youngest to take part: he infringes the rules of hierarchy, reverses roles, puts himself in the position of an underling by rolling on his back. As if by miracle, the timid little creature suddenly feels as if he had the strength of Hercules, and all cheered up joins in a wild game. With a cat, the puppy acts in a very enterprising way. But a misunderstanding often comes between the two partners: while the feline, always reserved, takes flight, the doggy, thinking, conversely, that this is an invitation to play, dashes after him and makes his quarry angry. A good sport, the puppy is not discouraged by that. He tries his luck again.

*Is it the child or this German Shepherd that's giving the invitation to play? Ball, stick, or tracking games—these are the puppy's favorites—and there are plenty of excuses and opportunities, especially in a yard where even the sprinkler hose will do.*

**The puppies who are most energetic in games are shepherd dogs, hunting dogs, Boxers, and little domestic pet dogs. The worst players? German Mastiffs and Pyrenean Mountain dogs.**

## Jumping Isn't Playing

For puppies that have to learn certain disciplines such as tracking, defense, hunting or agility drills, play is a basic principle.

Is a puppy good at catching? You encourage him to bite into a rag. Is he a born game tracker? Every future hunting dog has retrieving in his education program. Running, jumping, leaping...these forms of play prepare the puppy for agility drills.

he presents his treasure, and if you try to grab it he squeezes it between his teeth and runs off with it. In fact, his offering is merely bait. The puppy will do anything for a game.

## OPEN AIR GAMES

Playing with a ball has passed its tests: it's the young dog's favorite diversion. You throw the ball, the puppy catches it, then keeps it or brings it back depending on how he feels. He trains for racing, develops his muscles, and untiringly keeps on going. The ball game is a trifle humdrum for the master, but it's wildly amusing for the puppy. Be careful not to use the ball exclusively. The player might become the pet aversion of summer visitors by hurling himself on every ball on the beach. Games with a stick, as old as the hills and never likely to go out of fashion, are just as well liked by puppies. You throw a piece of stick that he catches in the air, and if you applaud him he lets himself be guided and asks for the stick again.

The tracking game makes him ecstatic. You let him sniff a handkerchief impregnated with your odor, then you hide. His superdeveloped sense of smell gives him every chance of discovering your hiding place with no trouble at all. It's child's play for him.

The puppy gladly accompanies us in our sporting activities: walking, jogging…. Even if it's not a game any more, he never misses a chance to have fun: he comes and goes, stops, turns aside, retraces his steps. While his master goes ahead in a straight line, he takes the longest way around, making the trip four or five times longer!

## INDOOR GAMES

When storms are raging in the wild, and when you live in town, you do have to invent some indoor games. You hide the ball under a sofa or under a dresser. The puppy finds it, brings it back, his tail quivering, and yaps as if to broadcast the news of his success.

He also likes educational games, on condition that they are suitable for his age. The principle is simple: these games must remain something that's done for

*The same urge to play unites the child and this Bearded Collie. In the young dog, this desire increases up to the age of six months and any opportunity is good for running, jumping, poking his nose into things, sharing a snack, or getting into mischief.*

*You throw the object, he catches it then keeps it or brings it back depending on how he feels; the games are interminable, and this German Shepherd never seems to get tired of the same ones.*

*Without changing the game, this Fox Terrier changes toys and swaps his for a pine cone.*

*Catching his tail, that's the new game for this writhing Golden Retriever. Could he be a bit frustrated?*

enjoyment, restraints being reserved for lessons that must be learned by heart.

### At Three Months: "Give a Paw!"

This game, for a very young puppy, is easy to learn because it corresponds to a spontaneous, natural gesture. Often a young dog, trying to attract his master's attention, sits at his feet and holds up his paw to give him a tap on the leg. You need only take this opportunity of holding the paw and saying to him: "Give your paw!" The next time, you make it happen: crouching down, you hold out your hand and give the order. At the very beginning, the exercise needs to be repeated three or four times a day. When the puppy is a few months older, you can make the test harder by practicing changing paws. After the left (most dogs are left-handed) he gives the right, then sometimes one, sometimes the other.

### At Five Months: "Play Dead"

For the first session, you wait for the boisterous creature to settle down, exhausted after a walk. He naturally lies down on his flank, with his legs stretched out. While holding him in this position, with one hand on his flank and the other keeping his head on the floor, you say: "Play dead," at the same time stroking him frequently and firmly. At the second session, you give him the order to lie down, then you make him lie on his flank and you stroke him. If he obeys the eye and hand command "lie down," he must remain immobile when you pull him by his collar. After two sessions, you take him by his leash: he's inert. A regular actor? But you mustn't forget his tip at the end of the session: that is to say, his reward.

### At Ten Months: "Sit Up and Beg"

This position—buttocks on the floor, back straight and vertical—is only possible if he has a well-formed skeleton because it requires great stress on the hip joints and the spinal column. The rule is the same as for giving a paw, but this time you take hold of the two front limbs. Then with one hand you support his lower back and with the other you raise the hindquarters. Beware! This exercise, easier with small-sized puppies, must not last longer than 5 to 10 seconds.

## SUCH FUNNY GAMES!

Sometimes things are not very clear in our little showman's head. Some of his amusements seem more related to pathology than to games, others reflect his canine instincts more than a liking for fun.

### He Chases His Tail

This is new: all he thinks about is catching his tail. What contortions he has to get into to achieve this! But however hard he tries, he cannot get hold of this "toy." He rotates faster and faster, like a regular top, then stops, overcome with giddiness. Then off he goes again on his crazy chase. This game is not like the others: it denotes frustration!

To see him amusing himself like this, you'd think he is short of toys. Yet he has everything. The fact is that he hasn't enough to do. Alone in a house with which he isn't yet familiar, separated from his brothers and sisters with whom he once played at catching, nibbling, chasing, and fighting each other in the famous tussling that made him so happy, now he's bored. Affection and stroking in profusion are the best remedy to prevent his losing his head.

### No Pity for the Slippers!

Another peculiar game: he attacks slippers, and anything else he finds on the floor as well. In a few minutes, Winnie the bear has his eyes pulled out, the socks are in shreds…. The young puppy is full of devilment! The fact is that between the ages of 4 and 6 months, he's cutting his adult teeth.

And then, slippers exert a strong attraction over him: they are so wonderful, always on the floor, gaping open, easy to grab, and pull to pieces! They are like prey, and after the age of 3 months, the young dog feels like hunting. Since he's clumsy and inexperienced, it's in his best interests to start with some easy booty; what's more appealing than a slipper?

## Dangerous Games

When he's tiny, the puppy must be supervised during his games. Accidents are no rare event, in the house as well as in the yard. The intrepid creature has a mania for putting everything in his mouth: he is capable of swallowing erasers and pins. Even his rubber ball can suffice. Beware! Our adventurer is not afraid of even the worst tricks: running out through a half-open doorway, or burrowing into a plastic bag in which he might suffocate.

## A Gift at His Feet

When our boisterous friend shreds a slipper, one's reflex is to grab the wreckage. That's like taking the food out of his mouth! Anything left on the floor corresponds in his canine mind to the big chunks of meat deposited by adult dogs living in the wild.

The slipper on which he exercises his fangs is like the food his master gives him. Hence his crestfallen look when he's lectured after his "offering."

So some manufacturers, being shrewd psychologists, have put on the market a chewing toy in the shape of a slipper.

# *The Young Dog's Menus*

*Two months, four months, eight months: a menu for every stage of life. The puppy needs to have completed his growth cycle to go on to the adult diet. And the more he has to grow, the longer the stages are and the more diversified the menus, whether he is nearly a year old or will soon be 18 months. Meat or fish, rice or flakes, anything will do, provided that the young dog's meals are perfectly balanced.*

*Mealtime is a feast for the puppy...As for his master, he has to supervise the rations and the ingredients according to his dog's breed, age, and later on, his activity.*

## FROM 7 WEEKS TO 4 MONTHS

You'd almost need a slide rule to measure the proportions needed by the puppy. The needs corresponding to the various growth stages are very precise. Hungrier for protein than at the adult age (25% instead of 20%), the young dog must not be short of glucides, either, in order to have energy, nor vitamins and minerals to strengthen his body. Nourishing one's pet properly also means taking into account his activities and the external conditions. A young Greyhound preparing to race will get a larger serving of fats than a puppy of the same size staying quietly at home. You don't give the same ingredients to a dog that's going to do a maintenance sprint as to a young sled dog starting out on a long and arduous course. Of course, age is a deciding factor in the daily ration, but weight, which varies with every breed, as shown in the table below, is an even more significant one. Growth is spread over 8 to 18 months, sometimes even up to 24 months for the large breeds. The puppy's growth curve can be charted by evaluating the average daily increase (ADI) in ounces. The progression varies from 2 oz. (60 g) per day for a puppy of small to medium-sized breed to 14 oz. (400 g) for a puppy of large breed. Between 2 and 4 months, only the smallest dogs, such as the Pekingese or the Dachshund, reach peak growth. According to calculations established by veterinary nutritionists, the ration must be composed to a large extent of meat (45%), equal parts of rice or cereal flakes (23%) and green vegetables or carrots (23%), to which is added 9% of vitamin enriched mineral supplement. These proportions are valid for both commercially produced foodstuffs and home-prepared food. One important detail: when you cook up little dishes for your puppy, you must complete them daily with the vitamin enriched mineral supplement (already included in "canned" food). This addition comprises dried yeast (30%), oil (30%), and a vitamin-enriched mineral compound (VMC) available from veterinarians. It is so indispensable that a puppy is given twice as much of it as an adult dog.

### Home-prepared Food

This job requires great availability on the master's part: it takes time to shop for the foods, measure out the proportions, and then cook them. For instance, to properly cook the rice, which must be absolutely digestible, you must allow 25 to 30 minutes. You also have to be vigilant about hygiene, both in the preparations and at serving time. Residues attract flies and cockroaches which spread microbes around. Leftovers must be removed and the food dish carefully washed. Then the puppy will not be contaminated and will not have digestive problems.

Fortunately, the young puppy is not demanding about variety in menus. Unlike the kitten, he is no gastronome: the same dish is always a feast to him, and that is very handy. The homemade mash invariably contains the same ingredients in the same proportions.

Between 2 and 4 months, the daily ration for the puppy, who is going to achieve 40% of his adult weight, amounts to twice the maintenance needs of a dog that has finished growing.

| GROWTH TABLE FROM TWO TO FOUR MONTHS [weight in pounds (kilograms)] | | | | | | | |
|---|---|---|---|---|---|---|---|
| AGE (in months) | PEKINGESE | DACHSHUND | FOX TERRIER | COCKER | COLLIE | GERMAN SHEPHERD | GERMAN MASTIFF |
| 2 | 2 (0.8) | 3.5 (1.6) | 6.5 (3.0) | 8.5 (3.9) | 9.5 (4.3) | 19.5 (8.9) | 31 (14) |
| 3 | 3 (1.3) | 6 (2.6) | 10.5 (4.8) | 14.5 (6.5) | 19 (8.7) | 32 (14.5) | 48.5 (22) |
| 4 | 4 (1.7) | 8 (3.7) | 14 (6.3) | 18 (8.3) | 27 (12.2) | 42.5 (19.3) | 64 (29) |

## Meals à la carte

What's on the well-fed puppy's menu? A good quantity of cooked meat (45%), or cooked fish with the bones removed, for the indispensable protein input; well-cooked rice, rich in starch and energy-producing, or cereal flakes (23%), the same amount of green vegetables, containing vitamins and calcium, to aid digestion. An essential little supplement: one cooked egg once a week. Don't forget that the vitamin-enriched mineral supplement, composed of corn oil (for the liver), brewer's yeast (for the fur), and vitamin-enriched calcium, sold in pharmacies, is indispensable for the bones. The supplement amounts to 9% of the puppy's ration, the equivalent of about a teaspoonful for a Yorkshire Terrier, 2 teaspoons for a Dachshund, a tablespoon for a Chow Chow, 2 and one-half tablespoons for a Greyhound. Lastly, the young dog, very sensitive to dehydration, must always have a bowl of fresh water available.

*In his bone, this Akita Inu finds sulfur, calcium, and phosphorus...and he satisfies his need to bite.*

Between 2 and 4 months, the puppy goes through an "intense self acceleration" phase. He achieves 40% of his weight, has four meals a day, and eats twice as much as at adult age.

Commercially produced food already includes in its rations a vitamin enriched mineral supplement.

A puppy drinks one tenth of a cup per pound (60 ml per kilogram) of body weight, or 2 quarts (2 liters) for a 6.6-lb. (30-kg), 4-month-old German Mastiff, and half a quart (liter) for a Cocker of the same age.

135

*At four months, the puppy loses his milk teeth and swallows them. Like this Westie, he nibbles everything: his permanent teeth are coming through.*

**A young puppy needs 0.5–0.6 oz. (30-40 grams) of meat per pound of body weight, and his energy needs are 260 kcal if he weighs between 4.5 and 9 lbs. (2 and 4 kg), and 2,800 kcal if he weighs between 88 and 110 lbs. (40 and 50 kg.)**

## Forbidden Foodstuffs

Potatoes and fruit are to be strictly forbidden, because they irritate the intestines. Some other foods are toxic to the puppy: mushrooms, for instance, especially when raw, in particular the Amanitas (phalloid, fly agaric, gyromitra) and morels. And what about bones? They do indeed give the young dog sulfur, calcium, and phosphorus, and meet his natural need for biting. But rabbit and chicken bones must be forbidden, because they are too small and sharp and cause pharynx and esophagus lesions. If bones are given in too large a quantity, they may cause intestinal obstruction or serious constipation.

As for sugar, it provides almost on its own the explanation for obesity in dogs. An 11-lb. (5-kg) puppy who eats two sugar cubes a day puts on 0.2 oz. (5 grams) of fat. In 3 months, his fat reserve amounts to 1 lb. (0.5 kg). On this sort of diet, no young dog can possibly keep his shape.

For instance, a Dachshund that at the age of 3 months weighs 6 lbs. (2.8 kg), (compared to 15 lbs. 7 kg) at adult age, must consume 22 oz. (620 g) of home-made food a day (compared to 11 oz. (310 g) at adult age: see the "Daily puppy ration" table, page 143). His meals, of which there are four, consist of 280 g of meat, 140 g of rice or flakes, 140 g of green vegetables, and 60 g of vitamin enriched mineral supplement.

### Prepared Food

What with moist foods—stews, small individual packs, and cereal flakes—and dry foods—puppy biscuits are available now—there is a huge choice insuring the puppy proper feeding. You can also find foods for reconstituting with liquid, very well suited to the young dog's teeth. Meat, corn, pasta, rusks, wheat, rice—all carefully proportioned and suitable for puppies over 2 months old.

These foods, based on by-products from meat packing plants, are subject to labeling requirements. Labels state average contents in dry matter, protein, fats, cellulose, total ash (noncombustible minerals) and additives. The daily ration is stated on the packaging: you need to refer to it because it takes the puppy's size into account.

Exceeding the recommended amount would start our friend on the road to obesity, a frequent illness that overtakes one dog out of every four, according to the British doctor Josephine Wills.

If you are interested in scientific calculations, you will see for instance that for a 4-month-old Dachshund who has achieved 50% of his adult weight and weighs 8 lbs. (3.5 kg), mature maintenance needs will be multiplied by 1.75, according to Professor Roger Wolter, author of *Diététique du chien et du chat* (Masson Publishers (*Diatetics for Dogs and Cats* [French]). The young dog, who will eat 6.5 oz. (190 g) of biscuits at adult age, consumes 11 oz. (330 g) at this precise stage of growth. If he prefers the individual moist packs, he absorbs 33 oz. (960 g) of moist food compared to 19 oz. (550 g) as a mature dog!

## FROM 4 TO 8 MONTHS

Life gets easier at this time: the young dog has only three meals a day now. Depending on the breed to which he belongs, his growth is about half over or in its final stages. A Newfoundland, for instance, is only halfway there by this time. The puppy's appetite and needs are declining. Let's look at the example of a 5-month-old Cocker (see page 143): he has reached 70% of his adult weight (he weighs over 20 lbs. [9 kg]); his maintenance needs are multiplied by 1.5 and he eats 25 oz. (720 g) of homemade dog food: 11 oz. (340 g) of meat or fish, 6 oz. (160 g) of rice, the same amount of vegetables and 2 oz. (60 g) of supplement. A month later, our pup is at 80% of his permanent weight: he now weighs 23 lbs. (10.4 kg.) If the commercial menu has been chosen for him, he absorbs 13.5 oz. (390 grams) of dog biscuits (mature maintenance requirements are multiplied by 1.35).

Does he prefer stews? His ration is approximately 40 oz. (1,160 g). Balanced feeding is the master's main concern: there must be neither excesses nor deficiencies in the puppy's food.

If it is too low in proteins and trace elements, it causes defects in bone growth, such as osteoporosis; too rich in meat and consequently in phosphorus (the amount of calcium is proportionate to the amount of meat supplied), and it causes nutritional hyperparathyroidism and osteofibrosis if at the same time it also contains vitamin A. Overfeeding, the cause of osteo-chondrosis, also creates digestive problems: flatulence, constipation, and diarrhea.

Strange behaviors result from all this. Anxious, aggressive, the puppy goes into coprophagia (he eats his excrement). He may also have allergies and get eczema-like disorders with itching skin. Lastly, if he is inclined to obesity, he may fall victim to osteoarthritis and diabetes mellitus. All these ills, which weaken the young dog and render him vulnerable to microbial attacks, must be avoided.

### Indispensable Nutrients

Canine feeding standards have been established that set the percentage of proteins, fats, mineral substances, etc. that play a specific role in the body.

### Proteins

Proteins promote growth and develop immunity and resistance to stress; they are found in meat (beef stew meat, cheek, ribs, red offal [variety meats] such as heart, liver, and spleen), fish, and eggs.

### Carbohydrates

They supply energy and exist in starchy foods, sugars, and cereals.

### Lipids

They are indispensable for exertion, and provide more energy than carbohydrates. In equal quantities, they

| AGE (in months) | PEKINGESE | DACHSHUND | FOX TERRIER | COCKER | COLLIE | GERMAN SHEPHERD | GERMAN MASTIFF |
|---|---|---|---|---|---|---|---|
| 4 | 4 (1.7) | 8.0 (3.7) | 14 (6.3) | 18 (8.3) | 27.0 (12.2) | 42.5 (19.3) | 64 (29) |
| 5 | 5 (2.4) | 10.0 (4.4) | 16 (7.4) | 20 (9.1) | 33.5 (15.2) | 51.0 (23.3) | 79 (36) |
| 6 | 6 (2.8) | 11.5 (5.2) | 17 (7.9) | 23 (10.4) | 38.0 (17.4) | 58.0 (26.5) | 90 (41) |
| 7 | 7 (3.2) | 12.0 (5.6) | 18 (8.2) | 25 (11.3) | 41.0 (18.7) | 64.0 (29.2) | 101 (46) |
| 8 | 8 (3.6) | 13.0 (6.0) | 19 (8.6) | 26 (11.7) | 44.0 (20.0) | 69.0 (31.4) | 108 (49) |

GROWTH TABLE FROM FOUR TO EIGHT MONTHS [weight in pounds (kilograms)]

supply twice as many calories. They are absolutely indispensable: the puppy, whose developing body uses up huge amounts of calories, derives them from fats such as the animal fats found in meat and from vegetable fats, which contain essential fatty acids, valuable for the skin and coat (see pages 170 and 175).

## Vitamins

They have been scientifically calculated by nutritionists: 10 international units (IU) per pound (22 per kilo) of body weight are needed by the young dog. Any excess is harmful and may cause osteodystrophy (bone diseases). A distinction is made between hydrosoluble vitamins, which are water-soluble, and liposoluble vitamins, which are fat-soluble. Among the latter, vitamin A, or retinol, stands out: it ensures growth, safeguards the sight, protects the skin, and allows the body to fight infectious diseases: it is found in liver, lungs, veal and pork, as well as eggs and tuna fish. Vegetables such as carrots, spinach, and lettuce contain provitamin A. Vitamin E or tocopherol, along with selenium, acts as an antioxidant for cells: it is present in cereals, meat, and oil. Vitamin K allows coagulation of the blood. Vitamin D, derived from fatty substances called sterols, binds calcium and phosphorus to bones. The vitamin D group is found in variety meats and eggs. Water-soluble vitamins are also necessary for the performance of the body's great vital functions. They include among others the vitamin B group:

—Vitamin $B_1$, also called aneurin or thiamin, allows assimilation of carbohydrates and prevents nervous and cardiac disorders; it is found in cereals, brewer's yeast, variety meats, and egg yolk.

—Vitamin $B_2$, or riboflavin, prevents eye lesions; it is present in liver and brewer's yeast.

—Vitamin $B_5$, or pantothenic acid, allows the assimilation of fats: it is very common in vegetables, red meat, variety meats, yeast, and cereals.

—Vitamin $B_6$, or pyridoxin, permits assimilation of fats and proteins; it exists in cereals and whole-grain rice.

—Vitamin $B_{12}$ or cyanocobalamin, plays an essential role in the maturing of red blood cells. It is contained in liver.

—Vitamin $B_9$, or folic acid, promotes the formation of red blood cells: it is found in spinach, variety meats, meat, liver, and yeast.

Vitamin H or biotin is also mentioned; inositol, a growth factor; choline, which helps prevent fatty degeneration of the liver. Vitamin C, found in green vegetables, is not indispensable to the puppy since he produces it himself via his digestive flora. Finally, vitamin P or bioflavonoids, which increase blood vessel strength and ensure growth, exist in cereals and brewer's yeast.

## Minerals

Calcium, which ensures the building of the bone structure, is found in dairy products and cheeses, but also in tap water. Phosphorus is involved in the constitution of the nervous system and is associated with calcium in bone formation; it is found in meat, fish, and eggs. Magnesium exerts a sedative action on the nervous system, and like calcium, it regulates neuromuscular balance and is found in oat flakes.

## Trace Elements

Iron, contained in meat and spinach, allows oxygen to be carried from the lungs to the tissues. But it plays its part only in the presence of copper, which is present in liver, beef, and whole-grain cereals. Iodine, which is found in green beans, ensures proper functioning of the thyroid gland. Finally, zinc permits healing of wounds, and like selenium, promotes growth.

## FROM 8 MONTHS TO I YEAR

At this age, the puppy can make do with two meals. The growth of a medium-sized dog like the Dachshund is practically complete at one year. Beyond that date, he has only 20% of his adult weight left to achieve. At 12 months, a Dachshund eats 13 oz. (370 g) of homemade dog food, including 6 oz. (170 g) of meat, 3, oz. (80 g) of green vegetables, the same amount of rice, 1 oz. (40 g) of vitamin enriched mineral supplement. If his menus consist of dog biscuits, his daily ration is 8 oz. (230 g) per meal—4 oz. (115 g)

*One snack, all right; two, shouldn't eat bread; three, hello trouble! This Bearded Collie is in danger of losing his shape if his master doesn't keep track of the daily rations.*

morning and evening. If he prefers the moist food, he will eat 23 oz. (660 g) divided into two meals.

### Rules Governing Commercial Foodstuffs

Since 1947 prepared foodstuffs have been subject to a use code which must be observed by professionals. Dry foods exist in the form of cereal and vegetable flakes and extruded, compressed, and flattened biscuits, with a moisture rate below 14%, which allows the product to stabilize and prevents proliferation of bacteria, yeasts, and molds.

Moist food, with humidity under 70%, is sterilized. As for semimoist products, they keep at room temperature.

The range of prepared menus broadens again with the addition of other products that must be distinguished from each other: whole foods, which suffice for the daily ration, and food supplements, with substances in high proportions.

Foodstuffs with special objectives, also known as "life cycle" products, are designed for a specific stage in the puppy's growth. A fair number of them have been flourishing on the market the last few years.

Pedigree Pal closely follows the puppy's growth and offers one product called Formula for Junior and one called Junior Plus. Techni-Cal (the Pet Food Company set up in Canada) offers a product called Croissance [Growth]. Pro Plan, or Ralston Purina, presents Growth; New Lines sells Puppy for puppies and juniors.

Science Diet Canine Growth products from Hills, Specific from Leo Laboratories, Eukanuba Puppy (and Junior for large-breed adolescents) from Iams, which have the advantage of insuring the puppy's optimal growth and protecting him from diseases, are also available.

From the huge array of foodstuffs you can also select treats: mini-snacks filled with marrowbone, dried beef or chicken squares, cookies, doughnuts, fried fish, heart-shaped flavored candies, reconstituted bones, etc. In bars, sticks, patties, chips, hearts, flat cakes, waffles, discs, rounds, sausages and various tablets, these very tempting treats must be dispensed in moderation: they amount to a calorie input that's over and above the daily ration!

### Additives

Growth factors, preservatives, and antioxidants, which prevent fats from becoming rancid, additives exist in many forms: flavoring, coloring matter, artificial sweeteners, emulsifiers, jellifying substances, foam reducers, etc. They are often used as over generously in dog foods as they are in foods meant for human beings.

## BETWEEN I YEAR AND 18 MONTHS

One meal can be enough at this age: that's handy for masters who are not easily available to feed their young puppy twice a day.

But it all depends on the stage reached by your pet. Paradoxically, though small dogs have grown up by this time, those belonging to large breeds are slower growing up. They are still a long way from the adult stage.

After one year, a young German Shepherd weighing about 65 lbs. (30 kilograms) still needs to eat twice a day until he's 14 months old. His food allowance (his adult ration is multiplied by 1.2) is 36 oz. (1,040 g) and includes 16 oz. (460 g) of meat, 8 oz. (240 g) of green vegetables, 8 oz. (240 g) of rice, 4 oz. (100 g) of supplement.

Beyond 14 months, when he exceeds 80 lbs. (36 kg), he can have just one meal. That's when he will get the adult ration, already less copious: if he is used to dog biscuits, he consumes 18 oz. (520 g) per day; if he prefers moist food, he can have 54 oz. (1,530 g).

### The Young Dog's Behavior with Food

The puppy is a glutton: he throws his food about and swallows it without chewing; a fast food adept, he hurls himself on his food like a starving creature without so much as glancing around.

In a group, if he is the dominant one, he automatically appropriates the food dish to be the first to eat.

*Between 8 months and 1 year, the puppy can make do with two meals. Then commercial foods are an ideal solution for the master, especially since the largest brands have extended their lines and offer foods suitable for every type of puppy. This Hungarian Pointer does not have the same needs as a Pekingese or a German Mastiff.*

| **GROWTH TABLE FROM EIGHT MONTHS TO ONE YEAR** [weight in pounds (kilograms)] | | | | | | | |
|---|---|---|---|---|---|---|---|
| **AGE** (in months) | **PEKINGESE** | **DACHSHUND** | **FOX TERRIER** | **COCKER** | **COLLIE** | **GERMAN SHEPHERD** | **GERMAN MASTIFF** |
| 8 | 8.0 (3.6) | 13.0 (6.0) | 19.0 (8.6) | 26 (11.7) | 44 (20.0) | 69.0 (31.4) | 108 (49) |
| 9 | 9.0 (4.0) | 14.0 (6.3) | 20.0 (9.0) | 27 (12.2) | 46 (20.8) | 73.0 (33.1) | 114 (52) |
| 10 | 9.75 (4.4) | 14.5 (6.5) | 20.5 (9.3) | 27.5 (12.6) | 48 (21.8) | 755 (34.3) | 119 (54) |
| 11 | 10.0 (4.5) | 15.0 (6.8) | 21.0 (9.5) | 28 (12.8) | 49 (22.2) | 77.0 (35.1) | 125 (57) |
| 12 | ADULT WEIGHT | ADULT WEIGHT | ADULT WEIGHT | 29 (13.0) | 50 (22.7) | 785 (35.7) | 132 (60) |

*For these little crossbreeds, it is age and weight that determine their food ration and their activity, which is rather light, all said and done, in their basket.*

**From 8 to 12 months, the puppy goes through a "self-decelerating" phase and achieves 80% of his adult weight.**

**After 12 months, the puppy goes through a slower growth rate period until he reaches his permanent weight.**

According to Dr. Chris Thorne, of the British Research Centre at Waltham, his taste is more or less pronounced according to his breed: so the Labrador and the King Charles Spaniel will eat anything at all without showing the slightest preference.

Fortunately, acquired experience influences the young dog's behavior in connection with food: for instance, he will avoid any foodstuff that has made him ill in the past.

His favorite weakness? Foods containing a large amount of protein. He prefers foods of animal origin to those of plant origin. Among them, he enjoys primarily beef, pork, and chicken; in second place liver; he can make do with horsemeat, he will not turn his nose up at lung and will accept spleen; as a last resort he will eat vegetables.

He prefers canned meat to fresh meat: he likes cubed meat better than ground meat. He likes cooked meat better than raw, and according to the expert Houpt, he prefers moist foods to dry foods.

As a very young dog, he has a weakness for sugar, and if he could choose the time, he would party at night rather than in the daytime.

Lastly our little glutton may have a big defect known as pica, which makes him swallow everything he finds, not just crumbs fallen from the table, or bones thrown in the trash, but also the handkerchief left lying on the sofa and the eraser on the

| GROWTH TABLE BETWEEN ONE YEAR AND EIGHTEEN MONTHS [weight in pounds (kilograms)] | | | | | | | |
|---|---|---|---|---|---|---|---|
| AGE (in months) | PEKINGESE | DACHSHUND | FOX TERRIER | COCKER | COLLIE | GERMAN SHEPHERD | GERMAN MASTIFF |
| 12 | ADULT WEIGHT | ADULT WEIGHT | ADULT WEIGHT | 29 (13.0) | 50.0 (22.7) | 78.5 (35.7) | 132 (60) |
| 13 | | | | ADULT WEIGHT | 51.5 (23.4) | 79.0 (35.9) | 136 (62) |
| 14 | | | | | 53.0 (24.0) | 79.5 (36.0) | 141 (64) |
| 15 | | | | | ADULT WEIGHT | ADULT WEIGHT | 145 (66) |
| 16 | | | | | | | 154 (70) |
| 17 | | | | | | | ADULT WEIGHT |

# PUPPIES DAILY RATION

| BREEDS | ADULT WEIGHT [lbs. (kg)] | PERCENT-AGE OF ADULT WEIGHT | ACTUAL WEIGHT [lbs. (kg)] | AGE (months) | NUMBER OF MEALS | DRY FOOD [oz. (g)] | MOIST FOOD [oz. (g)] | HOME-MADE FOOD [oz. (g)] | MEAT or FISH 45% | RICE or FLAKES 45% | GREEN VEGE-TABLES 23% | SUPPLE-MENT 9% |
|---|---|---|---|---|---|---|---|---|---|---|---|---|
| **DACHSHUND** | **15** **(7)** | 40 | 6 (2.8) | 3 | 4 | 13 (380) | 38.5 (1,100) | 22 (620) | 10 (279) | 5 (143) | 5 (143) | 2 (55) |
| | | 50 | 7.5 (3.5) | 4 | | 12 (330) | 34 (960) | 19 (540) | 9 (243) | 4 (124) | 4 (124) | 2 (49) |
| | | 70 | 10.5 (4.9) | 5.5 | 3 | 10 (280) | 29 (820) | 16 (460) | 7 (207) | 4 (106) | 4 (106) | 1 (41) |
| | | 80 | 12 (5.6) | 7 | | 9 (260) | 26 (740) | 15 (420) | 7 (189) | 3.5 (96.5) | 3.5 (96.5) | 1 (38) |
| | | 100 | 15 (7) | 12 | 2 | 8 (230) | 23 (660) | 13 (370) | 6 (167) | 3 (85) | 3 (85) | 1 (33) |
| adult ration | | | | | 1 | 7 (190) | 19 (550) | 11 (310) | 5 (140) | 2.5 (71) | 2.5 (71) | 1 (28) |
| **COCKER** | **29** **(13)** | 40 | 11.5 | 2.5 | 4 | 20 (580) | 60 (1,720) | 34 (960) | 15 (432) | 8 (221) | 8 (221) | 3 (86) |
| | | 50 | (5.2) | 3 | | 18 (510) | 52.5 (1,500) | 29 (840) | 13 (378) | 7 (193) | 7 (193) | 2 (76) |
| | | 70 | 14.5 (6.5) | 5 | 3 | 15 (430) | 45 (1,290) | 25 (720) | 11 (324) | 6 (165.5) | 6 (165.5) | 2 (65) |
| | | 80 | 20.3 (9.1) | 6 | | 14 (390) | 41 (1,160) | 23 (650) | 11 (292) | 5 (150) | 5 (150) | 2 (58) |
| | | 100 | 23.2 (10.4) | 13 | 2 | 12 (350) | 36 (1,030) | 20 (570) | 10 (257) | 4 (131) | 4 (131) | 2 (51) |
| adult ration | | | 29 (13) | | 1 | 10 (290) | 30 (860) | 17 (480) | 8 (216) | 4 (110) | 4 (110) | 1 (44) |
| **GERMAN SHEPHERD** | **about 70 (32)** | 40 | | 3 | 4 | 36 (1,040) | 107 (3,060) | 61 (1,740) | 28 (783) | 14 (400) | 14 (400) | 5 (157) |
| | | 50 | 28 (12.8) | 4 | | 32 (910) | 94 (2,680) | 53 (1,520) | 24 (684) | 12 (350) | 12 (350) | 5 (136) |
| | | 70 | 35 (16) | 5.5 | 3 | 27 (780) | 80.5 (2,300) | 46 (1,300) | 20 (585) | 11 (299) | 11 (299) | 4 (117) |
| | | 80 | 49 (22.4) | 6.5 | | 24 (700) | 79 (2,060) | 41 (1,170) | 18 (527) | 10 (269) | 10 (269) | 3 (105) |
| | | 100 | 56 (25.6) | 14 | 2 | 22 (620) | 64 (1,840) | 36 (1,040) | 16 (468) | 8.5 (239) | 8.5 (239) | 3 (94) |
| adult ration | | | 70 (32) | | 1 | 19 (520) | 53.5 (1,530) | 30 (870) | 13 (392) | 7 (200) | 7 (200) | 3 (78) |

**Calculating method**

*The adult dog's maintenance ration is multiplied:*
*by 2 up to 40% of adult weight;*
*by 1.75 up to 50% of adult weight;*
*by 1.5 up to 70% of adult weight;*
*by 1.35 up to 80% of adult weight;*
*by 1.2 up to 100% of adult weight.*

desk. The cap off the ballpoint pen and the ink cartridge don't even put him off.

When doing gastrotomies, veterinary surgeons sometimes discover a regular Aladdin's cave: coins, safety pins, and other treasures.

In fact, this anomaly is not so very surprising if you look at the puppy's natural context. Unfamiliar with the rigid schedules imposed by human beings, he eats anything: horse manure, a dead rat, a bit of green grass—hence the French name for couch grass, "chiendent" or dogtooth [which is not, as formerly thought, a vermifuge (something that destroys or expels parasitic worms); instead the puppy who goes looking for this rough grass gets a stomachache].

In the house, the passion for playing vacuum cleaner is dangerous. The puppy risks mouth and tongue irritations, vomiting, choking, gastritis, a perforated intestine, intestinal obstruction, chronic enteritis, and fecal impaction. So he absolutely must be corrected, either through homeopathic treatment or by some gentler method, such as diversion or play.

You will have to experiment to see what works with your puppy. Some dog owners have found success through the use of behavioral techniques, such as shooting the animal with a water gun and saying "No!" when catching the pet "in the act." Others "booby trap" the puppy's favorite "target" (such as the garbage pail) with things that will be too unpleasant for the animal (like cayenne pepper). If the dog doesn't respond to anything, you may have no other choice but to be diligent at keeping things picked up and put away.

*The dominant pup in this Boston Terrier litter has taken over the food dish so he can eat first. Young dogs are gluttons who will eat almost anything, with a preference for foodstuffs of animal origin and for sugar.*

## Allergies

Beef, cow's milk, fish, and less often eggs are the main allergens to which the puppy may react. Proteins, for instance, lose their antigenic power when they are cooked and are no longer digestible. Skin problems (in 3% of cases), digestive signs (15% of cases) are the most common symptoms of these allergies. A 48-hour low or starvation diet is imperative before offering the puppy a substitute food plan.

The canine feeding standards as defined for adult dogs by the National Research Council are as follows: proteins, 32%; fats, 13%; mineral substances, 8%; fiber, 3%; calcium, 1.3%; phosphorus, 1%; magnesium, 0.10%; iron, 320 mg/kg; copper, 35 mg/kg of iron; manganese, 80 mg/kg; zinc, 2,000 mg/kg; iodine, 3.8 mg/kg; selenium, 0.43 mg/kg.

A small breed dog does not eat very much. He must have exercise to ever "feel faint with hunger."

Lack of appetite may indicate the presence of worms or the ingestion of some foreign body.

*When a puppy eats everything he comes across (including plastic bottles that these Braques seem to be enjoying) he may be affected by pica. He absolutely must be corrected of this bad habit, which may turn out to be dangerous for his intestines.*

# A Healthy Puppy

If the puppy's health is perfect, it's because every weapon has been used and every precaution taken to protect him from disease: vaccines, antiparasitic products, disease detection, body hygiene, and lifestyle hygiene.

But many an incident threatens the intrepid puppy: wounds, burns, heatstroke, electric shock, poisoning, insect stings, snakebite. The rash young creature's master has to learn how to get him out of trouble very quickly. In some situations, help from the veterinarian is absolutely necessary.

*Vaccinated against fatal diseases, the puppy can go adventuring in the yard or in town. However, he is never safe from bacteria, germs, parasites, and worms. These young Tibetan Terriers still have to depend on their master's vigilance to make it through these dangers.*

| CALENDAR OF PUPPY VACCINATIONS | |
|---|---|
| AGE | DISEASES |
| 2 months (8 weeks) | Parvovirosis<br>Infectious hepatitis<br>Leptospirosis<br>Canine distemper<br>Parainfluenza |
| 3 months (12 weeks) | Parvovirosis<br>Infectious hepatitis<br>Leptospirosis<br>Canine distemper<br>Parainfluenza<br>Rabies |
| 4 months (16 weeks) | Parvovirosis<br>Infectious hepatitis<br>Leptospirosis<br>Canine distemper<br>Parainfluenza |
| Yearly | Parvovirosis<br>Infectious hepatitis<br>Leptospirosis<br>Canine distemper<br>Parainfluenza<br>Rabies |

**A puppy living in a group must be vaccinated against kennel cough as soon as he is 4 weeks old, then at 7 weeks, and get a booster every year.**

## Rabies and the Coyote

Coyotes play an important role in the transmission of rabies to the domestic dog population. For instance, a rabies outbreak that began in 1988 among the coyote population in Texas led to a declaration of an emergency quarantine in that state. Efforts to combat such outbreaks include rigid travel restrictions regarding domestic pets, mandatory annual vaccination of all domestic dogs 12 weeks and older, and the use of aircraft to drop vaccine-impregnated bait into those regions where coyotes cohabit.

## VACCINATION

Vaccination immunizes the puppy against fatal diseases: canine distemper, infectious canine hepatitis, leptospirosis, parvovirosis, rabies, and parainfluenza. As soon as the deactivated or attenuated microbe is injected, the young animal develops antibodies. But initial vaccination must always be followed by regular booster shots. If this schedule is not observed, our pet is no longer protected!

### Viral Diseases

#### Canine Distemper

The virus that causes this disease was discovered at the beginning of this century by the biologist Carré. Frequent in the puppy of under one year old (see page 76), but also in the adult dog, among canines such as the wolf, the jackal, and other species (otter, mink, ferret, badger, seal) it is transmitted by mere contact. After an incubation period of 4 to 7 days, it affects the respiratory system, multiplies in the tonsils and bronchial tubes, the lymphatic system and the blood, before spreading to tissues and organs. Canine distemper, which shows up first with the appearance of fever and red eyes, then shows symptoms identical to those of parvovirosis, which makes it more difficult to establish a diagnosis. The young dog refuses food, his eyes are teary; he has diarrhea, he coughs; his breathing is labored, his nose runs, and he fidgets and keeps turning around. This redoubtable illness appears in a number of forms: pulmonary, digestive, cutaneous, ocular, or nervous. The patient, who looks like an old dog, must be isolated. Treatment can be considered, but it does not guarantee that there will be no aftereffects, such as epileptic seizures. Prevention is insured by vaccination: a first injection can be administered at 2 months of age, with the second 3 to 4 weeks later, followed by a booster every year.

### Infectious Canine Hepatitis

This illness, due to canine adenovirus, is transmitted by urine. The puppy has a high fever [104–106°F (40–41°C)]. His tonsils are inflamed, he has digestive disturbances (diarrhea, vomiting, dehydration) and eye problems (conjunctivitis, corneal infection). But he might also die (page 76) without showing the slightest symptom, because the disease progresses so rapidly. Vaccination is done as of 8 weeks, in two injections one month apart. The booster is given every year.

## Parvovirosis

Often fatal, this form of gastroenteritis (viral infection of the digestive tubes), caused by a *parvovirus*. Although epidemics have almost disappeared, occurrences are still severe. Contamination occurs through direct contact. Exhausted, anorexic, the puppy is prostrate, vomits, and suffers from bloody diarrhea. He can be vaccinated as soon as he is 8 weeks old. The two vaccine injections are given 1 month apart. The booster is given every year or in some instances, every 6 months.

## Rabies

This disease, due to a *rhabdovirus,* is transmitted by bites. Excretion of the virus in the saliva of a rabid puppy begins 3 to 15 days before the appearance of symptoms. They appear after an incubation period of 15 to 60 days. The puppy's behavior changes: he salivates, has attacks of dementia, his voice is not the same, he becomes paralyzed. Vaccination is given at 3 months of age in one or two injections followed by boosters.

## Bacterial Diseases

### Kennel Cough

This highly contagious tracheobronchitis particularly affects puppies in group living situations. It appears as a sequel to a number of infectious agents such as the distemper virus or the hepatitis virus, but it is a bacterium (*Bordetella bronchiseptica*) that is essentially responsible for the ailment. It occurs through contamination, or after some post-weaning stress, or else after a sudden chill. The puppy, who loses his appetite, has a runny nose and runny eyes. He has a very typical dry cough, occurring in fits. Death is sometimes the outcome of this feverish state.

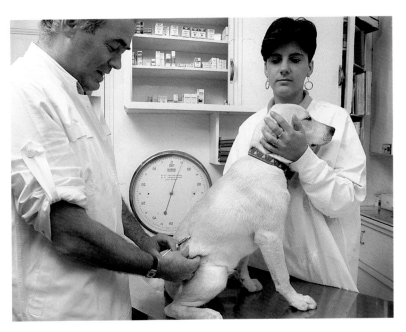

*After the vaccines, you need to think about the regular boosters without which the puppy is no longer protected.*

After the first injection of vaccine, which may be given at 4 weeks, and the second, which occurs 3 weeks later, the young dog must have annual boosters to be fully protected. This vaccine is usually reserved for those puppies continuing to live under group conditions or those that visit the kennel often.

### Leptospirosis

This is a very serious disease, also known as canine typhus, which develops in insanitary places: the germs of the leptospirus genus are present in the bodies of rats and field mice. Through their droppings, the rodents contaminate the puppy. He may also be infected by licking the urine of another dog who is sick or by drinking foul water. The young hunting dog is particularly exposed to this disease, which appears in a number of ways. The digestive form is very serious: the puppy has a high temperature [104°F (40°C)]; he is very depressed, has hemorrhagic gastroenteritis, and severe renal insufficiency. The hepatic form makes the skin and mucosa very yellow, and then, in

## Scratches and Pasteurellosis

Less frequent than in cats, this disease, due to a pathogenic bacterium called pasteurella, is transmitted by licking, biting, or scratching. Does the puppy have a wound? If he touches it with his tongue, it becomes very painful. The affected part becomes red and very swollen. The infection spreads and affects nearby joints, and ganglions appear near the bite.

**Not all collars or antiparasitic products are suitable for a puppy less than 3 months old. Some can be toxic and even fatal to a small animal. Check with your vet if you are unsure.**

## How to Remove a Tick

This acarid must not be allowed to remain active for more than 48 hours. Up to 1 in. (2 cm) in size after its meal—compared to ¼ in. (0.5 cm) unfed—it is a parasite on the puppy, drawing his blood and transmitting microbes. To remove the tick, you need to first kill it. It does no good to pull it out suddenly: the head may remain hooked in. You will have only half the parasite and the part left in the dog will form an abscess or a cyst. So you apply cotton soaked in insecticide to the intruder for 5–10 minutes.

Then you extract it, using tweezers. If you are afraid of missing the target, you can use an antitick pad (impregnated with insecticide), which on mere contact pulls out the parasite and kills it.

4 to 6 days, draws the puppy toward coma and death. Complications such as encephalitis and myocarditis are frequent and often fatal. Vaccination is done at 2 months in two injections 1 month apart. Boosters are given every 6 months or every year. Watch out: this zoonosis is transmitted to human beings by licking or biting. The leptospiri then enter through the skin, as soon as there is a wound, or via the mucosa, that is to say via the eye or the mouth.

### Parasitic Diseases

#### Piroplasmosis

If a pair of ticks, emerging from the undergrowth, settle on the puppy's body and meet a protozoan (*Babesia canis*) an infection is started. Unable to help himself, the hapless dog experiences the first onslaught of babesiosis [Texas fever], also known as piroplasmosis. He is depressed; his temperature exceeds 104°F(40°C). His urine is brownish. He is anemic. If treatment is not given, his skin and mucosa become yellowish (icterus). He is soon suffering from renal and hepatic insufficiency.

#### Stop Female Ticks!

Among the numerous species of ticks, there are two that attack dogs: *Rhipicephalus sanguineus*, a domestic tick that lives in attics and doghouses, and *Dermacentor reticulatus*, a wild tick that develops in natural settings, on plains and on lake shores. Their special feature is that they hook onto their hosts: they bury their heads in his skin just like harpoons, then live at the base of his ears, between his toes, or under his abdomen, for about 10 days. Long enough to get a good meal! When the female—she's the culprit!—is satiated, she lays between 3,000 and 5,000 eggs. For 3 to 6 days, each larva will develop and change into a nymph. The nymph will find a home on another dog, and on reaching adulthood will hook onto its host.

#### Lyme Disease or Borreliosis

Another tick, *Ixodes ricinus,* makes the puppy ill. In the course of its meal of blood, it transmits a bacterium

(*Borrelia burgdorferi*) to the animal; the latter, running a high temperature, loses his appetite and has aches in his joints and muscles.

In 1990 an anti-Lyme disease vaccine was put on the market by Fort Dodge Laboratories. The treatment consists of two IM injections 2 or 3 weeks apart. The puppy must be over 3 months of age and have an annual booster.

## ANTIPARASITIC PRODUCTS

Sprays, shampoos, and powders are legion for combating the myriads of parasites that assail the puppy. Every year veterinary laboratories, in search of advanced technologies, put revolutionary products on the market. Effectiveness, duration of action—the best score is 7 months—and ease of application are all irresistible advantages. Why do without them? Easy to use, these insecticides are available in tablets, atomizers, sprays, aerosols, and pipettes. They not only make it possible to treat the animal, but also hidden corners, hallways, cars, and small rooms. Among the latest products there is a great invention: a methoprene-based insect growth regulator, which destroys eggs and larvae spread around the house. These up-to-the-minute products are environmentally friendly: they contain no CFCs, they protect the ozone layer and do not give off any unpleasant odors.

### Against Ticks
#### Ehrlichiasis
The domestic tick (*Rhipicephalus sanguineus*) transmits this disease. But the real culprit is a parasite, rickettsia (called *Ehrlichia canis*) which after a 10-day incubation period infects the blood. The puppy runs a high fever—104°F (40°C)—and loses his appetite. Listless, he presents disorders due to poor coagulation of the blood. Hemorrhaging results from a reduction in the number of platelets, called thrombocytopenia. Though treatment with antibiotics is one resource, it is better to take preventive measures by destroying ticks outdoors and providing your puppy with an antiparasitic collar.

### Against Fleas
#### Flea-bite Allergy
It is the flea's saliva that causes flea-bite allergy dermatitis. The puppy is in living hell: he licks himself, his skin weeps, he bites himself…. His fur gets thin and breaks off across his abdomen, on his back, and on the tips of his paws. Eczema and microbial lesions and infections may occur if veterinary treatment is not given. Prevention is better than cure, with the use of an antiparasitic product.

### Against Worms
#### Tenia (Tapeworms)
Starving, the puppy harboring tapeworms gorges himself in vain: he doesn't get a single ounce of food: the worm absorbs all nutritive substances. Made up of segments 6–12 in. (15–50 cm) long, it can be detected through its rings that look like grains of rice, deposited near the puppy's anus. The puppy has digestive problems: his stools are soft, he is constipated, and licks his hindquarters. As he derives no benefit from his food, he has growth problems.

## Where Are the Fleas?

They are everywhere. Nesting in fur, tucked in between floorboards, in wall-to-wall carpeting, under the leg of a chair. When the temperature is mild and the atmosphere damp, from spring to autumn they proliferate. There is not a second to lose. As soon as they have found a host, they stuff themselves with blood and lay eggs, over and over again: a total of 2,000 in the course of their existence, disseminated in the puppy's basket and also in the carpeting and the floorboards. Three weeks later the larvae are born, protected in a cocoon called a pupa. They need a scant week to turn into chrysalides. When they emerge, it's an invasion! For one flea can be hiding 500 others. In one month, 10 fleas produce a colony of 250,000 individuals: eggs, larvae, and pupas! They are everywhere!

*After a country walk, this Whippet's master will have to inspect fur and ears. Ticks, fleas, and plant spikelets may well make their way into them and cause itching and diseases.*

**Seventy percent of puppies aged 3 to 6 months are affected by worms, compared to 97% from birth to 3 months. A puppy may have worms without any external contamination.**

## Cat Fleas versus Puppies

There are over 2,000 varieties of flea, but the one that attacks puppies is the cat flea (*Ctenophalides felis*). It is reddish brown; its body is elongated, flat, and 2 to 3 mm long. Its activity time is distributed as follows: 1% on the puppy's neck, 99% in the arms of the armchair. In less time than it takes to tell, it turns our pet into a fleabag. It tickles? It makes him scratch? It's worse than that: he is at risk of serious illness. For the little insect that climbs up when it is in the larva stage eats the eggs of *Dipylidium Caninum*, the dog tapeworm.

Worming is the only way to combat tapeworm infestation. The worming product, which will have been administered in the first week, then every 2 weeks until weaning, will be repeated every month until 6 months of age. Then the process will be repeated twice a year. But frequency must be increased—up to four times a year—for a young dog who frequents farms and woods. The process is easy: there are tablets, syrups, and pastes that can be administered by syringe or dropper directly into the animal's mouth or by mixing them with his food.

### Echinococciasis

This disease occurs when the puppy has consumed the viscera of animals contaminated by a tapeworm of small size. The parasite lodges in the small intestine and drops its eggs to the exterior. The problem caused the puppy by echinococciasis is almost insignificant; but on the other hand, it is a very serious illness for human beings. The latter may be contaminated in two ways: either by caressing a puppy, or by eating wild blueberries, raspberries, or blackberries soiled by rodent excrement. Initially, it is the fox that hosts the parasite, whose eggs, expelled in fecal matter, contaminate mice and field voles. Everything is linked together: the places frequented by these little wild animals are infested. The worm's larvae migrate to the liver and form cysts that set off serious problems. The huge hepatic cyst develops like a veritable cancer; a kind of metastatic growth forms in various organs. There is a dual lesson to be learned here: wild berries should not be consumed without rinsing them in water and one's puppy must be wormed!

### Trichuriasis

This is an illness which mainly affects puppies raised in a group. It is due to the presence of trichurides, small round worms that dig into the walls of the large intestine and the cecum. This nematode (*trichuris vulpis*) is whitish, or pinkish when engorged with blood. It is 1.5–3 in. (4 to 7 cm) in length. The larva becomes adult in 2 or 3 months. The puppy becomes infected by absorbing the eggs evacuated with the stools. Chronic diarrhea, often bloody, indicates the presence of the worms.

## Medications Against Heartworm
### Dirofiliariasis

This disease is called heartworm disease. It is caused by *Dirofilaria immitis*. This worm is transmitted by a larva-carrying mosquito called Culex, which is common all over the world, even on icefloes.

The worm measures 6–12 in. (15 to 30 cm) in length and settles in the heart and the pulmonary artery. Infested, the puppy becomes thin, is out of breath, and coughs. The only known means of preventing it is special heartworm preventive medication, with ivermectin or milbemycin as the active ingredient, prescribed by the veterinarian in spring and in summer.

## Mosquito Repellents
### Leishmaniasis

This disease, known as "Riviera leprosy" is caused by a protozoan (*Leishmania donavani*), which lives as a parasite on white blood cells, and is itself transmitted by a small mosquito. This tiny, humpbacked, hairy insect lays its eggs in chinks in tree-bark and walls. As evening falls, the female sets out to find warm-blooded animals. If she happens to sting a sick dog, she absorbs his parasites and inoculates them into our puppy. The puppy loses weight, his muscles atrophy; he is sad-faced, his skin is dry and covered in dandruff; the hair around his eyes disappears and his claws grow abnormally long. Ulcers appear and develop around his nose and ears. An unpleasant odor emanates from his skin. In most cases, the puppy has both keratitis and conjunctivitis. At present, leishmaniasis can only be stopped with repellents, effective weapons against mosquitos.

### Trombidiasis

This disorder is common between June and October, when the trombidion larva is active; this is a tiny acarid also called harvest bug, harvest tick or harvester, harvest mite or chigger. Though the acarid is harmless, its orange-colored larva, which is no more than 0.25 mm in size, insists on feeding on the puppy's skin and lymph. It becomes active at the end of summer and settles between the toes, on the eyelids, ears, lips, or anus, where it remains for 4 days. For 3 weeks its saliva causes severe itching.

## HYGIENE
### Preventing Infections
#### Ingrown Claws

This painful ailment affects puppies whose claws are too long. The claws of an indoor pet are not sufficiently worn down, and, therefore, curl over on themselves and stick into the skin. Sometimes the young dog tries to pull them out, but he is clumsy and can only remove a part, and the rest of the claw becomes infected. It is best to cut the dog's claws regularly.

## Worm Colonies

There are many worms that infest puppies: flat worms or cestodes like the tapeworms, round or nematode worms like the trichurides. Among the latter must be counted the ancylostoma [type of hookworm], 1 millimeter long, and which, secured to the intestinal wall, causes a dark-colored diarrhea and anemia. The ascarids, white or pink, 4 in. (10 cm) long, lay large numbers of eggs (5,000 to 15,000 per gram of excrement) and bother the puppy, who does not grow properly; his fur is dull and his appetite is capricious, minerals and vitamins being absorbed by the worm. His sense of taste is affected too: you see him eating earth or the excrements of other animals. His breath is very foul; sometimes he has hiccups. His intestines, invaded by the armada of ascarids, are blocked up. The young animal, bloated, has diarrhea and attacks of dizziness or over excitement. The parasite settles in organs like the liver, and in the muscles, lungs, and brain. If you stroke your pet, you will not escape this infestation either!

*There are many worms that infest puppies. To eliminate them, regular worming is indispensable from the first week on. Tablets can be mixed with food or a syringe or dropper can be used as for this Husky. After six months, the operation is repeated twice a year so that the puppy will be spared.*

 **Beware: conjunctivitis can be a symptom of distemper.**

**A spikelet or a foreign body may cause otitis.**

**Puppy claws growing abnormally long are sometimes a sign of leishmaniasis.**

## Conjunctivitis

This painful disease is characterized by redness of the eye and constant blinking of the eyelid. An ailment of the conjunctiva—the second protective layer of the eye after the eyelids—it is sometimes due to improper growth of an eyelash, often to the presence of irritating parasites. The puppy's eye must be regularly cleared of impurities.

## Gingivitis

This is an inflammation of the gums, due to the presence of tartar, a yellowish deposit that contains staphylococci. The puppy's mouth gives off an unpleasant odor. Proper buccodental hygiene avoids this ailment.

## Otitis

This is the most common ear pathology affecting our faithful companion. Some breeds, such as the Poodle or the Cocker, whose ear canal is covered with hair and rich in sebaceous glands, are predisposed to it. It is an inflammation of the external auditory canal, caused by parasites such as the mite that causes mange, by bacteria, or by yeasts. The puppy feels a sharp pain, shakes his head, whines; his appetite declines to the point that anorexia is to be feared. White secretions appear in his ears and pruritus soon occurs. Cleaned weekly, his ears escape these infections.

## Ear Mange

This illness, also called otacariasis, often affects young dogs. It is due to the presence of an acarid (*Otodectes cyanotis*) which feeds on skin debris and lives as a parasite in the ear canal. The puppy shakes his head and scratches his ear, which is full of blackish brown cerumen. The ailment is contagious from one puppy to another. So ears must be inspected frequently and always kept clean.

## Body Mange

This ailment is due to a tiny acarid, invisible to the naked eye—it measures less than a half-millimeter—

*This Boxer is not feeling like himself. Maybe he just has a case of indigestion? But perhaps he has a viral, bacterial, or parasitic ailment? The vet's diagnosis will permit the disease to be identified and the young dog to be restored to health by prescription of effective treatment.*

the mange sarcopt. From the laying of the egg to the adult stage, this parasite has a very short cycle: growth takes no more than 2 weeks. It burrows into the skin, but it may also remain at the surface of the dermis and spread the ailment over the body. The puppy develops eruptions, especially on the face, limbs, and ventral area. He looks as if his coat is moth-eaten and covered with scabs. This disease, unremarkable to begin with, is transmittable from one individual to another. It may become very serious if it

is not treated. Grooming is what prevents the puppy from becoming infested.

### Ringworm

Various sorts of funguses called dermatophytes cause ringworm: *Microsporum gypseum, Trichophyton mentagrophytes* and *Microsporum canis*. The latter, the most common, feeds on the keratin in skin and hair. The puppy loses his hair in circular patches ½–1 in. (1 to 2 cm) in diameter. This mycosis is benign, but is

*No "casting" and no advertising for these show-off Shelties. The fact quite simply is that with their fluorinated bones, they don't have a thing wrong with their teeth!*

 **Psychotherapy, homeopathy, acupuncture, osteopathy . . . a puppy can be successfully treated with alternative medicines, in full swing in veterinary clinics.**

## Good Hygiene

A puppy that loses his fur outside of molting time (which occurs twice a year) is having some sort of growth problem. Perhaps he is the victim of parasitic ailments caused by ticks, fleas, bugs, mange sarcoptes, or maybe acarids like the Demodex. Good hygiene is therefore indispensable. It enables the skin to protect the system and insure the body's defense against germs, microbes, and other attacks.

transmittable to human beings. The treatment, based on anti-fungal products, is lengthy, and requires the young dog to be kept away from others. His fur requires regular maintenance care.

### Demodecia

This is due to a parasite, *Demodex,* an acarid of the arthropod family, like spiders. It develops in follicle channels in sebaceous glands, and finds a favorable environment in young dogs. When it smothers a hair, the animal loses its fur. Unlike ringworm, demodecia does not result in nummular (coin-shaped) but rather in "eyeglass" depilation localized around the eyes. This ailment is unrelated to alopecia, another skin disease, which indicates a growth problem.

### Pyodermatites

These skin diseases caused by development of staphylococci, in particular *Staphylococcusintermedius,* are classified as two categories: superficial pyoderma, localized on the skin surface of the skin or at hair roots, and deep pyoderma, serious dermatitis appearing in the form of furunculosis and showing up as hypodermal inflammation in the inner thigh area.

Among superficial pyodermatites, a distinction is made of junction line pyodermatites, which occur on lips and affect dogs with pendulous lips, such as the Cocker, the Setter, and the German Shepherd. They also appear on the tail and the face, in particular in brachycephalous breeds with heads as broad as they are long, such as the Bulldog, the Pug, the Pekingese, and the Shar-Pei. Impetigo is also one of the superficial pyodermatites and is often encountered in young dogs affected by a lesion or a pustule developing under the horny layer of the epidermis. Lastly, some forms of folliculitis, which cause severe itching, show up as pustules and affect in particular short-hair breeds such as the Boxer. The coat then takes on a moth-eaten look.

### Tetanus

Rare among canines, this disease is due to a bacillus called *Clostridium tetani,* spread around in earth, manure, and horse droppings. The incubation period varies from a few hours to about 10 days. In the dog's system the bacillus produces a toxin that affects the nerves and the spinal chord, giving rise to nervous disorders.

The animal seems to have gone mad, his body becomes rigid, and his body temperature rises.

This disease is certainly often the consequence of a wound, and finds a favorable environment in any open or infected sore. But it also occurs when indispensable hygiene measures are lacking. How can you see and clean your animal's wounds if the coat that hides them is never inspected?

## Food Hygiene to Fight Illness and Microbes
### Aujesky's disease
This ailment is due to a herpes virus and shows symptoms similar to those of rabies. The virus affects the nerve centers and causes encephalomyelitis. A number of problems result: salivation, paralysis, behavior modification, … . The puppy will even go so far as to mutilate his head. To avoid this, ban raw pork and variety meats from his menu.

### Obesity
It's a worldwide problem. It affects Cockers and Labradors as much as it does Dachshunds. Over-consumption of food must be avoided and regular walks help the puppy to stay in shape.

### Osteofibrosis
Very frequent in puppies, this demineralization of the bone structure is caused both by an excess of phosphorus and by a lack of calcium, resulting from an "all meat" diet. The puppy has trouble holding himself upright. He is dispirited and sickly. His bones are deformed and so fragile that he is afflicted with spontaneous greenstick fractures.

### Seborrhea
This is a skin anomaly that appears when the dog has an oily skin. The sebaceous glands, located near the hair

*Can water from a stream be stagnant? This young Yugoslav Shepherd is completely fooled. Watch out for leptospirosis!*

root and distributed over the whole of the body (with the exception of the nose and pads), secrete an abnormal amount of sebum. The puppy's coat looks shiny and oily: it emits an unpleasant odor. The origin of this ailment may be due to a diet too rich in carbohydrates and lipids.

### Urticaria
This allergic reaction may be caused by substances in contact with the skin, or by consumption of poorly tolerated foodstuffs or medications. In a few minutes, the skin is covered in blisters and the puppy is itching. In places the hair is on end and the skin all swollen. It may happen that the young dog is afflicted with giant facial urticaria (Quincke's edema), which gives him a "hippopotamus face"; asphyxia is to be feared. Warning: foodstuffs likely to cause an allergy must be eliminated!

## DETECTION
### Tumors
Tumor does not always mean cancer. Skin tumors are the most frequent ones (68%), before mammary tumors (25 to 42%), which can be avoided by ovariectomy of

young bitches under three years of age. Next come testicular tumors, then tumors of the mouth, and finally bone tumors. Early detection is of fundamental importance. Any lump exceeding ½ in. (1 cm) in diameter must be removed: operation-related risks are low compared to the risk of cancer.

## INJURIES
### Skin Wounds
#### How to Stop Bleeding
With a sterile gauze compress or a clean handkerchief, pressure is exerted on the affected area. Ordinarily the seepage stops after two minutes. If it does not, a tourniquet must be used; you can make one yourself or obtain one from a pharmacy.

#### How to Clean a Wound
Begin by cutting away the hairs surrounding the injured part. Then examine the wound: if you find a foreign body, remove it with tweezers. Then disinfect the wound, from the center outward, with a compress soaked in hydrogen peroxide or Dakin's solution (alcohol is not a good disinfectant). One last precaution: apply a dressing so that the puppy does not lick himself. When the wound is large—over ½ in. (1 cm)—take the puppy to the veterinarian, who will suture it.

### Eye Injuries
Warning! These injuries may be serious ones. If the eye remains closed, the puppy may have a corneal lesion. The proper eyewash must be used. The injured pup may also have a foreign body in his eye. If it is only a speck of dust or an eyelash, the intrusive object can be gently removed with the corner of a clean handkerchief; then the eye is cleaned with an isotonic antiseptic solution or some physiological serum. But any object that has entered the globe of the eye may have a traumatizing effect: a spikelet, a thorn, an insect, a bit of gravel, … . In each of these cases it is best to apply a moist compress over the closed eye and take the puppy to the veterinarian.

### Nose Injuries
No doubt about it: if a young dog is bleeding from his nose, a spikelet must be stuck in it. The grassy spike may be removed with tweezers. Then an icepack is applied to the nose to stop the bleeding.

### Injuries to the Teeth
The puppy likes to play with pebbles or pieces of hard wood. That is how he may end up breaking his teeth. As soon as bleeding becomes visible, hydrogen peroxide-soaked cotton is applied to the wound. But if the break is serious, the incautious little creature is in danger of becoming infected and having an abscess. In that case, the tooth must be extracted by a veterinarian specializing in orthodontics.

### Ear Injuries
While fighting among themselves, puppies bite each other regardless of the strength of their fangs, and ear injuries are frequent.

These wounds are disinfected with a compress soaked in hydrogen peroxide, then a dressing is applied. The ear is kept folded by means of a stretchable bandage fastened with adhesive medical tape.

But the undisciplined little animal gets his paw to it and pulls it all off. So an Elizabethan collar must be bought or made (out of a plastic bucket from which the handle and bottom have been removed). This odd-looking outfit, though effective, certainly displeases him. However, he has to get used to it.

### Foot Injuries
Wounds between the toes are cleaned with cotton pads soaked in hydrogen peroxide. Then a gauze compress is applied, and the foot is wrapped in a bandage twisted over every two or three times around. The dressing is secured on each side with adhesive medical tape.

## THE MASTER'S KNOW-HOW
### Making a Splint
All it takes is a violent movement or a jolt for the puppy to start limping. Luxation of the patella [dislocation of

*By constantly playing with pebbles, nibbling them like a mad creature, it happens that the young dog breaks his teeth. The wound must then be disinfected and if need be, the tooth must be extracted by a vet.*

## The First Aid Kit

It can be a cosmetic bag or a plastic box with an airtight lid, lightweight, strong, and easy to carry around. It contains: a pair of tweezers for extracting thorns and foreign bodies from ears, nose, and eyes, or for removing impurities from a wound; scissors for cutting gauze; a roll of adhesive medical tape; some disposable sterile syringes, for dispensing an antiseptic product onto wounds; some antiseptics for cleaning up wounds (some 90° alcohol, 5% by volume hydrogen peroxide, Dakin's solution, an eye lotion); some sterile gauze; some absorbent cotton; a medical thermometer; a small flashlight for examining ears, the mouth, or wounds; a tourniquet for reducing severe bleeding [a 12-in. (30-cm) length of thick elastic will do]; lastly, a cold pack that can be found at the pharmacy, useful for halting bleeding and for contusions, sprains, and heatstroke.

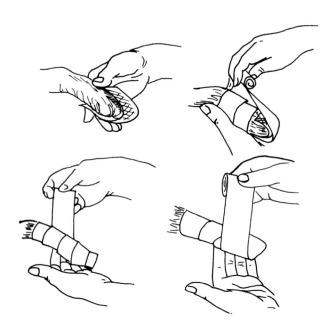

the kneecap] is frequent, in particular in small-sized breeds such as the Poodle and the Yorkshire Terrier, but it may also be congenital in origin. The puppy limps intermittently, and from time to time holds his paw up.

How can his discomfort be alleviated when you're out on a walk? Even though no bandages and no medical adhesive tape are available, you can still create a makeshift splint: you immobilize the limb by wrapping it in a handkerchief or a scrap of fabric (a tuft of grass will do the trick as well).

Splints that are notched at each end with a knife to thread a piece of string or a shoelace are just three bits of wood laid flat on the injured limb. Then string is wound around them two or three times and a knot is tied.

### Making a Muzzle

A muzzle is useful when a panic-stricken injured puppy is affected by the reflex to bite. But he must have his mouth closed while he is being helped. If you are in the open countryside, you can make a muzzle with a strip of fabric 40 in. (1 m) long and 1 in. (2 cm) wide. Over the nose you tie a nice tight square knot, then a second identical one underneath, and a third behind the ears.

### Transporting an Injured Puppy

The method of transportation varies according to the animal's size: a tiny puppy can be carried in a basket or a sufficiently large cardboard box (he must not be hunched up, because it would make his injuries worse); a medium-weight puppy will be safer in a wooden box. Be sure that you place your animal gently inside his refuge: bumps and sudden movements must be avoided. Spread a cloth along his back, then slide an end of the fabric under his front paws, head, and neck; place the other end under his side, abdomen, and back paws.

Lastly, lift the animal's shoulders and chest while stretching the fabric firmly. With the four corners of the cloth, you can thus make a hammock. For a large-sized puppy, you need to have ready a strong plank

## Removing a Spikelet

Ears, mouth, nostrils, and eyes are all sensitive places where spikelets get caught: spikelets are components of the ears of a graminaceous plant also known as "rat barley" (*Hordeum murinum*). As it makes its way along the hearing canal or through the nasal fossae, the "thief" or "traveler" can cause serious problems. If it stays between the puppy's toes, it causes an abscess and treatment by the veterinarian is necessary.

that you hold by its sides. You put one arm around his neck, the other around his abdomen, and you lift him while pulling him flat against you. Then you set him on the stretcher, one hand under his shoulder and the other under his thigh, while sliding him gently onto the blanket or the wooden plank.

If he is fidgety, immobilize him with three strips of fabric, one in front of his thighs, the second over his sides, and the third around his shoulders.

## EMERGENCIES
### Burns
The puppy is in danger of burning himself if he goes near fire, boiling liquids, very hot metal objects, or hot tar. The injured area is protected with gauze: never use anything greasy. Then take him to the vet's right away.

### Shock
Difficulty in breathing, sudden weakness, pale mucosa: the puppy is in shock. He has probably

experienced some physical or emotional trauma, heatstroke, infection, or poisoning. What is to be done? Lay the puppy on his side: the head is extended so that he can breathe more easily, and positioned lower than the rest of the body in case he vomits. Then the little animal must be kept warm.

In case of respiratory arrest, pull his tongue forward and rub the end of his nose.

### Heatstroke
On very sunny days, the puppy may pass out and tremble all over, particularly if he is shut in a car parked in the sun. His temperature very quickly

exceeds 107.5°F (42°C). If something is not done quickly, he will die. You must plunge him into a very cold bath or apply cloths filled with ice cubes to his head. If he does not come to his senses in less than ten minutes, he must be taken to the vet's as a matter of emergency.

### Displacement of Stomach
This is a very serious incident. The stomach has become twisted and the puppy is in shock.

This happens while on a walk, after a meal: the puppy is suddenly nauseous; his abdomen becomes dilated. You must go immediately to the nearest veterinarian, who will restore the stomach to its proper position. To avoid this incident, do not have your young pet run immediately after his meal.

### Poisoning
Vomiting, diarrhea, convulsions, and death through cardiac arrest threaten a puppy who has licked or swallowed a toxic product, in the kitchen or in the yard.

The poison ingested must be identified and you must make haste to call the local poison center, which will inform you of the antidote.

But be warned! You must be careful not to act without due consideration: you should not make your puppy vomit nor give him milk, because fats promote the absorption of soluble toxins. Only the veterinarian is in a position to intervene and administer a treatment appropriate to the situation described by the master.

If the puppy has ingested rat poison, he will be afflicted with generalized hemorrhagic syndrome. Blood will be found in the stools, urine, and vomit.

*To cool his body down, this puppy, who does not perspire, breathes very fast and pants.*

**The Collie is very sensitive to sunburn. If you see a pink, hairless mark on his body, you must keep him in the shade and apply a "maximum screen" sun cream to him.**

## Heat and the Puppy

A sudden rise in the puppy's temperature [up to 107.5°F (42°C)] under the influence of heatstroke is explained by the nonexistence, more or less, of any perspiration system; only his pads are supplied with perspiratory glands, but with no thermo-regulatory power. So as soon as the temperature exceeds 86°F (30°C), the puppy starts breathing very rapidly to cool his body. The inspiration and expiration motions that usually occur 30 to 40 times per minute increase to between 300 and 400!

To combat anticoagulants, the puppy is treated with products based on vitamin K1 or else with blood transfusion. If he has swallowed glucochloral-based mole poison, the puppy sinks into deep anesthesia, followed by coma...and by death. Unfortunately there is no known specific antidote for this poison.

Intensive medical resuscitation, continued until the hapless animal throws up the toxic product, may get him out of trouble. Only emergency treatment can save him if he has sampled strychnine, metaldehyde, or crimidine, which are very fast-acting. Valium, barbiturates, and perfusions are sometimes helpful.

## INCIDENTS
### Insect Stings

Bees, wasps, and hornets relentlessly attack the puppy's head, muzzle, and paws. These insects' stingers must be removed with tweezers. Then a vinegar-soaked compress is applied to reduce the swelling in the affected area. If the puppy is allergic to these insects, he must be taken to the vet's, where corticoids and a preventive treatment for the summer months will be administered. That leaves animal spines. The little busybody may stick his paw on a hedgehog or a porcupine. After giving him a sedative, you can remove these spines with tweezers. The rash little creature may also take on a stinging caterpillar or a toad, whose skin contains irritants.

He whimpers, his mouth is inflamed. You must quickly plunge his mouth into a bowl of cold water, or spray water into the mouth without letting him swallow it. Finally, take him to the veterinarian, who will prescribe antihistamines.

### Snakebite

If the puppy ventures into thickets on his own, he may have unpleasant encounters with a venomous snake. You suddenly see him leap up, howling, and then start licking himself furiously and come back trembling all over and nervous, sometimes losing consciousness. Two fang marks, a few millimeters apart, reveal a viper bite. The area is swollen. Without delay, put

## TOXIC PLANTS

| PLANT | SYMPTOMS | PLANT | SYMPTOMS |
|---|---|---|---|
| **Aconitum napellus**<br>Napel aconite<br>(leaves, seeds, roots) | vomiting, diarrhea, convulsions, and death by cardiac arrest | **Ilex aquifolium**<br>Holly (berries) | vomiting and abundant diarrhea |
| **Aquilegia vulgaris**<br>Columbine—(whole plant) | vomiting, diarrhea, convulsions and death by cardiac arrest | **Ipomoea purpurea**<br>Ipomoea [inc. morning glory] (seeds) | hallucinogenic effects |
| **Buxus sempervirens**<br>Boxwood (leaves) | gastrointestinal irritation | **Iris**<br>Iris (bulb) | intestinal irritation<br>abundant diarrhea |
| **Clematis**<br>(entire plant) | gastrointestinal irritation | **Lathyrus**<br>Sweetpea<br>(seeds and fruits [pods]) | nervous symptoms (paralysis, convulsions) |
| **Colchicum autumnalis**<br>Autumn crocus<br>(entire plant) | gastrointestinal irritation muscular and respiratory paralysis | **Lupinus**<br>Lupin (entire plant) | hepatic disorders<br>respiratory and cardiac disorders |
| **Conium maculatum**<br>Hemlock (entire plant) | trembling, convulsions, gradual paralysis, weakened respiration, death by cardiac arrest | **Narcissus**<br>Narcissus (bulb) | gastrointestinal irritation<br>excessive salivation |
| **Convallaria maialis**<br>Lily of the valley<br>(entire plant) | gastrointestinal irritation, slowing of cardiac rhythm | **Narcissus<br>Pseudo-Narcissus**<br>False narcissus"; jonquil, daffodil (bulb) | gastrointestinal irritation<br>excessive salivation |
| **Crocus**<br>Crocus (bulb) | gastrointestinal irritation | **Nerium oleander**<br>Rose-laurel<br>[common oleander]<br>(entire plant) | gastrointestinal irritation<br>nervous and cardiac disorders |
| **Dieffenbachia**<br>Dieffenbachia or poisonous arum<br>(stems, leaves) | severe irritation of the mouth, esophagus, stomach, intestines | **Parthenocissus quinquefolia**<br>Virginia creeper (fruits) | gastrointestinal irritation |
| **Delphinium**<br>Larkspur<br>(leaves and seeds) | vomiting, paralysis of limbs, weakened respiration, slowing of heart rate | **Philodendron**<br>Philodendron<br>(leaves and stems) | gastrointestinal irritation |
| **Euphorbia**<br>(entire plant) | gastrointestinal irritation | **Ranunculus acris**<br>Buttercup (stem and sap) | severe irritation on contact (mouth, esophagus, stomach, intestine) |
| **Euphorbia pulcherrima**<br>Poinsettia or scarlet euphorbia<br>(leaves and flowers) | gastrointestinal irritation | **Rhododendron**<br>Rhododendron<br>(leaves and stems) | vomiting |
| **Galanthus nivalis**<br>Snowdrop (bulb) | gastrointestinal irritation abundant salivation | **Taxus baccata**<br>Yew (leaves and seeds) | gastrointestinal irritation trembling, convulsions, cardiac and circulatory disorders, death |
| **Gladiolus**<br>(bulb) | gastrointestinal irritation abundant diarrhea | **Tulipa**<br>Tulip (bulb) | gastrointestinal irritation |
| **Hedera helix**<br>Ivy (leaves and stems) | gastrointestinal irritation nervous and cardiac disorders | **Viscum album**<br>Mistletoe (berries) | gastrointestinal irritation, nervous symptoms, abundant salivation |
| **Helleborus niger**<br>Hellebore (entire plant) | gastrointestinal irritation cardiac disorders | **Wisteria**<br>Wisteria (seeds and flowers) | gastrointestinal irritation |
| **Hyacinthus**<br>Hyacinth, bluebell (bulb) | gastrointestinal irritation | | |
| **Hydrangea macrophylla**<br>Hydrangea<br>(leaves and flowers) | stomach pains, vomiting, diarrhea | | |

## Taking the Puppy's Pulse

The respiratory rate fluctuates between 18 and 20 respirations per minute. In the puppy, cardiac pulsations are 110 to 120 per minute. At adult age, they vary from 80 to 100 in the case of small-sized dogs, from 70 to 80 for a heavy dog. You can take the dog's pulse by pressing your ear over his heart and applying your thumb to the outer surface of his thigh and the index and the second finger to the inner surface. You will then discover the pulse in the femoral artery.

 **A cool damp nose is not a sign that a puppy does not have a high temperature.**

**The tourniquet, used only in cases of extreme emergency, must never be kept in place for more than a quarter of an hour.**

**To lower a puppy's temperature, you can give him a cool bath.**

a tourniquet an inch or so above the injury and disinfect the wound. There is no point in making an incision to extract the venom by aspiration: that activates the circulation; nor is it a good idea to inject an antivenin, for that could set off a serious allergic reaction. So you must get to a veterinarian immediately.

### Electric Shock

An accident happens fast. The puppy chews electrical wires and gets an electric shock. Even if he seems unhurt, he may have deep burns on his tongue or gums. He is in danger of infection and being unable to feed himself. So he must be taken to the vet's.

## Toxic Household Items from A to Z

Here in alphabetical order is everything that constitutes a danger for our young animal: antifreeze; antirust; antiseptics; chlorine bleach; colored pencils; crayons; depilatory creams; detergents (dishwashing liquid, laundry soap, automatic dishwasher products); fire-extinguishing foam; fungicides; gasoline; glues; hair dyes; herbicides; ink; insecticides; lacquers; matches; metal polishes; mothballs; mouse poison; nail polish; paints; paraffin; pens; perfumes; plants; polishes, waxes, and other cleaning products; rat poison; refrigerants; scouring products; shampoos; snailbait; suntan oils and creams; tar.

## Taking Temperatures

Ask a friend to hold the puppy. Then push the end of the thermometer deep into the animal's anus and hold it there for three minutes, which is a long time for our impatient little pup! The easiest way is to use an electronic thermometer that gives an audible signal as soon as the rectal temperature has been established. When does he run a fever? When his system is invaded by germs, viruses, or bacteria that disturb his thermoregulatory system. High temperature is sometimes uneven: it remains dead level in cases of distemper, rises suddenly in cases of parvovirus.

*To make the pill go down, the medication is buried in a tasty morsel. A real treat!*

# Keeping Clean and Grooming

The little dog scratches and licks himself, but his grooming leaves something to be desired! His master's help is required for taking care of his eyes, ears, pads, and claws. His coat in particular needs special care: brushing, untangling, shampooing. Dental health depends on a special dentifrice, shaped like a bone, chewable at will. Beautiful, clean, bathed, and shampooed, the puppy, too, can look like a show dog, thanks to grooming secrets.

*Grooming a dog is not a luxury, it's a necessity, a first step toward health, especially if he has abundant shaggy hair like this Schapendoes.*

*Brushing*

*Untangling*

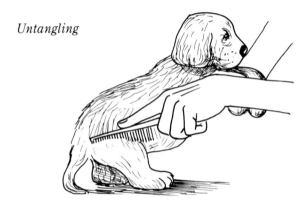

## A Disposable Glove

For grooming your young dog, you can use a wash glove for dogs, available from stores. Impregnated with a lotion specially designed for the puppy's skin and fur, it is hypoallergenic, removes unpleasant odors, washes gently and refreshes. The glove is rubbed over the back, abdomen, chest, thighs, and paws. The puppy doesn't need to be rinsed off because the lotion is removed by evaporation. In half an hour, the coat is dry, flexible, and silky. As good hygiene requires, the glove is thrown away after use.

## Anatomy of a Hair

A hair is a flexible filament. It consists of a living component, the root, arising from the pilose follicle, and a dead component, the shaft, located above the skin surface. The coat is made up of longer, stiffer hairs, which ornament the fur, and horizontal beard hairs. The longer hairs give the coat its shiny appearance and provide thermal insulation. Each hair has a sebaceous gland, which secretes sebum, and a sweat gland.

## THE MASTER TOUCH

The first step toward beauty: grooming. From head to foot, the dog's body is gone over with a fine comb. Dandruff is tracked down, dust is removed, flanks are dusted off. Eye discharges are stopped. Bad breath is a signal: the teeth need to be inspected. A runny ear reveals the presence of microbes. Lastly, if the young dog is dragging himself along on his rear, his anal sacs are bothering him. Grooming must not leave anything out, starting with the fur.

### The Coat

Brushing and untangling are two elementary operations. Well-kept fur must be aired: loose hairs and unsightly, unhealthy knots are eliminated, for there is nothing sadder than having to cut or clip a coat that's become impossible to untangle. There would be visible gaps in the puppy's fur. It's better to prevent matters from getting to such a point.

### Brushing

You always brush according to the direction in which the hair grows, from the back toward the abdomen, and from the head toward the tail. But there are a few exceptions to the rule: a Bobtail [Old English Sheepdog], a Pekingese, and a Borzoi, who have a lot of hair, are brushed in the other direction; all you need do to the short hair of the Dachshund or the Boxer is give it a rubdown. A damp glove or a chamois leather are all it takes to remove the dust. Lastly, a dry towel will make their coats shine. How often you brush varies according to breed: twice a year for the short-haired puppy, in spring and in fall, which is molting time and when hairs fall out; every day for a long-haired puppy like the Afghan Hound; at least once a week for a wooly, silky coat like that of the Poodle. Some days the brushing session is superficial: tangled hairs, called matts, remain behind the ears, in the armpits, under the tail, and in the inguinal area (groin)… A comb must be used to get rid of all these stubborn knots and allow the fur to be properly aired.

## Untangling

After brushing comes the indispensable untangling time. Lock by lock, with the comb, all the knots are undone. Sometimes the teeth of the comb get hung up without getting results. There's no point in pulling: you only upset your pet and break off his hairs. It's better to use a cream or a detangling spray: if you coat the lock of hair with this product, the knot dwindles away in your fingers quicky, and the hair becomes smooth. Rinsing in clear water eliminates any greasy or oily look. At the end of the session, don't forget a light combing in the hidden areas, inside the external ear and on the inner surface of the thighs.

## Bathing

After brushing and untangling, it's bath time. Be careful not to get water into the puppy's eyes and ears! The first shampoo gets rid of grease, and the second one gives the fur volume, color, and shine. Conditioner comes after the second rinse, then you begin to comb and brush your puppy with the third rinse water, which you keep at 77°F (25°C). You rub the fur down: finally, you spread a small amount of detangling product over it and you carefully comb the dog before one last rinse to remove the substances in the detangling product.

## Drying

With a very gentle hair dryer, on low heat, you dry the puppy starting with the neck and rib cage. To make the coat shine, spray on a glossing product that seals up splits in the hair and protects from external attacks.

## Grooming Equipment

Good grooming does depend on the master's know-how, but also on the equipment used. Tools must be chosen according to the animal's fur and their own quality. The comb and brush must be suitable for the texture of the hair and never damage it: a brush that sends hair flying in all directions is only fit to be thrown in the trash. It is unsuitable for the puppy's coat, and

*The puppy would certainly prefer to dry himself by rolling in the grass. But in winter or when his master wants the puppy's coat to shine, the hair dryer is more practical.*

**On vacation or when you're in a hurry, the puppy may be given a dry shampoo.**

### In the Bath

A bath is the best guarantee of cleanliness. All puppies, however, do not need it: the pilary secretion of the shepherd, for example, protects him against bad weather; it is also unnecessary to bathe the Collie, Pekingese, Bearded Collie, and Bobtail [Old English Sheepdog] unless they come back coated with mud from their country outings. By contrast, long-haired puppies must be bathed every 1½ months, sometimes even every week. A dry shampoo is better for hard-haired dogs.

*There is a suitable brush or comb for every type of coat.*

**A puppy must never be bathed during a vaccination period. He can have his first bath one month after the second booster vaccination.**

**The under-hair, which gives the puppy's fur its vital strength, must not be removed in large amounts.**

| NUTRIENTS NECESSARY FOR COAT MAINTENANCE | |
| --- | --- |
| NUTRIENTS | FUNCTION |
| Essential fatty acids<br>Biotin<br>Zinc | Renewal of the epidermis |
| Vitamin B₆<br>Essential fatty acids | Sebum secretion |
| Iron<br>Iodine<br>Copper<br>Biotin | Fur color |
| Proteins<br>Sulfurated amino acids<br>Essential fatty acids<br>Trace elements | Fur growth |
| Essential fatty acids<br>Vitamins A, B₂, H | Combatting inflammations |

whatever it is made of will not do. For preference, select a boar-bristle brush, the advantage of which is that it will not be rough on the fur, will brush without pulling the hair out, and will leave the coat smooth and clean. Brushes equipped with nickel-plated ball-tipped bristles also allow untangling that does not irritate the puppy's skin. The ideal comb is equipped with teeth rounded at their tips. If the puppy belongs to a long-haired breed like the Briard or the Afghan Hound, choose a rake comb, with a perpendicular handle, which is the easiest to hold. When untangling becomes a chore, you can try an untangling tool with blades. It does not much matter what it is made of—metal or horn. But on the other hand, the spacing of the teeth is an essential criterion: fine spacing is suitable for fine hair and a fairly thin coat; medium spacing is right for normal hair and a dense coat; wide spacing is ideal for thick hair and a very dense coat.

## Toiletries

Veterinary cosmetology respects coat types and the animal's skin. A wide range of products designed for puppy grooming is available. Thus, the same shampoo is not used for mixed fur as for long fur. One should also know the amount of lipid secretion (lipids are composed of sebum and keratinous elements) so as to avoid using substances that are irritating for the puppy's skin. Shampoo, cream, lotion, spray, toilet powder, and conditioner are not luxuries, but grooming products. They have a triple function: the upkeep, embellishment, and care of the dog's fur. Each type of coat and breed needs its own shampoo: with protein for a Yorkshire Terrier, bracing for an Old English Sheepdog, a Borzoi, a Collie, a Pekingese, a Bearded Collie, a Husky, and a Malamute. As the height of refinement, there is a shampoo for each coat color. Did you know that a young black Labrador is better looking when he is washed with a charcoal shampoo?

The natural products fad is in full swing, from freshness shampoo to green apple in the shampoo to white nettle for greasy hair, by way of antidandruff shampoo, very useful for a puppy while he is cutting his teeth or after parasitic ailments or skin diseases like dermoepidermatites. His pretty fur is indeed sometimes covered in tiny specks of unsightly white dust: dandruff. Should you shampoo once or twice? Two applications are needed: one to remove the dirt, and the second to make the coat shiny. Two different shampoos are recommended, incidentally: one protein-based, the other with jojoba oil, for instance. These "beauty" products are practical and save time. A quick spray on the puppy's coat and the brush glides over his fur. No more long-drawn-out brushing sessions! For untangling, spray and lotion eliminate the tangled locks in two steps and three motions.

## Eye Care

Once a week, the outline of the eye must be wiped with clean gauze. The gauze is soaked in lukewarm boiled water, or a physiological serum, or even an eye lotion. This antiseptic eye solution avoids the irritations to which the puppy is exposed as he runs in the wind, particularly in the country.

## Ear Care

The hairs covering the entrance to the external ear and the auditory canal, which are abundant in some breeds like the Poodle, the Yorkshire Terrier, and the Bichon, need to be cut. By getting stuck to ear secretions, these hairs may cause formation of a plug and blockage of the auditory canal. The cerumen, consisting of sebaceous secretions and sweat secretions, is eliminated naturally in the puppy, but the self-cleaning power may sometimes become reduced. The cerumen is then produced in unusually large amounts. It can be dissolved with the help of an ear product: the ears are massaged with this product and the dirt loosens on its own: the puppy shakes his head and evacuates the debris. This method is much safer than using a cotton tip, which if misdirected packs the dirt down instead of pulling it out. Obviously the external ear must not be forgotten: every week, with cotton soaked in lukewarm boiled water or an ear lotion, all the folds are cleaned, and then dried with cotton.

It is not advisable to wash a puppy less than 6 months old. dry shampoo will suffice, followed by a rubdown with a terry-cloth towel. After the age of 7 months, the puppy may be bathed regularly: every 2 or 3 months if he lives in the country, once or twice a month if he lives in town.

*Though not so meticulous as the cat's, a puppy's grooming is still effective. It is left up to the master to inspect eyes and ears, which the puppy cannot reach. Any unusual drainage must be reported to the vet, because it might be a sign of disease requiring treatment.*

171

## White Fangs

The dog toothbrush, on sale at the veterinarian's or at your local pet store, is provided with extra-soft bristles to protect supersensitive gums. The head makes a 135° angle with the handle. That is practical in use, whatever the position of the puppy, who must be accustomed very early to its use.

## Nothing Wrong with His Teeth!

Veterinary laboratories have invented several dentifrices for dogs. The irresistible toothpaste with the wild taste, reminiscent of feasts of meat and other tasty treats, the mint-flavored dental gel with the meaty aftertaste, and the artful, famous chewing bone: while the puppy chews, nibbles and salivates, he cleans his teeth without knowing it. This product, which dates from 1982, has opened the way for other inventions. Among the latter, there is the 100% natural ox-hide bone, which has become the first fluorinated dentifrice for dogs. Of course it has a beefy taste!

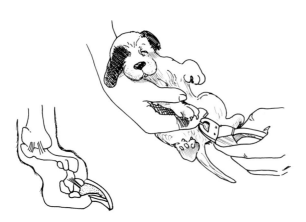

## Tooth Care

Once a week at least, you must clean the puppy's teeth to prevent tartar formation. This unsightly deposit, located at the junction of gums and teeth and due to the fermentation of scraps of food, is the source of many problems: later on it will cause loosening of the teeth or lesions on the gums. As an adult, a canine often needs to visit the vet, who will remove the dental plaque by an ultrasound process. So it's best to follow a good buccodental hygiene routine from early on, to avoid caries and destroy bacteria.

## Care of the Pads

To rid the puppy of the dirt that gets stuck between his toes, you have to cut the hairs at the same length. This simple bit of grooming, of which the frequency will vary according to the number of times he goes out or for walks, is very important. At the end of a stroll, the pads need very close examination, for they may be harboring bits of glass, spikelets or maybe little stones, which hurt your pet and may result in infections and cause abscesses.

## Care of the Claws

If they are too long, continuously growing claws may hamper the puppy when he walks. This is of particular concern for city dogs who do not wear down their claws on the ground as their country counterparts do. So the claws need to be cut with clippers, or a special drop-action clipper for dog's claws. You hold the end of the paw in one hand, then with the other you clip the tip of the claw, being careful not to cut it too short, because you might hit a vein (the gray part on the diagram opposite).

## Care of the Anal Sacs

This operation, unpleasant though it is, still has to be scheduled every month. It involves "clearing the anus," that is, squeezing the anal sacs located on either side of the anus. A nauseating brown liquid, which the puppy has not managed to expel on his own, now comes out of them. Very bothered by this excess, the

*In order to observe the breed standard, the master of this Maltese Lapdog must wrap each lock in tissue paper and finish the brushing with a toothbrush. Thus spruced up, the puppy will perhaps win the certificate of admissibility to the standard championship.*

## How to Have Charm

The dog's natural world has a sort of similarity to a fashion parade. Some dogs wear hose (markings located on their extremities) or are made up with beauty spots (markings on the inner angle of the eyebrow). You see some wearing a dark mask, the Boxer for instance. As for coats, some prefer suits: the English Cocker wears trousers; as for the German Mastiff, he never goes out without a tie—a white marking that shows up against his black fur—and he also wears socks on his front paws: more casual, the Basset Hound is seen in pajamas, and the slack, relaxed skin on his rump shows us two big pockets of a sort, hanging on the calves of his legs. The length of coats goes to both extremes: the Hungarian Shepherd's fur is 11 in. (27 cm) long; the German Shepherd's is 1.5 in. (4 cm). As for the naked Mexican dog, he finds himself...stark naked. Every puppy has its own special look: a center hair part for the Lhasa apso, a pony tail for the Shih Tzu, a topknot for puppies inconvenienced by having big locks of hair over their eyes, etc.

puppy may show his discomfort by rubbing his hindquarters along the ground as if he were itching. Action must be taken to avoid infection.

## LIFE AS A SHOW DOG

Grooming is the guarantee of beauty and elegance. Jacuzzi, blower, grooming table, drying hutch, to say nothing of clippers, combs, carding brushes, and scissors (straight, tapering, or sculpting) make up the panoply. At the grooming salon, care is taken to observe the standard for each breed. Remember that the certificate of admission to the beauty championship has been transformed into the certificate of admission to the standards championship [CAC]. The groomer therefore makes every effort to approximate his "model" to the standard of beauty, and in order to do so, to disguise the puppy's flaws, from rotundity to defects in his muzzle. Any puppy who lies down on the antislip runway, whether he has a pedigree or not, has been made to look his best: a Poodle has a choice among the Bolero cut, the Zazou cut or the Saint-Tropez cut (with ringlets around the paws); a Yorkshire Terrier could not possibly escape having hair curlers put in!

### Canine Perfumes

The final grooming touch is perfume. Some veterinary laboratories have created complete ranges of deodorants in the form of lotions or sprays, and deodorizers that eliminate unpleasant odors from baskets.

But bothersome secretions also come from the mouth, which can be treated with menthol, and the ears, which can be cleaned with ear lotion. After this refined grooming, the puppy has earned his toilet water: a sweet perfume for a little bitch, a fruity perfume—more muscle in it—for the male!

## Such a Lot of Colors!

In Italy, the really stylish thing to do is to match the color of one's dog's coat to the color of one's shoes or car: golden yellow, salmon pink, pastel green, or sky blue! It has made the grooming expert Oscar Ripamonti forget what the dog's natural colors are. And yet, in the range of breeds, the palette is varied and the shading subtle. The deep black of the Labrador, the Giant Schnauzer, and the black Cocker is different from the jet black of the miniature Pomeranian, the slate color of the Briard, and from the bluish shade (a dilute black) of the Chow Chow. White is genetically impossible according to dog experts, but the creamy white of the Samoyed, the Terrier, and the Komondor contrasts with the dilute yellow of the Westie. Yellow dresses the puppy in a coat of light: pale yellow for the Labrador Retriever, golden for the Cocker Spaniel. Tawny animals dress up in subtle shades: light or dark for the Boxer, flame in the Brittany Griffon, sometimes buckskin, apricot, reddish, wheat gold, or sable when diluted as the Whippet's coat is. Sometimes cherry, sometimes mahogany, such are the shades of the characteristic red of the sumptuous Irish Setter. Plain coats, two-tone coats, tricolor coats, even "quadricolor" coats. Combinations of colors are numerous in our dog friends: a tawny coat with charcoal (tawny and black on the tips of the hairs), a brindled coat with crosswise stripes in the Boxer, diamond patterns in the Mastiff, patchwork in the Welsh Corgi, piebald with a speckled background in the Pointer.

*Is there any need to turn to dyes when perfectly naturally, within the same breed, the same litter even, as with these Cocker Spaniels, varied colors are embellished with spots and speckles and other designs?*

*We promise, we swear! These three harlequins have not overturned the inkpot. Their coats, in bad-student's-blotting-paper style, are entirely natural for German Mastiffs.*

## Nutrition and Beauty

Foodstuffs play an important part in the beauty of the coat and the health of the skin. A puppy deprived of essential fatty acids (EFA), present in wheat, corn, and sunflower germ, shows a dry skin: wounds take a long time to heal. If the puppy loses his hair and his luster, if his skin is scaly, it's certain that he has a protein deficiency. So he needs fish, eggs, and meat rich in amino acids. To have a beautiful coat, the young dog must not lack vitamins either. They contribute to hair and sebum formation, they promote pigmentation, renew the epidermis, and activate the bacteriological defense system. It takes only a biotin or vitamin H deficiency for hair to lose its color and skin to become too dry. Proportionate consumption of butter, liver, and foods of plant origin enable the problem to be remedied. Lastly, the puppy needs milk, wheat germ, and yeast, all rich in vitamin $B_6$, and also animal fats, green vegetables, and oil-bearing plants. Nourished in this way, he is armed to escape skin problems. There remain the famous trace elements: for lack of zinc, skin thickens, hair loss is a sure thing (especially around the lips, ears, and pads); deprived of copper and iron, a pretty pup with ebony fur becomes reddish and covered with stringy hair; without iodine, the puppy has soft, thick skin from which the hair has been lost.

# Preadolescence

*Whatever his size, the puppy coming up to adolescence is acquiring confidence and trying to have things his way. He is tortured by a desire to take the master's place: already disturbed by the opposite sex, he is giving us all sorts of trouble and is starting to go on the loose. How can we get him back on the right path and prevent his setting up an irreversible hierarchy?*

*Adventuring is part of the program. The age of love affairs will soon be here, with preadolescent dogs following their noses and running off on their own.*

*Nothing can slow down this Golden Retriever when he's on the run. However, he risks encountering danger on his way if his master is not vigilant. Little love affairs are not the only reason for running away: there is also lack of affection, jealousy, etc.*

 **At 4 months, the puppy's motor activity begins to decline.**

**At 5½ months, development of the young dog's brain is complete.**

## THE HIERARCHY-ESTABLISHING PHASE
### (from 13 to 16 weeks)

Who gives the orders? Who obeys? From the age of three months on, the puppy knows his place among his own kind. To keep his rank, he sometimes has to fight, at the risk of a few injuries. The highest ranked assumes the privilege of attacking when he likes, whom he likes. Even though the competitive spirit may move his adversaries, he is always the one who retains the priority. You can recognize the boss among thousands: he's the one showing his teeth and growling...His adversary, tail between his legs, fur flat, body crouched, trying to make himself as small as possible, accepts his inferior position, always ready to obey. To each his own rank. It's a code: among dogs, one is either dominant or dominated.

The first spends his time putting the second in his place: the latter has the job of appeasing his superior, whose anger is ever increasing. If the boss raises his hackles, the underling keeps calm. His fur remains smooth, as if he were naked, completely open to the dictatorial whims of his interlocutor. The stronger dog has only one thing on his mind: making an impression. To show his status, he performs the flank ritual. He gives his neighbor a sudden bump, whether the latter is standing up or lying down, and he keeps the pressure up. His method? Get across the pathway as if to prevent his adversary from entering it.

Rooted to the spot, he stays still as a statue of salt, well positioned to observe his underling's every gesture and every motion. If he does not succeed in intimidating him, he performs the mounting ritual: arching his back, he places his front paws on his underling's shoulders. This scenario is merely a charade intended to impress, no more, no less. As if to attack, he prepares to leap: it's a trick that has the intended effect, for the other dog backs away. Then the stronger one acts out the ambush scene, crouching down...or pretending to.

The body attitudes of each of them reveals a well-established hierarchy. Among dogs, this scheme of things is immutable, but the boss insistently stresses his authority. No question of letting himself be dethroned! He has a distinct presentiment: some day or other, his subordinate will get the notion that he wants to reign. It is this image of a conquering, ambitious puppy that persists in cohabitation with the master. During the whole hierarchy establishing phase, the young dog aspires to gain his stripes and send his master to the bottom of the ladder. If nothing is done to make his efforts fail, he will gain ground. How can we put the clock back to the right time?

## A Boss Mentality

For the young dog, nothing is more logical than to try to take over the controls. The parallel is established right away: just as he tried, among his own kind, to get the best place, he tries in the same way, with human beings, to reverse the roles. In the beginning, a little bit of a dog trying to lead us by the nose is touching! On walks, he's the one who decides which way to go. He sets off to the right or left, stops at the intersection, takes his time; in the country he sniffs the ground, then starts again when he feels like it, retraces his steps…It's simple, his master is on the end of the leash, obeying at every quarter turn! Does this young dog really have such a strong personality, or is his master lacking in that department? If we do not react very quickly, the dog will become intolerable as he grows up. He starts by settling into our armchair and gradually goes on to occupy all the hierarchical positions that should be forbidden him. Have we granted him a corner on the bed? He will never be willing to leave it again because he has made it his personal territory. The sweet, pretty puppy drowsing at the foot of the bed becomes increasingly encroaching. If he is of a large breed, you can expect to be putting up with a 75-lb. (35-kg) heavyweight on your comforter, ready to growl when you want him to move over!

## He Puts up a Resistance

Even before adolescence, a puppy like this does not take long to make it clear that he's at home here. To mark his territory clearly and to indicate his

*Top: This English Setter has indeed learned the leader-subordinate lesson. From there he sits to attention!*
*Bottom: Who's giving the orders? Which of these two Hungarian Pointers is obeying? At the age of three months, among dogs, the hierarchy is clearly established.*

**By seven months, the dog must know how to obey the order "lie down." The words are repeated when he has settled down on his abdomen, but he can also be forced to assume this position by giving him the order to lie down.**

179

*Nobody can change anything in this scenario. There's inevitably one little Borzoi who's trying to become the boss.*

## The Wolf Camp

The sense of territory is very marked among wolves. The dominant male is located in the central point. Around him strut the subdominant adults, whose rank is awarded by the boss. They are surrounded by the young males. Then come the wolfcubs, both sexes together. But the circle would be incomplete if there were no "scapegoat" dominated by all—this is the famous outcast that you find for instance in cat societies. On the female side, the dominant wolf need not envy her male counterpart. She occupies exactly the same position. The subdominant females assemble around her, followed by the younger ones. Lastly the wolfcubs fall into line—males and females—owing obedience to the whole extended family.

Among dogs, a big boss dominates the pack and rules the troop. He is sustained in this role by a superdominant male, placed just beneath him and equal to the superior female, whose authority is immense. It is she who has the last word over the subdominant males. The latter are not powerless, however: they reign over females of their own rank, who themselves dominate the young males to whom the very young females must submit.

dominance, he urinates on the carpeting. As of that moment, the master has become his underling. The young dog no longer knows how to obey. When we give him an order, he puts up a resistance. Assuming a threatening stance, he shows his teeth, lifts his upper lip, lowers the bottom lip. His mouth is open, the corners of the lips stretched forward: he is ready to bite. On the alert, ears pricked up and pointed forward, he is watching his adversary for the slightest hint of aggressiveness to set off an uproar. The tail between the legs, sign of allegiance, has been replaced by the upright whip, as with his own kind. This is the way he emits odors from the anal area to assert his identity. Leader of the pack and head of the line, he fully intends to remain so. If he tail quivers, he's getting angrier. On his head and shoulders the hair rises, forming crest and mane. He growls and glares.…

### Putting Him in His Place

Where does his dominance come from? Behaviorists have been wondering about this: have we paid him excessive attention and thus raised him to godlike status? Is he too isolated, thwarted in his desire for freedom? Has he been a victim of psychic traumatization? Has it been hard for him to tolerate moving house? Is he unhappy over the death of a loved one? Is he comfortable at the kennel? Is he bored at home?

Even though he properly assimilated the "subordinate-leader" lessons as of his seventh week, he cannot escape a serious revision that consists of three main courses: elevation (he is taken by the scruff of the neck and lifted off the ground), inversion (he is turned over on his back or else lifted up in a lying position), and pronation (he is laid down on his side and his back paw is lifted so as to uncover his abdomen).

Lastly, he is at an age to go on to the "lie down" lesson. Lying stretched out on the floor, in the "battle lost" position, his throat exposed, he recognizes his submissive attitude. As soon as he opens his thigh, victory! He's finally admitting that you're the boss.

What organization!

## THE RUNAWAY AGE
### (as of 3 months)

A new whim: our puppy takes off by himself, at the risk of being endangered on the roads. This behavior nevertheless shows that he is now capable of managing on his own, without his master. Our young adventurer is impelled by his canine instinct: he wants to locate prey, explore his territory, and extend it.

If, when springtime comes around, he has reached the age of 5 or 6 months, he is going to experience a big thrill: it's the season of love. The bitch gives off pheromones, and the male, even at a distance, perceives all the unusual and intoxicating odors. It is understandable that, at that time, canine escapades break records. But sex is only one incentive for running away.

## MALE AND FEMALE
### (from 4 to 5 months)

The young males get on their mother's nerves. They are there, sniffing the anal area, bewildered, nostrils dilated. The bitch can no longer stand their presence close to her flanks. She banishes them from her sight when they begin adolescence. On the other hand, she grants a certain indulgence to the calmer, steadier young females. That is how, in the wild state, two clans are formed—males on the one side, females on the other—instituting two hierarchies.

## LIVING IN A GANG
### (from 5 to 6 months)

Anyone who loves me, follow me! That could be the puppies' motto. The hierarchy-establishing phase is succeeded by the period known as gang-organizing time, which marks the end of the juvenile phase. To live in a pack, everyone remains firmly on his position. Watch out for disputes! Assemblies are frequent: they all come together in the same district, they go off to conquer new places, males on one side, females on the other.

With the master, a new team is formed: the human being is the head of it, and the puppy is at his command.

*Initial approaches between two Fox Terriers of opposite sex. In the wild, males and females make up two clans with well-established hierarchies.*

**In no case must a lesson situating the puppy's rank with respect to his master ever be confused with entertainment or games.**

## SENSE OF TERRITORY
### (at 7 months)

In the wild, it's gang living that causes the dog to mark out his territory. Tiny but perfectly structured, this space gathers all the members of the pack into circles. Dogs are placed according to their social rank. The center area welcomes the chiefs. As on the master's property, you have to show your credentials to get in. But the other dogs are always keeping an eye on things and the weaker ones have the mission of watching and giving the alert. As soon as an intruder approaches the territory, they bark, threaten, show their fangs. What a dog's job! The sentinels ensuring the gang's safety have a chance of being upgraded. However, the center, domain of the lords, is not accessible without permission from the bosses.

# Language

He whines, gives shrill cries, growls. You might say he mews, too. A little later on, he yaps or yelps. And, of course, he barks. But what do all these dog vocalization patterns mean?

From his tail to his ears, his body also expresses his emotions. The young dog is able to make himself understood by his own kind, by us, and...by the cat.

He also reveals himself in his various behaviors: he lets his tongue hang out, lifts his leg, bumps into everything in his path...The dog's code is a thousand leagues away from ours. His attitudes and his behaviors always have a meaning, good or bad, that we need to be able to interpret.

*With his eyes, ears, tail, fur, back, and paws, the young dog shows his state of mind and his wishes. It's up to his master to find out about this language.*

## VOCAL LANGUAGE

The more the puppy grows, the more he gives tongue. He emits many more sounds than his peers in the wild. But not all breeds are equally talkative and noisy: though the Cocker and the Dachshund have pretty good "volume," the Chow-chow and the sled dog keep a mute on; as far the Basenji, with his special larynx, he has a toneless voice: you can't hear it.

To vary his repertoire, the puppy, who enjoys changing his tone, plays on duration, frequency, volume, and rhythm. To go from one register to another, he also has some mechanical sounds at his disposal: panting and chattering his teeth. A whole range of vocal sounds expresses his emotions: moaning, shrill whining, groaning, mewing, yapping, growling, howling, coughing…and barking of course. That's not all: to tell more about it, he can make up a clever mixture. The sounds are superposed and you hear a sort of growling bark, a howling bark, or a yapping bark. In canine musicology, you would call them mixed sounds. The puppy does not deploy all his vocal wealth just for the pleasure of making a noise or to express himself. You need only lend him an attentive ear to perceive that the concert has nothing to do with background music.

Howling, for instance, is not an ordinary sound. It's the wolf's only means of expression. Among canines it is frequent with the Samoyed, the Malamute, and the Husky. It is not heard at night, but at dusk, emitted by a number of dogs locating each other. In the wintry countryside, at evening, when a dog howls "at death," it's because he is alone, too isolated, and wants to be reassured. If another dog, a few hundred meters away, answers his calls, communication is established. The dialogue continues, interminable. Howling is a very infectious means of expression. When he moans, a puppy is telling about his pleasure and how happy he is to live close to his mother and to play with his brothers and sisters. Yet it is the very same cry that will betray his discomfort, later on.

By giving shrill cries, he demonstrates that he is in pain. When he growls, he is in a bad mood; deep, cavernous rumblings from his throat are threats. His voice is deep when he is sure of himself. Sometimes the sounds grow softer, less muted, less surly: then he is said to be grumbling. If he is not sure of himself, sounds which were almost shrill disappear into a yapping bark, a sign of impatience and feigned threats. If he needs to defend himself or warn his people, his bark is muffled.

Barking is the dog's ordinary call: often incorrectly, it is confused with threatening. However, if he repeats his "woof" to the point of monotony, and even being annoying, the young dog is anxious and uncertain. When he barks upon a stranger's visit, of course he wants to inspire fear, but at the same time he is asking to be relieved of his own fright. At this precise moment, he has visions of other dogs coming to his side, as happens in the extended canine family in the wild. That really is a puppy's way of doing things.

The little canine barks are every turn when he is very young: because he's happy, because he doesn't have everything he wants, or even just because he's playing, chasing his peers as if he were pursuing prey. Barking regularly keeps pace with group activities.

With human beings, the dog has other reasons for barking: he greets his master when he comes through the doorway, he invites him to play; he also lets it be known when things are not all right in his doggy life. For barking is not just a hymn to joy: it's also a distress signal and we need to be able to understand it. Fortunately it's easier to guess what is happening with our pet when we look at him. The whole truth comes out in his body language.

## BODY LANGUAGE

With his eyes, ears, tail, fur, back, and paws, the dog can show how he feels and what he wants. Is he being nice, or on the alert? His whole body gives him away, just as much as his sign language does. If he wrinkles up his face, we fear aggressiveness. You can read the corners of his mouth like an open book: when they are raised and his ears are pricked up, the puppy is bursting with boldness. Have a care: from one minute

*The puppy has at his disposal a huge range of sounds for communicating. If he howls "at the dead" it means he's all alone and wants to be reassured. Depending on subtle differences, barking expresses, anxiety, joy, or encouragement to play.*

to the next, he might even attack. On the other hand, if the corners of his mouth are pulled back, our dog is not feeling calm. He is utterly panicked when they are fully stretched to the point of curling over into a sort of hem. With his tail, the puppy reveals what he wants and what he is feeling. Since he was seven weeks old, he has known that by wagging it he delivers a message. He tested this invention while he was still a suckling: right and left, with his pendulum-like tail, he made his bothers and sisters understand him; it was also by this means that he begged his mother for food. Then as the days went by, he discovered that through his tail he held the key to language.

Because of the various tail positions, because of the motions and impulses he gives his tail, the dog can hide nothing from us. If he thumps his tail, it means he is preoccupied by two different states of mind, and

isn't sure what to do. That happens when his master returns to him: the joy of being with him again is mingled with the fear, rooted in him like a weed, of disappointing him.

The frequency and manner of wagging his tail also supplement his way of expressing himself. The little dog who is demonstrating his obedience wags slackly and limply. Conversely, if he is very agitated, or even aggressive, he lashes his tail stiffly and with determination. Is he holding it up high or at half-mast? If he wags if toward the ground, he's feeling that he's at the bottom of the ladder; if he hoists it skyward, thus marking his self-confidence, he feels he's the boss.

That's not all: he also gives his anal sacs a vigorous lashing, to bring out the odoriferous substances that reveal his state of mind and constitute a form of language in widespread use among dogs. Sometimes,

*When he approaches a strange object or another animal with his tail held high, this young Vendean Briquet Griffon shows that he is not at all impressed.*

As he grows up, the puppy's repertoire is gradually reduced to only three or four vocalization patterns, half as many as when he was in his infancy.

## He Knows All About Us

A puppy is perfectly capable of reading a person's intentions. His sense of smell is an information service: in the odor of the perspiration and in the acidity of the skin, he detects the effect of emotion hormones. His eyesight does not mislead him either: signs and gestures, which reveal feelings and opinions, are easy-to-read messages for a canine used to communicating and expressing himself in this way in his clan.

too, he puts his tail between his legs: a sign of insecurity, fear, and forced submission. In that case, none of his feelings must show, no trapped odor can escape. Placing his caudal appendage between his legs is the equivalent of veiling one's face in the human world.

### The Dog and Us

With us, our dog friend often uses his tail to make himself understood; he carries it low when he comes to greet us, showing us his pleasant side. If he is exquisitely polite, he offers his forepaw. When we inspire him with respect, he dips his colors, tail and ears well down, seated on his hind legs. As he recognizes his master, he crouches three-quarters of the way down. As proof of total submission, he tucks his tail between his legs, then lies down. He is all ours, he surrenders and tries to say so by wagging his tail.

When the time comes to beg us to play with him, he places his muzzle on our arm. Play, ever again: hindquarters raised, his tail like a crescent moon, his back bent, his front paws folded back, and his ears pricked up, he drums with his paws. He's full of joy! In his rapture he licks our mouths. When in order to protect his master he wants to point out something unusual happening in the house, the puppy is no longer the same: befogged by his mission, he raises his tail at the same time as his ears to give the alert. Eyes glued to the strange object, he can see nothing else. Is he afraid? He remains silent and tucks his tail under his belly. Sometimes he loses his temper. His anger is easy to see. There is one sign that is never misleading: he nibbles the edge of someone's trouser leg. Be careful: he might suddenly go on the attack. His body is all stiffened up, his tail in the air, the fur on his back raised, and his ears pricked up. Flews stretched, he seems to have a sneering smile, showing that he is ready to leap. If he has to defend himself, his tail stays horizontal. His ears are flattened, his back arched. That's not groaning you hear, but growling. But if something attacks him, he cries "Uncle," lying down on his back, legs apart, displaying his genitals. The puppy's language is perfectly clear to his peers, but not always correctly interpreted by human beings. Thus it is that very friendly attitudes of his sometimes earn him unjustified reprimands, for his conduct is the same with everyone, those close to him as well as strangers. The soggy kiss with which he favors his master by way of greeting may be very displeasing to friends, who right away take him for an ill-mannered creature. He doesn't know that he may be annoying when he barks a number of times to invite people to play. Crestfallen, the poor wretch is sent away with an authoritarian "Lie down!"

## Dogs Among Themselves

Nothing has changed since the time of their ancestors. The language of dogs, for all breeds as a whole, is universal. Through his signs and attitudes, the dog asserts his rank in canine society and communicates with his own kind.

### Meeting

To get to know each other, dogs sniff at each other without observing each other. As a matter of fact, staring is provocation: if the bolder one looks his counterpart right in the eye without having introduced himself first, he is committing a serious insult which leads to a scrap. After a pause spent sniffing each other, with ears pricked up, an approach is made with measured tread. They walk discreetly around each other and sniff each other's hindquarters. Exchange of visiting cards: each emits a spray of urine. The ice is broken.

### Greeting

As a sign of politeness, the ears are flattened and suddenly contract. The corners of the lip raised rearward, they decide to give each other a broad smile ("You like me, I like you"). Everything's perfect: the doggies can just play together now. If there are no affinities between the two dogs, each of them simply goes back where he came from.

### Threatening

When two dogs dislike each other, they vie as to which can be more intimidating. Tail raised, hackles raised,

*One dominant dog, one underling. The hierarchy is established as of the first meeting.*

*If the dominant dog shows that he is somewhat authoritarian, the underlying submits completely by presenting his vulnerable neck.*

*To make each other's acquaintance, dogs sniff each other without looking each other in the eye.*

*When contact has been established, the puppies can play.*

## Unchanging Puppy Ways

All his life, a dog retains the attitudes he had as a young puppy. By wiping his tongue across our faces, he is repeating the sequence for asking for food and maternal affection. Sometimes it happens that he licks his sexual organ: this is also a childhood memory, for his mother calmed him down by licking him there. Is he lying on his back and waving his front paws? He wants to be tickled, as in the days when the mother dog massaged his abdomen before swallowing his excrement. Is he putting his paw on his master's knee? In his earliest infancy at the time when he was still being suckled by his mother, he used to press his paw against her nipples, seeking a caress or a tidbit.

The puppy does a lot of begging: he's asking for mercy, tail tucked under, ears laid back, when he lies down on his back. That's how he cried "Uncle!" to his brothers and sisters when he was losing the fight.

*Though the dog's language isn't the same as the cat's, some gestures are ambiguous: this cat does not seem at all pleased to have a newcomer in his territory!*

Depositing excrement is another form of marking, more common among wild canines, such as the coyote, the jackal, or even the spotted hyena.

## Between the Dog and Us

You can hardly imagine to what extent human beings impress a dog. Our upright stance intimidates him: he feels really tiny at our feet. So a crouching position is recommended for approaching an anxious dog. In addition to this, you should not focus your gaze and never stare him in the eye!

For the dog, unlike human beings, never look straight at someone's eyes. This is a sign, not of hypocrisy, but of submission. If he stares at us, it means he's threatening us.

Why does he suddenly feel like attacking? Certain postures set off this reflex—when we lean over him, for instance. A few clothing-related details also make him distrustful: the peak of a cap casting a shadow over a face; dark glasses veiling the messages he uses to unmask us, etc.

frowning forehead, flews pulled back, they walk around each other. Then they growl: the tension is rising. Most of the time there is no declaration of war and they remain on equal terms. They each continue on their way again, lifting a leg and taking their eyes off each other.

### Farewell to Arms

When two dogs cannot stand each other, war is inevitable. The two enemies place themselves in a T-formation, the stronger one along the vertical line, right in the middle of the other one. Sure of himself, the dominant dog has his heckles raised, his ears pricked up, his tail in the air, and his mouth half open. He may be content with a threatening attitude: head up, eyebrow raised, eye dilated. He stretches his neck out, all his teeth bared, his tail on the horizontal. But he may also stiffen his body, and put his head and then his paw on the underling's neck, grab his muzzle and growl. Will the adversary yield? If he does consent, he looks away, flattens his ears and pulls his neck in. Then he lies down, rolls over on his side, his hind legs parted skyward and his abdomen exposed. He offers his neck and throat and urinates a little. It's all over: he's laying down his arms. Without violence or biting, this is a very common combat procedure.

### Fighting

To come to blows using their teeth is the last recourse for dogs who have not been able to make peace upon meeting. This is the only outcome dictated by their agnostic behavior (behavior for resolution of a conflict with another animal). Each of them tries to dodge the other's jaws while attempting to topple the enemy by striking him with his paws. They grab each other by the neck, the withers, the shoulder. Whichever of them manages to throw his adversary to the ground and keep him there by threatening to bite is the winner.

## Between Dog and Cat

Are they really enemy brothers? Among them, mischievous games and velvet paws are more frequent than scratches and bites. Though the first meeting is a regular conversation between deaf folk—the body language not having the same meaning for both—dog and cat get along well together afterwards. When they are raised together, they experience youthful errors together (slippers in shreds, vases in pieces) as well as learning how to be clean and finding out about the master's punishments and signs of affection. They have the same enthusiasm for play. So it's a perfect partnership.

## GAIT

From the time he's three weeks old, the puppy stops dragging himself around on his stumpy little legs like a seal on the sand, and practices a number of ways of walking. He keeps pace, like a good dog; he merrily trots along on forest walks. Then expanding pent-up energy takes precedence over the restrictions on too well-behaved a dog, and he's off at the gallop! A regular slalom champion, he moves like lightning, weaving in and out among the trees. These three gaits are valuable ways of expressing himself.

Change of direction: as he's running headlong, he suddenly changes direction, though we don't know what's prompting him. This is a common tactic with a hunting dog in full pursuit of prey that zigzag as they flee, and whose motion he follows closely.

Carried along by the excitement of the game, he takes off from the ground to leap after the ball. A single relaxation of the powerful muscles of his hindquarters and he is projected into the air, leaping three times his own height! His aerodynamic form is perfect. He runs, he stops, he jumps as if for a takeoff; he flies forward, forelegs folded, then in full ascension, folds his hind legs. Way up there, his eyes fixed on the ball, he starts his descent, with his hind legs under his body. He plunges into the second phase of the jump, with his tail acting as rudder. Before he falls to the ground, he stretches his front limbs as far as they will go, with the back ones extended behind. No trouble with the landing: his legs have hardly touched the ground when he pulls the hind legs under his body

*The dog has three gaits: walking, trotting, and galloping. This Tibetan Terrier, a champion racer, carried away by the game, can beat records and jump up to three times his own height.*

## Upright Like a Bear

In his surveillance job, the dog sometimes stands upright, exactly like marmots responsible for alerting their peers. It's known as the "bear position." Resting on a promontory or a little branch as light as a feather, in perfect balance, sniffing the air, he has his eye riveted on the horizon.

So this miniature Continental Spaniel (Papillon) does not lose sight of the football game in progress or is it something else that has caught his attention?

189

*Even if he doesn't feel like urinating, the dog lifts his leg. Trees, posts, bushes, lamp posts…. He has a preference for vertical objects. This is how he marks his territory and lets his peers know about it.*

**Defecation is used to differentiate among clans which may include up to eighty individuals. In order to impregnate places thoroughly with their odor, canines scrape the earth with all four feet. In this way they add the scent of the glands located on the ball of the foot.**

**By marking, the dog warns of danger, guarantees his safety, and protects his young. He avoids social conflicts and organizes his romantic appointments.**

close to the other two. Such speed! In his wild run, he has not wasted one-tenth of a second.

## DOG MANNERS
### A Sense of Territory

In the mind of a puppy, the house that shelters his master is a sacred place: it's the central place indwelt by the thinking head of the pack. Whether his place is "near God" or far behind, among powerless dogs, his mission is always the same: to keep watch and give warning in order to protect the boss. By barking, he marks his territory and sets the barriers stopping outsider dogs from coming in. The warning has been given: nobody had better walk on his flowerbeds! Intruders of the canine species are in any case perfectly able to translate the sounds he makes according to their intensity, broadcast amplitude, register, frequency, timbre, and harmonics. They'd better just behave themselves.

### He Urinates on Upright Objects

It's another way of marking his territory. The young puppy, who was used to finding reassuring odors in urine, now uses this practice to say that he has made himself at home. It all starts at puberty, between 7 and 9 months, or during the second or third time of coming into heat, in young bitches. The bigger the dog gets, the more he tries to appropriate and hold on to a territory. Trees, posts, bushes, lamp posts…vertical objects are what he prefers for setting the boundaries. The odors, nose-high, arouse the curiosity of his peer, who deciphers in them clear, precise messages, regular signboards affixed to a fence: "No entry," "Private game preserve."

From the urine, the dog quickly finds out about the "marking" peer's private life; it's obvious to his nose whether he's dealing with a male or a female, a puppy or an old dog. He knows all about the health and sexuality of the messenger, as well, when he came by, and lastly, what his hierarchical position is. Is an alarm signal, a threat, or an invitation involved? Depending on his interpretation, he is careful not to go into the property, private or otherwise, or else, on the contrary, he is at pains to add his own marks. If he's dominant, he raises his hackles and strengthens his personal odor by rolling, for instance, in a putrefying animal carcass. If the message left is an enticing proposition, he cannot let the opportunity slip and deposits his urine too. He is ready, right off the bat, to marry the unknown seductive female.

## He Lifts His Leg

Even if he doesn't feel like urinating, the dog lifts his leg. When he's facing another dog, this position shows his rank in the canine hierarchy. Does he lift his leg horizontally, like three-quarters of males? We are dealing with a dominant, very touchy about his territorial rights. If he encounters the slightest resistance, he'll attack: the other dog must very quickly get into the submission posture. Does he keep his leg down? His temperament is calm and resigned. He's an underling.

The crouching position is revealing, too: leg up, we are dealing with a superior female; down, she's a subordinate. Marking by a bitch in gestation is peculiar, especially before she gives birth. The mother-to-be scratches the ground as if making a nest, deposits a few hairs, then urinates in a very uncomfortable position—backwards, with her hind legs in the air. She does this over and over again, indefatigably. She marks intensively.

## He Jumps to Greet Us

The sight of his master rejoices his heart. How could he possibly hide his joy? He stands up on his hind legs, bouncing up and down like a ball. He is certainly showing how happy he is, but he is actuated to behave like this for a very simple reason: he's not very tall, and is trying to put himself at the same height as his master. He is trying to catch his eye. Is he being paid enough attention?

In the pack, the dog jumps to greet dominant members. With us, he cannot behave like that, such manners are not those of a civilized dog. It may be that

*For these two Briards who have nothing to drink, putting out their tongues is the only way to lower their body temperature.*

he is expressing some sexual impulse in this way, or what is more serious, that he wants to dominate his master. In that case he does not jump toward the face but at the throat, paws placed on the chest and shoulders. Beware! Danger! This has nothing to do with a demonstration of affection.

## He Hangs Out His Tongue

Running after the ball that's speeding miles away, what an effort! The puppy comes back panting, with his tongue hanging out. Why does he show us this fleshy organ, "mobile thanks to 17 striated muscles, innervated by the great hypoglossal nerve" according to the Larousse Dictionary?

Because he is perspiring! Our dog friend, unlike human beings and horses, is not endowed with sweat glands. He does not, like the cat, have the possibility of

*He digs and digs, this West Highland Terrier. His head is in the dirt because a treasure is hidden in it: his bone.*

refreshing himself by licking. Letting his tongue hang out is the only way he has found to feel less hot, if he has no water available. He reduces his body temperature by inhaling air, but for that the temperature has to be lower than 100.4–102.2°F (38–39°C)—his body temperature. During heatwaves, the problem is a crucial one. The dog has no recourse: the more he pants, the more hot air he swallows, and the more running will lead to disaster, risking heatstroke.

### He Hides His Bone

Treated with fluorine or made of ox hide, the bone you give your pet is like a little sweetmeat at the end of a meal. As in the wild, impelled by the food-burying instinct, he will inter his provisions. He scrapes with his front paws, then, in the hollow, deposits his bone, and with his muzzle—unlike the cat, who uses his paws—covers his treasure with earth. Even if he is well nourished, the dog has not rid himself of this ancestral gesture, a sign of great foresight: this is how the canine in the wild sets up his pantry after dismemberment of the prey, before hard times set in.

## CRAZY DOG ATTITUDES
### He Clings to Our Legs

This practice is frequent in the prepubescent puppy. When he was tiny, this was how he used to express the hierarchical pattern with his peers: the one who clings to the other one's body shows his dominance, asserts his authority. If he takes the master's moving leg for a doggy, it shows that he is missing the company of his own kind. But this attitude is not a practice of a well-mannered dog. If a stop is not put on his outbursts, our pet will become threatening.

### He Growls at the Mail Carrier

The attitude of the hurrying person who deposits the letters, turns, and hastens away arouses the hunter's instinct. For the dog, any fleeing object suggests prey and provokes as desire for pursuit. The mail carrier's rapid motion arouses his aggressiveness. In this scene he perceives the same nervousness that reigns when dogs meet and want to fight each other. In this case, the first one who backs off reveals his fear, admits his weakness. For the dog, that's exactly what the mail carrier does, inadvertently putting the canine in a position of strength.

### He Is Jealous

Let's call it frustrated, instead. As a result of some annoyance, the young dog is no longer as amiable and happy as before. Something has upset him. He has probably not been stroked like the other dogs in the household. He slips his head in between his protector's hand and the other dog in vain, it leaves his master cold as marble. This indifference provokes a diplomatic incident, followed by scrapping and grinding of fangs. The dogs shove and threaten each other. Yet the master is not there, they're as thick as thieves.

## He Wrecks Everything

Drapes in rags, chair legs scraped bare, moccasins chewed to shreds...be warned, the little dog is not feeling like himself. Is he not getting enough exercise? Is he lonely?

If he keeps on acting like a demolition crew as he grows up, there may be a problem: such behavior isn't normal. You need to fix up a quiet corner for him in the house, a den where he can use up his excess energies on a old blanket, for instance.

## He Is Scared

Suddenly he comes to a dead stop and stiffens up; the puppy is afraid. His ears are down, his tail tucked between his legs...He's all shrunken and shaking. In his terror, he urinates where he is. Panic makes him crazy: he does not hesitate to fly at the throats of dogs four times his size! In a mild state of anxiety, he can still overcome his apprehension, remain vigilant, and react quickly.

But if he's trembling, if he's turning his head in all directions, his mouth half open and his breathing rapid, his situation is more disquieting.

Anxious, he cannot leave the house without trembling: a falling leaf, sends him into veritable torpor and you can't get him out of his hiding places, either.

His fear is sometimes inexplicable. On the other hand, we can prevent other kinds of anguish due to nonadaption (e.g., a country-dwelling puppy suddenly projected into urban living). A phobia can also result from a bad experience like a car accident.

## He Is Aggressive

The gentlest of puppies are capable of biting. All it takes is for him to be afraid and he'll become incapable of analyzing a situation. He scratches himself, nibbles things, and coincidentally, bites.

It's the beginning of the end. As in a fair number of animals, aggressiveness in the dog occurs at the time of hierarchy establishment or on an occasion when some danger threatens the territory.

*Is this gentle Collie capable of biting? Fear may make any dog aggressive.*

Outside of that, it is not a natural phenomenon. Our puppy probably had a bad experience with some slice of life, or poorly assimilated some lesson. Does he have enough time for playing and using up his energies?

## He Doesn't Feel Safe

He makes life impossible for us. At the slightest sound, he jumps and barks; he is constantly overcome with fear. As if to get rid of his "uneasiness" he licks himself excessively, until he bleeds; he hides and trembles. Of course some genetic cause may be at the origin of his condition: his mother may have been disturbed during gestation, for instance. Or he may very simply not have been reassured enough or held in someone's arms when he was very little. Without affection, a young dog cannot fully develop.

# The Puppy in All His States

A perfect alliance of bone and muscle, the dog's body is all flexibility, made for jumping, galloping, and all-terrain running. Combining fur and the right temperature, his system can face up to cold and tolerate heat. With this well-built body and sharp senses, the puppy is ready for any exploits.

*Thanks to their insulating coats, these six athletically built Alaskan Malamutes can tolerate severe cold.*

*Motor muscles, flexor muscles, extensor muscles...Ideal architecture for these two German Pointers.*

Depending on the look and length of the limbs, a distinction is made among the medium-bodied type, to which the hunting dogs and shepherds belong, the short-bodied type, characterizing the Mastiffs and small domestic pet dogs—Pekingese, Pug, and French Bulldog—and the long-bodied type, which includes the Greyhounds and some Collies and Terriers.

## Successful Balneology Treatments

In Italy, at Bornio (Lombardy), in France, at Salles-en-Béarn (Pyrénées-Atlantiques), and in the US, at Calistoga, California, where the hot mineral springs are again being used, four-legged patients are not afraid to jump into the water.

Growth problems, joint lesions, arthrosis...all these ailments can be treated thanks to thermal cures. Muscle re-education does wonders in these waters rich in sulfate, bicarbonate, calcium, magnesium, phosphorus, and sulfur.

## A WELL-BUILT BODY
### Skeleton and Musculature

Bones and muscles make up an ideal architecture for hunting and racing. Motor and flexor muscles located at the level of the neck and withers, extensor muscles close to the spinal column, etc. The puppy is built like an athlete. His spinal column, flexible and powerful, also endows him with great motion capability: it consists of seven cervical vertebrae, thirteen thoracic vertebrae, seven lumbar vertebrae, three sacral vertebrae, and about 20 coccygeal vertebrae.

But more than to his back, it is to his loins, and his neck and withers, that the puppy owes his amazing flexibility. Like the cat, he has no clavicles: his forelimbs have no real articulation with his trunk and allow him to spin around. On the other hand, his feet are ridged: five digits on the forepaw, including a dewclaw, and four on the hind foot. He may have round, oval, elongated, or simply normal feet, unless he is "cat-footed" or "hare-footed."

His head consists of the skull bones (the occipital, parietal, and temporal bones) and the facial bones (the maxillary, frontal incisor, nasal, zygomatic and mandibular bones). The latter differ from one dog to another. So a champion is judged according to his stop (the line separating the skull and the face), the line of the forehead running down to the end of the nose, and the brow line separating the ears.

But a beauty prize is also determined from the withers, connecting the head and trunk to the neck, from the back, the curve of the lower back, and the croup. Vertically, which stresses the direction of the limbs with respect to the floor, is also reviewed. The ideal is that the line starting from the point of the shoulder and passing over the forearm, carpus, and digits should be vertical. If it deviates outward, the dog is described as "too open." If the reverse, the animal is "too closed" or his hindquarters are "too close together." The direction of the front paws is no trivial matter either. If they happen to close slightly together inward, the dog is said to be "knock-kneed"; opening outward, he is called "bowlegged." When the forearm and the elbow turn outward, they are "lyriform." Even the metacarpus causes objections to be raised. Is it long, very sloping, when seen in profile? The puppy is then "long-jointed," If it is short and vertical, our friend is "straight-jointed," a description that is common as concerns Terriers.

## Fur and Temperature

Thanks to his insulating coat that traps the air, the puppy is equally well protected from the heat and from the cold. A sled dog, used to being in the Far North, can tolerate a temperature that falls below −70°F (−57°C). His fur is very precious: the beard hairs, forming a fine smooth-looking down, insure thermic insulation and maintenance of the body temperature, despite external variations. The longer the fur, the warmer the dog. Between long hair and short hair, the temperature may vary from 33–34°F (0.5–1°C). Being homoiothermal [warm-blooded] the doggy has an internal temperature of 101.3°F (38.5°C) all the time. However, it does fall slightly, early in the morning, and rises again in mid-afternoon. If it falls below 98.6°F (37°C) or exceeds 102.2°F (39°C) something abnormal is occurring in the dog's body.

Another factor comes into play in body temperature maintenance: the respiratory rate. Faster in the puppy than in the adult dog, and more accelerated in dogs of large size, it varies according to the animal's age and activity.

# A WELL-FILLED HEAD
## Dentition

A puppy's age can be guessed from his teeth. The development of the set of teeth—periods of teething and replacement of the milk teeth—is the same for all dogs, whether or not they use their fangs in playing with their brothers and sisters, whether they are the offspring of guard dogs, or were born to be peaceable. First event: at 3 weeks, the canine teeth come through. Immediately afterwards, it's the incisors and premolars' turn: now you can tell that the puppy is between 24 and 30 days old. He is barely 4 months old

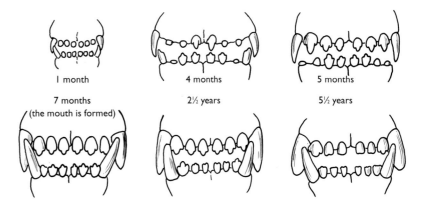

1 month     4 months     5 months

7 months (the mouth is formed)     2½ years     5½ years

Between 6 and 12 months, when the permanent molars come in, the puppy starts chewing again as he did at 3 or 4 months and even earlier, at 6 or 7 weeks. Look out for things left lying about! To help him cut his fangs, there's nothing better than a veal bone, a toy bone, or a dentifrice bone.

when his milk teeth fall out and the middle incisors are replaced. Two weeks later new intermediates (lateral incisors) and entirely new incisors located more toward the side take their places in his jaw. At 5 months, the puppy has his real canines, at 6 months his premolars, then his molars. By the time he's 7 months old, he can claim a full set of adult teeth. The lily-shaped, intact white incisors show that he is 1 year old. Three months later, the center lobe of the fleur-de-lys is damaged. Between 14 months and 2 years, the lower middle incisor is leveled; between 18 months and 2 years the incisors in the lower jaw are beginning to wear down. Soon the fleur-de-lys shapes of the upper incisors become harder to see, then disappear: the dog is 3 years old already. One year later, the incisors and intermediates, still in contact, are completely leveled. At 5 years, they are growing farther apart and are already starting to turn yellow.

At adult age, the dog has 42 teeth. Each half-jaw comprises three incisors, one canine, four premolars,

*The ear consists of three parts: the external ear (1), which collects sounds; the middle ear (2), which transmits vibrations; the inner ear (3), which transforms sounds and is involved in maintaining balance.*

**When racing, a young Saluki or other Greyhound, like a cheetah, may attain a speed of 45 mph (70 km/h).**

## Lovely Eyes

Bright yellow, nut-brown, light or dark, black...the dog's glance is in harmony with his coat and the end of his nose.

At an early age, all puppies have eyes as blue as a robin's egg. And though the Husky is distinguished by his blue eyes, he is the only one who keeps the youthful color. Being walleyed, which is due to loss of iris pigmentation, is a flaw.

two molars in the maxillary bone and three in the mandibular bone. The incisors play a minor role, but the premolars and molars, located behind the canines, are of capital importance: they cut up foodstuffs. We distinguish the precarnassials, the carnassials, and the postcarnassials.

### Sight

Dogs are somewhat myopic, in particular the Bulldog, the Pekingese, and the Boxer, all endowed with bulbous eyes. At a distance of 275 yards (250 m), the puppy cannot distinguish his master from a wooden dummy. He perceives details a little better at 165 yards (150 m). On the other hand, very sensitive to motion, he can catch a hand sign from over ½ mi. (1 km) away.

As concerns colors, the poor thing can't make them out well at all. His eye, protected by three eyelids, contains in the retina a large number of rods, 18 times more numerous than the cones that capture color. It is these rods that reflect the image in black and white. So does the dog maybe see his surroundings in pastel colors?

In the dark, his eyes shine. At night he can see like a cat. The back of his eye is lined with the *tapetum lucidum,* which intensifies light. His field of vision is excellent: he has an aperture of 270°. True, that's not so good as that of the horse (350°), but much better than that of a human being (180°).

### Hearing

Though the dog has very average sight, his hearing on the other hand is excellent, especially in certain breeds. It's a question of ear configuration: pricked up like those of a German Shepherd, they are a formidable advantage. On the other hand, hearing ability is diminished in a dog with long drooping, low-set ears, like those of a Saint Hubert [Bloodhound] or a Basset Hound. The dog is in fact capable, thanks to 17 muscles contained in each ear, of turning them toward sounds to pinpoint a noise. A single ear suffices to capture the emission of sound, but the pair is needed to evaluate wavelength differences.

The dog's ear consists of three parts: the external ear, which includes the pinna, a regular parabolic antenna, the auditory canal and the tympanum; the middle ear, composed of ossicles—the anvil (incus), the hammer (malleus), the stirrup (stapes); the internal ear, which receives the vibrations recorded by the middle ear. It is the internal ear, that transmits the information to the brain via the nerve fibers.

The dog has a hearing frequency up to 100,000 Hertz (compared to 20,000 for human beings). He perceives ultrasounds—the squeaking of a rodent under the ground or of a bat in the night. Our footsteps, for even better reasons, cause him to cock an ear long before we have stepped into the hallway. He hears the sound of leaves in the winter wind (10 decibels). It's easy to understand why the noise of thunder (120 decibels) is real torture to him. At 28 yards (25 m) distance, he hears a sound that we cannot detect beyond 5 yards (4 m). Does he take after the wolf, who can hear one of his peers howling 4 mi. (7 km) away?

## Nose

Such a sense of smell! The puppy's olfactory sense is a treasure: from the time he was born it enabled him to find his mother's nipple; later on to identify his path, people, and things. As an adolescent, he can tell where there's a female in heat for 6 mi. (10 km) around. His whole life depends on olfaction: it's the one last faculty that will remain with him in his old age.

What's his secret? The huge concentration of sensory cells: the dog's nose contains 220 million olfactory cells, compared to 5 million in human beings. His 200 square centimeters of mucosa, located in the nasal cavities, makes up the pituitary membrane and gives him an olfactory capability 100 times superior to ours. At detecting the butyric acid contained in perspiration, he is 100 times better than we are. Human perspiration, for a police dog, is as good as fingerprints. The dog has hundreds of opportunities in life thanks to his sense of smell: as a truffle dog, he can sniff out the precious tuber buried 12 in. (30 cm) deep.

*This English Setter enjoys a highly developed sense of smell, which makes him a good hunting dog. Some breeds, like the Bloodhound, can pick up the scent of an individual four days after he has passed by and track him for a distance of 45 mi. (70 km).*

## What Does He Dream About?

Barking, pedaling motions, whiskers quivering, wrinkling of the nose, ears being lowered, tail thumping...the puppy moving like that in his sleep is having a dream. Every six minutes, he can escape into the world of dreams. His brain stores up images of his experiences and reprints the behavior pattern. The puppy dreams of fights or has nightmares...

## Does He Have a Sixth Sense?

He knows when a storm is coming, hears seismic shocks; his sensitivity to changes in atmospheric pressure and variations in static electricity levels tell him before us about disturbances that are on the way; he finds his way back to his master after traveling hundreds of miles.... The fact is that the dog's brain, like that of the pigeon, is equipped with a micromagnet (in the form of magnetite in the nerve fibers). But you might also think that the dog has a sixth sense, from his amazing way of feeling things.

# Toward Adulthood

Childhood games are behind him; from now on, the senses rule. The young bitch has her first experiences of estrus, but she is not yet old enough to be impregnated. Of uncertain temper, she takes us on, has little appetite, and drinks when she's not thirsty. As for the adolescent male, he marks everything he comes across. Youth has to happen!

When adolescence is over, the young dog has not necessarily finished growing. But what a lot of things he has already experienced! When you have been lucky enough to know him as a tiny puppy, you are in a better position to understand him in adulthood. With the dog, one thing is certain: he will love us to the end of his days.

*Not all puppies are on the same schedule. Between the Dachshund who reaches his adult size at 12 months, and the German Mastiff who reaches his at 18 months, this Bloodhound will finish growing at around 15 months. A large part of his training will be done by then, and he will enter upon his life as a dog.*

## Sex and Orders

When the female is recalcitrant she sits down to show her disagreement. She sometimes accepts courting, but opposes being covered, which is an act of dominance. However, if the suitor is a superdominant, she may deign to get up. She stands to attention to receive the homage of her suitor.

**Adolescence is the time for sterilization for both sexes. The male may undergo castration (removal of the testicles). The female may be subject to a surgical operation (see page 55).**

## The Purpose of Marking

Just before mating, the young bitch keeps on marking the premises and leaving behind a thousand and one messages. They are the odoriferous chemical substances released by the sexual pheromones that are all powerful in canine communications. The hypophysis, located at the base of the brain, produces estrogenic hormones on a cyclical basis. stimulating the ovaries. The male is thus well informed as to his Dulcinea's condition. He drools, puts his tongue on the damp earth. He marks in his turn, generously, secreting the male hormone, testosterone, thanks to the glands located in the penis and around the edges of the anus. If he is a dominant, his odor is much stronger and the message lasts longer.

## A BIG CHANGE
### (as of 7 months)

The time of puberty has come. The physiological and behavioral differences between males and females make their appearance: each of them buries and forgets his babyhood. For him, it's constant marking: shrubs and stones sprinkled with his urine let his desires be known; for her, the transformations take longer.

### The Female

Puberty occurs with the appearance of the full genital cycle, from the age of 7 months or much later, around 14 or 15 months, in the case of a large-sized bitch. Earlier, the young female undergoes some hormone surges which indicate the start of ovarian activity. It results in the discharge of a few drops of blood. But this is false estrus, short-lived and not very intensive. The bloody discharge continues for 8 to 10 days. The bitch's vulva gradually increases in volume: this is proestrus. The males, perceiving exciting odors, are very much attracted, but irritated, she rejects them. Under no circumstances can she be impregnated during this period of time.

The pubescent bitch is very thirsty and urinates a lot, releasing chemicals that drive the males mad. These lovers are capable of traveling miles to meet her. They are not disappointed: while the vulva is distended, swollen, the young female allows herself to be approached by her suitors. Soon she has no more discharges. This is the beginning of the ovulation period, which will last between 10 and 15 days.

With us, the bitch is jumpy and displays a very different kind of behavior. Aggressive, capricious, she shows no interest in her meals, hardly touching anything and being very picky. She may also become timid, touchy and scared in the presence of other dogs.

The trouble is that the idea of making a getaway is constantly on her mind, because there is only one thing she wants to do: meet a male. If by any chance she happens to be free in the open countryside, she may be followed without the slightest embarrassment by 10 or so four-footed "hoodlums."

## The Male

Sexuality is completely different in the adolescent male dog. While the female may have sexual relations twice a year, the male can copulate throughout the year. So he is always in search of sexual relations. Aside from the few propitious days in spring and in autumn, which leaves 50 weeks of abstinence in a year, he is hardly ever satisfied. Sometimes, by the time he's 5 or 6 months old, he will indulge in sexual gestures on his cushion, a gesture he was already making at a month and a half when he mounted his brothers and sisters. At birth the sexual hormones are in place, but will not become active before 6 to 10 months.

## The Love Parade

The female is not always ready to accept the advances of the young beau. She attacks the male, chases him away, scolds him, bites him. She sits down as soon as he approaches and has quite made up her mind not to yield an inch. That goes on throughout proestrus.

After four days of ovulation, the parade can begin. The bitch runs toward the male, then backs off. If he has no idea what's going on, she struts about and hits him with her paws. He chases her, they meet. They sniff each other's neck and ears, their tails quiver. It's a good day for a love affair!

## Sex and Social Rank

In the pack, only dominant males have the right to mate. They choose females of their own rank. Those below it rarely mate, unless a superior male makes advances to them.

Lower-ranking females have a slower sexual operation, and their periods of estrus, which are low-key, are often synchronized with the estrus of high-ranking females. This curiosity of nature does the species many services: bitches of lower rank have false pregnancies and produce milk just when the dominant females are delivering their young. So the young puppies will never want for foster mothers.

As to underling males, they are completely inhibited in the presence of their chiefs and have no

*Lovers' meeting between two Dalmatians. The lovely lady isn't always ready to accept advances.*

After estrus, the cycle includes a third period, metestrus, which extends over a period of 3½ to 4½ months. This corresponds to the maturation and then the regression of the corpus luteum in the ovary. The bitch is now adult, capable of gestation and then lactation.

## False Pregnancy

This is a complex condition. Without ever having been impregnated, the bitch presents the same symptoms as if she were in gestation. She fusses over plush toys, guards them jealously, does not leave her nest. One astonishing fact: her nipples are all swollen and hard—milk is even seen leaking from them! As a matter of fact, the flow of milk is not an aberrant physiological phenomenon. When the bitch's ovaries are at rest (anestrus, or absence of estrus, lasts 5 months) the corpus luteum sets off lactation. Thus, after every ovarian cycle, the bitch is capable of feeding infants. That explains the adoption stories in which bitches, as foster mothers, suckle endangered kittens or rabbits.

desire to mate. From time to time, however, they attempt to improve their hierarchical status and put on their seducer's outfits. But they cannot fall for any bitches except young females of low status.

## END OF A GROWTH STAGE
### (as of 12 months)

Not all puppies are on the same schedule: the Miniature Spitz, the Dachshund, and the Scottish Terrier have finished growing by 12 months, the Cocker by 13 months, the Collie and the German Shepherd at 15 months, whereas the German Mastiff, at over 18 months, will still be filling out a bit and become a heavyweight at over 130 lbs. (60 kg).

### The Age of Sexuality

Long after 1 year, at 18 or 24 months depending on the breed, the young dog fulfills his reproductive role. His senses kindled by his partner in heat, he seizes the opportune moment to approach her and assert himself. A jet of urine and he is right beside his fair maiden. He places his paws on her back while she raises her croup, consenting: he locks her, she swings her tail sideways; he climbs on her back, grabs her with his two forepaws. The sexual act begins.

In the canine species, lovemaking may last a long time because of what is known as lockup. As if trapped by the female's contracted vagina, the dog cannot withdraw his penis of which the bulbous part, called the *bulbus glandis,* has swollen up like a balloon.

Male and female are thus bonded together, immobile. Standing upright, forelegs on the ground, one hind leg on his fiancée's back, the poor male has his body all twisted. Impatient, the bitch would like to free herself from this uncomfortable position, but the young leading man is having a good time. Duration of lockup: 5 to 30 minutes, sometimes 2 hours, during which the male experiences three phases of ejaculation. If British ethologist Desmond Morris is to be believed, he releases 1.25 billion spermatozoids the second time!

The bitch is in a bad mood, prisoner that she is. But her partner, who is capable of copulating five times a day, is probably unhappy that he cannot indulge in the sexual act more often... .

Indeed he does not often have the chance to meet anybody. "Wayward" bitches are not found everywhere . . . their masters try to keep them at home.

## DOG QUALITIES
### Memory

In the wild, memory is vital. The young dog must spot dangerous places and remember escape routes to evade a predator as fast as possible. It's a question of life or death. Thanks to his hearing and his sense of smell, which are highly developed, the dog retains unchanging memories of facts and things. Thus all his life he remembers what he has experienced, particularly between the eighth and ninth weeks, when his senses are heightened.

Every odor—it is said that there are seven primary odors from which various combinations are perceived— is recorded in the memory area located in the thalamus. Every sound is striking to him and enriches his auditory memory: the sound of the car's engine is referenced forever. Even a lengthy absence will not succeed in effacing the reactions of a dog listening for this familiar sound.

The dog also records the situations and signs that he has learned to decipher alongside his brothers and sisters. Gestures used in training him to be obedient or to signify a reward remain graven in his memory.

For the same reasons as visual memory, tactile memory is very important for animals living in a pack: they bump each other, rub against each other...their skins remember. Hence the capital role of caresses for a very young dog called upon to draw closer to human beings.

Lastly, the dog remembers facts. He does not forget in which corner of the yard he buried his bone, unlike the feather-brained squirrel.

### Instinct

Despite the education given him, the young dog retains his canine instincts, identical to those of the wolf cub who is unaware of the ascendancy of human beings.

## PHYSIOLOGICAL AND BEHAVIORAL DEVELOPMENT OF THE PUPPY

| | AGE | SIZE-WEIGHT | DEVELOPMENT | ACT |
|---|---|---|---|---|
| **INTRAUTERINE LIFE** | **14th day** | 2 mm | | |
| | **20th day** | 3 mm | First signs of limbs | |
| | **25th day** | 14 mm | Outline of nipples | |
| | **26th day** | | First sign of ear<br>Iris pigmentation | |
| | **28th day** | | First heartbeats | |
| | **30th day** | 19 mm | | |
| | **31st day** | | Hairs around eyes | |
| | **33rd day** | | Embryo reaches fetus stage: palate appears, digits, claws, eyelids, and sexual organ (male or female) appear. | |
| | **42nd day** | | Ossification of skeleton | Moves, reacts to maternal motion |
| | **45th day** | | Formation of fur | |
| | **53th day** | | Fur complete | Sucks, leaves curled position, straightens body |
| | **55th day** | Achieves 3/4 birth weight | | |
| | **58th to 62nd day** | Birth size | | |
| **BIRTH** *Neonatal or vegetative period* | **0 minutes** | Between 2 and 18 oz (80 and 500 g) according to breed 4 in. (10 cm) approx. | Short, sticky pink hair<br>Nervous system under development<br>Deaf, blind | First cry |
| | **5 minutes** | | | Crawls toward maternal abdomen |
| | **Few hours** | | No visceral motor capability<br>Cerebral cortex nonexistent<br>Body temperature: 96°F (35.5°C)<br>Has burrowing reflex | Swallows 1 g colostrum every 1 to 2 seconds<br>Has four basic sounds:<br>whimpers, gives shrill cries, mews, groans<br>Seeks softness and warmth |

205

| | AGE | SIZE-WEIGHT | DEVELOPMENT | ACT |
|---|---|---|---|---|
| **1st WEEK** | **1st day** | Loses 10% of his weight | Has cartilaginous skeleton<br>Has all his teeth in bud form<br>Well-developed sense of smell<br>Tactile faculties | Snuggles up to mother and brothers and sisters<br>Pushes back hair over nipples,<br>holds up head to suck<br>Distinguishes between feeding bottle teat<br>and his mother's |
| | **7 days** | Has doubled birth weight | Rectal temperature: 98.6°F (37°C) | |
| **2nd WEEK** | **9 days** | | Rectal temperature: 96.8°F (36°C) | Maximum mewing<br>Suckles 6 times a day |
| | **10 days** | | | Barks<br>Turns around and around in nest<br>Digs with nose |
| | **14 days** | | Eyelids open<br>Sees nothing<br>Perceives first sounds<br>Loses burrowing reflex | Explores nest |
| **3rd WEEK** *Primary socialization* *Imprinting* | **15 days** | | Reacts to unpleasant or painful sensations<br>Body temperature: 100.4°F (38°C) | Walks backwards |
| | **20 days** | | Formation of hearing<br>Upper incisors and canines<br>Control of urination | |
| | **21 days** | Toy dogs reach 5/6 of height | Control of defecation<br>Is startled when hands are clapped<br>Eyes follow person moving | Gets up on his limbs<br>Shakes head from right to left<br>Wags tail<br>Seeks out human hand |
| **4th WEEK** *Attraction phase* *Socialization* | **25 days** | | Acquires normal temperature: 101.3°F (38.5°C)<br>Sensory, auditory, and visual systems functioning<br>Incisors and molars come through | Wrestles with brothers and sisters<br>Grabs mouths<br>Walks<br>Emits first growls<br>Plays |
| | **28 days** | Weighs 7 times birth weight | Neurological maturity | Collective nap<br>On waking, leaves nest to urinate<br>Runs, climbs over obstacles<br>Wrestles, tries to bite<br>Hardly mews any more |

| AGE | | SIZE-WEIGHT | DEVELOPMENT | ACT |
|---|---|---|---|---|
| Training by mother | **5 weeks** *Aversion phase* | | Facial expressiveness and acquisition of visual code / Claws come through / Memory of facts | Curls lips back, puts everything in mouth / Learning to inhibit biting / Wags tail while suckling / Chases brothers and sisters / Adopts head to head and head to tail positions |
| Life in the pack | **6 weeks** *Critical phase* | | Peak of cerebral development / Prepares for weaning / Immature organization of pack spirit / Understands brothers and sisters' language | Sleeps by himself / First hint of sexual act during games / Snivels in mother's bosom / Eats on his own |
| | **7 weeks** | | The 28 milk teeth come through (at 52 days) | Stops suckling from mother / Tries to impose his will |
| 2 MONTHS | **8 weeks** | | | Is wary |
| | **9 weeks** | | Acquires adult sleep pattern (sleeps 14 hrs/day) | Fears unfamiliar things |
| | **10 to 12 weeks** | | | Has acquired independence, gives his paw |
| 3 MOS. | *Education by human being* | Growth peak of very small dogs | | Tries to abscond |
| 4 MONTHS | | Dachshund reaches 50% of adult weight | Milk teeth fall out, incisors, intermediates, and canines come in | Tests master's authority / Hierarchical plan established / Separation of the sexes / Mounts his peers |
| 5 MONTHS | | Cocker reaches 70% of adult weight | Brain development ends / Adult canines / Bitch comes into first heat | Arches body if back is stroked / Lives in a gang |
| 6 MOS. | | German Shepherd at 80% of adult weight | Molars and premolars | Chews things / Lives in a gang |
| 7 MONTHS | | | Set of adult teeth: 42 | Lifts his leg / Territorial sense / Urinates on things |
| 8 MOS. | | | | Plays more and more |
| 12 MOS. | | End of Dachshund's growth [15 lbs. (7kg)] | Teeth are white, intact | He is now an adult / Sexual activity |
| 14 MOS. | | | Lower incisor leveled | |
| 18 MOS. | | German Mastiff's growth ends [132 lbs. (60kg)] | Lower incisors worn down | |
| 24 MOS. | | | | Bitch can be impregnated |

First reflex: making sure of survival, an instinct of prime importance in the behavior of any animal. It gives rise to the preying instinct, linked to the need for food.

This is demonstrated for us by the still-tiny puppy, in the scene in which he "kills" a toy that has been shaken, torn to pieces, and destroyed. This instinct is monitored, modeled, and otherwise directed by the educator. Thus fetching is taught to a Retriever, control to a tracking dog, and obedience to the leader of a herd.

Very naturally, threats or aggression awaken the puppy's defensive instinct. When he's little, he defends his food dish, and refuses to let go of the toy that belongs to him. On the defensive, he shows two reactions: the instinct for flight, the only way out from the traps set by a predator, or the fighting instinct in response to an attack. The latter appears frequently in the games indulged in by very young dogs. Depending on the animal's future role—defense, guard, or house-pet—the fighting instinct is heightened or controlled.

All these instincts induce the dog to protect his territory and his master. So there is nothing unusual in his warning the household by barking, turning around and around before lying down on the tiled floor. All that is specific to the canine.

We cannot blame him, either, when he licks our faces: it's the ritual for the return of the adults, during which the younger ones come and rub against their relatives. How can we be angry with him if he sprinkles the house with a few drops of urine if another dog has encroached on his territory?

## Intelligence

It varies depending on the individuals: but in many cases, it is human beings who stimulate or conversely stifle canine intelligence.

The dog does indeed possess innate faculties and enjoys the influence of breed, the top of the class being the Poodle, the Chihuahua, the Cocker Spaniel, the Weimaraner, and the mongrel, but the master's role is capital. He must walk his companion and play with him to stimulate his brain. He also needs to avoid mixing types, for each dog has very precise abilities: you cannot expect the Afghan Hound to stop thieves, but on the other hand the German Shepherd is capable of detecting by unusual signs (whispering, hasty motion) the attitude of individuals who are up to no good.

Canine intelligence is a predisposition to meet new situations and to react for the best. In unexpected situations, the dog shows genius: he rescues sleeping children from fire without having received any commands at all. The amazing performance of the canine sense of smell does not explain everything: we cannot overlook the subtlety and shrewdness which characterize the dog.

## Fidelity

Lassie, Rin-tin-tin, and other dogs symbolize this quality. The word "faithful" sticks to the dog's skin and has earned him our lasting friendship.

Fidelity is the corollary of the pack instinct: the dog's life has no meaning except in a group, in its collective activities, in its exchanges with others. For him, any initiative is gregarious. He behaves in the same way in his human family, seeking a leader so he can settle down under his protection and give him absolute fidelity.

## If He Were a Human Being?

If he had the body of a man, at 12 months he would already be big brother to a baby; at 16 months, he would be like a young man. Unsettling thought!

*Early childhood with a Schapendoes, a wonderful pal who dries tears and brings laughter. Then one day the little clown is old enough to become a protector.*

| DOG'S AGE | HUMAN AGE |
|-----------|-----------|
| 6 months | 10½ years |
| 7 months | 11½ years |
| 8 months | 12½ years |
| 9 months | 13½ years |
| 10 months | 14½ years |
| 11 months | 15 years |
| 12 months | 15½ years |
| 14 months | 16 years |
| 16 months | 18 years |
| 18 months | 20 years |
| 2 years | 25 years |
| 3 years | 29 years |
| 4 years | 32 years |
| 5 years | 37 years |
| 6 years | 40 years |
| 7 years | 44 years |
| 8 years | 47 years |
| 9 years | 52 years |
| 10 years | 55 years |
| 15 years | 77 years |
| 16 years | 80 years |
| 17 years | 85 years |
| 18 years | 88 years |

**False pregnancy should not be unduly worrying. But you must not touch the bitch's nipples during this period of time. That would increase milk secretion. If lactation continues beyond 21 days, the bitch must be taken to the vet's.**

**Dominated by his master, the house dog does not seek to relieve his libido; this is the way it is in the pack, where mating is unthinkable for an underling.**

# The Practical Puppy

To live in safety today, the little dog must be vaccinated, have an identification tattoo, and always have his identity documents with him. They are his passport for going on vacation and crossing country borders. His master can also insure him against diseases and accidents and keep a notebook of useful addresses.

*Each of these Bearded Collies must have his papers and be vaccinated as well as tattooed to be properly protected.*

## PAPERS

Any transaction, whether concerning a gift or a sale, should be validated by documents attesting to the transfer of property and conferring an identity on the young animal.

These formalities provide a guarantee after the act of purchase: if the puppy is affected by redhibitory diseases, it should be the vendor's responsibility to indemnify the new owner. What documents need to be obtained at the time of acquisition?

• The sales certificate is signed by both the seller and the buyer. It shows the date of sale, the animal's identity, the sale price, the name of the veterinarian designated for the purchase inspection, the tattoo number, if applicable, the puppy's breed, his price, the function assigned him (domestic pet, guard dog, etc.), and if appropriate the vaccinations that have been performed. If a transaction involving no money is concerned, agreement must be reached with the person giving the dog to make out a certificate of proof of gift.

• The AKC papers, which will include the puppy's breed, sex, color, date of birth, the AKC registered names of the puppy's sire and dam, and the name and address of the breeder. If possible, request copies of the sire and dam's AKC papers prior to assuming ownership of the new puppy.

• As for the vaccination certificate filled out by the veterinarian, it is not mandatory in the strict sense of the word, but no serious breeding establishment would fail to provide it. Generally speaking, any puppy purchased from a breeder has been vaccinated. Thus, after the purchase visit (see page 95), the veterinarian merely has to establish the vaccination schedule and give the boosters. The practitioner therefore gives the master a health record notebook to be brought to each appointment.

## TATTOOING

More effective than an ID disc or a collar, tattooing is done by a veterinarian or by an approved tattooist: the latter cannot anesthetize the animal. The operation is performed on a puppy at least 6 weeks old, at the same time as the first vaccination. The instrument used is a dermograph, a sort of pen filled with ink, that causes a sheaf of neddles to vibrate on the skin. Letters and numbers are inscribed inside the ear or thigh, in indelible ink.

So the puppy has a real "tie that binds." His identification number is immediately recorded. In the future, acting on a call from anyone who has seen the lost dog, the automated central database or national canine directory can give not only the identity of the four-footed stray (name, sex, breed, age, and color) but also the name, address, and telephone number of his master. It's a way of protecting your animal: in the event of loss, if the dog ends up in the pound, his tattoo often enables him to escape euthanasia.

## INSURANCE POLICIES

They provide protection from two types of concern: the puppy's health costs and damage caused to others.

Whether staying in a kennel or visiting a third party, the little dog may commit a lot of blunders: he chews the legs of the Regency armchair, shreds the sofa cover, digs up the orchids, ... . His master is responsible for all the damage. The losses are covered by civil liability insurance and comprehensive home-owner's insurance. On the other hand, in a dogs' boarding kennel, the master is not held responsible for the damage caused by his pet.

As concerns health, it is worthwhile to get an animal medical-surgical insurance policy.

Most policies provide for reimbursement of the expenses occasioned by an accident or connected with nonelective surgical operations or major illness. Preventive therapies such as dentistry, flea control, vaccinations, and elective surgeries (i.e., neutering, tail docking) are generally not included in the basic coverage of these policies. Veterinary Pet Insurance, the nation's largest insurer, has written over 500,000 policies on pets in the United States. Other pet health insurers exist as well. Your veterinarian can assist you in making the right choice.

## TAKING HIM ON VACATION

It's best to avoid last-minute applications and allow a month before "D-day" for taking care of all the formalities and getting your pet vaccinated. It is imperative that everything concerning the puppy be in order; for health and legal reasons, verification on a required basis is done in the United States as it is in other countries. Even before making hotel reservations and buying the airline ticket, you need to be sure that anywhere you go, as regards customs inspectors and police officers, your pet will be able to show his credentials.

A trip to the vet's is indispensable. Documents need to be current. Depending on the lifestyle selected for the vacation, certain vaccines are recommended; if for instance you are taking your puppy to wooded areas, consider vaccinating against Lyme disease; anti-rabies vaccination is mandatory.

Besides the antirabies vaccination certificate (which you may be required to show at any time), a certificate of good health (very helpful when you are going through Customs) is usually required as well.

Obviously, these papers won't prevent the little devil from taking off on his own and getting into every kind of mischief! This is the time to make sure that your traveling companion is included in your "Head of family's civil liability" or "comprehensive" insurance policy.

### Vacations With or Without Your Puppy?

Most transportation companies provide for domestic pets to ride along. In cars on trains, on airplanes, on ships, the puppy will find his place. Arriving at his destination, he can also have a place to stay and food.

A list of pet-friendly hotels and motels can usually be obtained from travel organizations and car clubs such as American Automobile Association (AAA). Many travel guides available at book stores also list those locations where dogs are welcomed. In addition, your veterinarian or local boarding kennel may be able to assist you in locating a veterinarian (in case of emergencies) and/or boarding facility within your

*Pending use of the electronic chip, an indelible tattoo inside the ear provides a measure of protection for this young Dandie Dinmont Terrier.*

**A dog picked up as obviously wandering and wearing no identification marks (collar or tattoo) is considered a stray. After a brief stay in the pound, he is put down.**

## The Electronic Chip

This identification procedure is in use in the United States; a chip is implanted painlessly under the puppy's skin; it contains a code that is deciphered with the help of a reader.

213

*When traveling with your pet, be sure to bring along the appropriate papers.*

**Three documents should be carried with you on vacation: the vaccination record, the antirabies vaccination record, and the certificate of good health.**

place of destination. But problems arise when you are considering taking your puppy abroad, where some countries impose a quarantine. It's better to entrust him to good hands or board him.

In the event of the loss or theft of an animal while on vacation, you need to report it to the pounds, alert police stations, contact veterinarians and trades people (put up notices), inform the local press for notices in the "Lost Animals" columns, and call the specialized organizations, such as animal rescue groups.

## Traveling with Him

Going places with your dog will involve planning and preparation. The main issue on every trip with a pet should be maximizing the dog's safety and comfort. Because of their usually in-home lifestyles, most dogs should be crate-trained. This greatly simplifies traveling as the dog's bedroom/den actually goes with the animal. Crates also add to the safety of a dog while a vehicle, train, or plane is in motion.

Unless you are absolutely certain that you can purchase the same brand of dog food at your destination that your pet eats at home, be sure to include enough food in your luggage for the entire trip.

There have been many improvements in air travel for pets in recent decades. A dog in an airline-approved carrier is welcomed on most of the larger overseas and domestic airlines. (If your dog has something other than an approved carrier for its den/sleeping area, such carriers are usually available on a rental basis from the airlines. Call ahead to be certain.)

To enhance the ease and safety of your dog's traveling, there are some good "rules of the road" to follow:

• Long before you plan to travel by air—even before you make your flight reservations—contact the airline you plan to use for their most current regulations about traveling with a pet. Ask the airline for any hints or suggestions about how to insure the safety and comfort of your dog. Some smaller dogs may even be allowed as carry-on luggage, which lets the dog ride, in its carrier, in the passenger section with you.

- Consult your veterinarian about any reasons that your pet should stay at home. Puppies, older dogs, and pets in poor health should probably not make a long and potentially stressful trip. The veterinarian can also provide you with a health certificate, which most airlines require for pet passengers. This certificate must be dated no more than ten days before the date of your flight. You also could ask your veterinarian about the advisability of motion-sickness or tranquilizer prescriptions for your traveling pet.

- Your airline reservations should be made well in advance, making certain that the reservation clerk knows that you and your dog will travel together. If the dog can't ride as carry-on luggage and must be placed in the cargo/baggage compartment, book a direct flight— if possible—to your destination, which will not necessitate changing planes. Even if you have to drive to a hub airport, a direct flight is always preferable.

- If your dog has to ride in the baggage area, be certain to actually observe your pet being loaded on the plane, before you board it yourself. This is another reason that you should arrive very early for your flight.

- If you are traveling to another country, be certain that you meet all the entry requirements for bringing a dog into that country. Also be sure of the re-entry requirements you will have to face when leaving your destination and returning home.

- Double-check the airline carrier (your own or a rental) to make sure that the bolts holding it together are all tightened down and that the door and latch work correctly. Also make certain that the "conversion kit" for a water dish is attached so it can be filled from outside the carrier, if necessary.

- Prominently affix "Live Animal" stickers to the outside of the carrier. Be certain that you have attached a luggage tag with your name, address, and home phone number along with your destination and a phone number there.

- Include in the carrier a freshly laundered pad or blanket for the added comfort of your four-legged friend. Be sure to put in one of your dog's favorite toys to help lessen loneliness and boredom.

- Do not feed your pet for eight to ten hours prior to your flight's departure. You can water and exercise your dog up to two hours before flight time. In order to prevent your pet and its carrier from becoming a soggy mess, do not put any food or water (other than in the external conversion kit waterer) in the carrier.

- While airline personnel are generally quite service-oriented, you should always assume a firm, but courteous, attitude with them. Clearly assure them that you greatly value your pet and expect every standard of pet comfort and safety to be met.

- One breeder suggests taking a picture of your pet with you for identification purposes. Another puts a small lock on the carrier door (with an extra key taped to the top of the carrier under duct tape). Still another dog owner always photographs her pet as it is being loaded onto the plane.

- Be certain to get the names and employee numbers of as many as possible of the key people handling the transportation of your pet. (If things don't go well, you know who to blame; if things go well you know who to thank.)

Whether accompanying his master by air, by train, or by ship, the dog must always have his leash, collar, and if he is large, his muzzle. On the train, the dog may be allowed out of his basket to stay on his master's lap. The privilege is not granted him everywhere, however, and he risks finding himself in the baggage car.

On ships, your dog goes straight into the cabin, and depending on where he's headed, often he travels free.

Before boarding the puppy, a deposit may have to be paid to reserve his place. You should insist the keeper give you a receipt as well as a deposit certificate showing the placement date, the owner's name, and a description of the animal.

Your doggy friend is not welcomed everywhere abroad. He is subject to a 1 month quarantine in Canada, 4 months in Finland, Norway, and Sweden, and 6 months in the United Kingdom. He is forbidden to enter Iceland and Australia.

## USEFUL ADDRESSES

### Kennel Clubs

American Kennel Club
51 Madison Avenue
New York, NY 10010

Canadian Kennel Club
89 Skyway Avenue, Suite 100
Etobicoke, Ontario M9W 6R4

### Breeders

American Dog and Cat Breeders Association
    and Referral Service, The
33222 N. Fairfield Road
Round Lake, IL 60073

### Kennels; Pet Sitters

American Boarding Kennels Association
4575 Gallery Road, Suite 400A
Colorado Springs, CO 80915

National Association of Pet Sitters, The
1200 G Street, NW, Suite 760
Washington, DC 20005

### Humane Organizations

American Humane Association, The
63 Inverness Drive East
Englewood, CO 80112-5117

American Society for the Prevention
    of Cruelty to Animals
424 East 92nd Street
New York, NY 10128

Humane Society of the United States, The
2100 L Street, NW
Washington, DC 20037

## Puppy on Board

• A safety harness may save the puppy's life in a car, in the event of violent braking or an accident. It fastens automatically over the safety belt buckles and can be adjusted according to the puppy's girth [between 24 and 40 in. (60 and 105 cm)]

• A tranquilizer prescribed by the vet can reduce the puppy's anxiety, It's better not to feed him to avoid his becoming carsick. However, he must never be deprived of water.

• During the trip, you must frequently moisten the puppy's head and flews. He must drink at every stop.

• The puppy must never be left alone in a poorly ventilated car. He is at risk of heatstroke, which would be fatal for him.

## General Pet Information

Delta Society
PO Box 1080
Renton, WA 98057-9906

Morris Animal Foundation
45 Inverness Drive East
Englewood, CO 80112

American Pet Society
406 South First Avenue
Arcadia, CA 91006-3829

Animal Health and Nutrition Council
PO Box 184
Pennsauken, NJ 08110

American Veterinary Medical Association
1931 North Meacham Road, Suite 100
Schaumburg, IL 60173

Orthopedic Foundation for Animals
2300 Nifong Boulevard
Columbia, MO 65201

American Canine Sports Medicine Association
12062 SW 117th Court, Suite 146
Miami, FL 33186

Dog Museum of America
51 Madison Avenue
New York, NY 10010

Pet Food Institute
1200 19th Street, NW, Suite 300
Washington, DC 20036

Pet Information Bureau
1220 19th Street, NW, Suite 400
Washington, DC 20036

*Travel cages are available at the airport so that your dog can travel in the airplane's baggage hold.*

**Before leaving for foreign countries with your dog, all the information needs to be gathered from embassies or consulates. Antirabies vaccination is mandatory. The rabies vaccination certificate and the certificate of good health will usually be asked for at borders. Any puppy who sets foot across the Atlantic is subject to a health examination.**

*In the mountains, at the seaside, in foreign countries, a young dog is happy anywhere provided that his vacation has been prepared for.*

Pet Loss Foundation
16811 Edinburg Lane
South Bend, IN 46635

World Wide Pet Supply Association, Inc.
406 South First Avenue
Arcadia, CA 91006

### Hotlines
National Animal Poison Control Center
(Toll call 1-900-680-0000)

Pet Loss Support Hotlines
916-752-4200
708-603-3994

## USEFUL LITERATURE
### Magazines
*Dog Fancy*
PO Box 53264
Boulder, CO 80322

*Dog World*
29 North Wacker Drive
Chicago, IL 60604

*Natural Pet*
PO Box 42053
Palm Coast, FL 32142-8917

*Pure-Bred Dogs—American Kennel Gazette*
Official Publication of the American Kennel Club
51 Madison Avenue
New York, NY 10010

*Pet Life*
1227 West Magnolia Avenue
Fort Worth, TX 76104

## Books

AKC, *The Complete Dog Book* (Howell Book House, Inc., New York, 1992).

Alderton, David, *The Dog Care Manual* (Barron's Educational Series, Inc., Hauppauge, NY, 1986).

Bear, Ted, *Communicating with Your Dog* (Barron's Educational Series, Inc., Hauppauge, NY, 1989).

Bear, Ted, *How to Teach Your Old Dog New Tricks* (Barron's Educational Series, Inc., Hauppauge, NY, 1991).

Coile, D. Caroline, *Show Me!* (Barron's Educational Series, Inc., Hauppauge, NY, 1997).

Klever, Ulrich, *The Complete Book of Dog Care* (Barron's Educational Series, Inc., Hauppauge, NY, 1989).

Lorenz, Konrad Z., *Man Meets Dog* (Penguin Books, New York, 1967).

Pearsall, Milo, and Charles G. Leedham, *Dog Obedience Training* (Scribner's, New York, 1979).

Pinney, Chris C., DVM, *Caring for Your Older Dog* (Barron's Educational Series, Inc., Hauppauge, NY, 1995).

Pinney, Chris C., DVM, *Guide to Home Pet Grooming* (Barron's Educational Series, Inc., Hauppauge, NY, 1991).

Rice, Dan, DVM, *The Complete Book of Dog Breeding* (Barron's Educational Series, Inc., Hauppauge, NY, 1996).

Schlegl-Kofler, Katharina , *Educating Your Dog* (Barron's Educational Series, Inc., Hauppauge, NY, 1996).

Ullmann, Hans J., *The New Dog Handbook* (Barron's Educational Series, Inc., Hauppauge, NY, 1985).

Wegler, Monika, *Dogs: A Complete Pet Owner's Manual* (Barron's Educational Series, Inc., Hauppauge, NY, 1992).

Wrede, Barbara J., *Before You Buy That Puppy* (Barron's Educational Series, Inc., Hauppauge, NY, 1994).

Wrede, Barbara J., *Civilizing Your Puppy* (Barron's Educational Series, Inc., Hauppauge, NY, 1989).

### Afghan Hound

A coat of silver, platinum or gold, long, true-to-race, delicate head; bony hips, thin, curled tail. This Greyhound, a native of the Asian steppes of Mongolia is a true courser—he's known as "Tazi" in his home country. It means "speedy."

He also has a vocation as a hunter, but his very long, abundant and silky fur, forming wide pantaloons and requiring considerable upkeep, causes him to be considered a "for show only" Greyhound. In any case he does quite enjoy sofas and a drawing-room existence, but a love of the wide open spaces soon gives him a desire to run off on his own.

Proud, dignified, and independent, he is nevertheless easy to educate: an affectionate and understanding master contributes to his perfect balance and great sociability.

*AKC Group II*
25–27 in., 50–60 lbs.
(62–64 cm, 20–25 kg)

### Airedale

In the country of Yorkshire, along the Aire Valley, he's nicknamed "king of terriers." His earliest profession was otter-hunting, but he goes after rabbits and boar equally well, and even bear, in Canada. Well suited to guard and defense work, he is highly valued in the army and the police force.

The Airedale makes a very good pet: in educating him, his energy and independence need to be taken into account. With a square body, a long head, strong jaws, small v-shaped ears, bright eyes, and tail held high, he's a hardy creature. Above all he needs exercise, especially if he lives in a city environment. Lastly, this dog with his beard and mustache, with his black coat over a tawny red background, needs to be groomed: brushing every week, and shaving three times a year.

*AKC Group IV*
23 in., 45 lbs.
(60 cm, 20 kg)

*From the Airdale to the Yorkshire Terrier (opposite) from shepherds to hunters, from sled dogs to lapdogs, there are 114 breeds to choose from, to say nothing of crossbreeds and mongrels.*

## Akita

In the province of Akita, in the north of Japan, this sizable sporting dog is not a sled dog but a hunting dog. His forehead is wide, his ears are pricked up and bent forward, and his tail is curled over his back. He has a warm-tinted coat: it's brindled (black, red, and white) or else black, red and white, ornamented with white patches. Little inclined to barking, quiet and reserved, he's made for life outdoors.

The puppy's education requires patience and firmness. He's a good watch dog and guard, but not aggressive toward human beings; however, he loathes being teased by his peers.

*AKC Group III*
26 in., 85 lbs.
(70 cm, 38.5 kg)

## Alaskan Malamute

With his tail raised above his back or carried low "like a fox," a compact body, a wide skull, strong jaws, small, upright ears, this dog, in his warm, light gray or black cloak, looks like a wolf. Known in France since 1975, he was used at the end of the 19th century by the Eskimo Malamute tribe which was prospecting for gold in Alaska. Of calm temperament, and very independent, he is sociable, but he needs snow all the time.

*AKC Group III*
23–25 in., 75–85 lbs.
(59–64 cm, 34–38.5 kg)

## American Cocker

When he arrived in France in 1975, it was not in order to ply his trade as a hunter. This silky-coated dog, too fragile for scrubby undergrowth, became a stay-at-home: he had to abandon ditches and thickets to cultivate his image as a hero straight out of Walt Disney's animated movie "Beauty and the Tramp." His success transformed him into a pet dog. Easy to educate (he's not stubborn), the city Cocker now spends his time in homes and exhibition halls.

*AKC Group I*
13.5–14.5 in., 22–30 lbs.
(37–40 cm, 10–13 kg)

## American Staffordshire Terrier

This dog with his short, thick, multicolored coat with highly developed jugal muscles, with a strong supple body, must be educated with the greatest care. His ancestors were English fighting dogs who plied their trade in the United States in the 19th century. This stubborn animal must remain confined to his role as watchdog and guard dog.

*AKC Group IV*
17–19 in., 40–45 lbs.
(43–48 cm, 17–20 kg)

## Anatolian Shepherd

Short or medium-length fur. He is a native of the high plateaus in the middle of Turkey where his qualities as protector of the herds have been praised since time immemorial. This watchdog, of impressive size but of calm temperament, cannot make do without a yard.

25–28 in., 90–140 lbs.
(71–81 cm, 40–65 kg)

## Appenzell (a cattle herding dog)

Short, dense fur. This Swiss dog's ancestors were mastiffs accompanying the legions of antiquity. Energetic and lively, obedient during the training period, he is constantly on guard at his post.

19–23 in., 45–55 lbs.
(48–58 cm, 22–27 kg)

## Argentine Mastiff

This mastiff with a short white coat and short ears has energy to spare.

He is a former fighting dog who measured his strength against large wild animals and was brought into South America by the Conquistadors.

*AKC Group III*
23.5–25.5 in., 85–95 lbs.
(60–65 cm, 40–45 kg)

## Australian Shepherd

Mid-length coat, in various shades: blue-black, reddish-black, three-toned, black and flame. This very attractive dog's ancestors were shepherd dogs brought to Australia by Basques toward the end of the 18th century. After the United States, where he was introduced a century later, he became implanted in England. The Australian shepherd is not recognized by the FCI (Fédération cynologique internationale: International Federation of Dog Experts, headquartered in Belgium).

*AKC Group VII*
17–20 in., 48–60 lbs.
(45–58 cm, 22–29 kg)

## Barbet (a spaniel)

He is the ancestor of the Poodle, but his official place among retriever hunting dogs and game flushers is a reminder of his incredible speed in starting ducks. A native of North Africa, this dog with his incredible little beard has a curled tail. With a well-tempered character (but easy to educate) he has gone from a rustic lifestyle to a very citified existence. With his thick, dirty-white fleece, his moon-like head and his eyes round as marbles he adopts a city-dog look, wearing, like the precious Poodle, the "lion" cut! With hindquarters shaved and pompoms around his ankles, it is much easier for him to swim. Finally, this water dog, with his relaxed nature, playful and jovial, is predisposed to agility training.

21.5–23.5 in., 45 lbs.
(55–60 cm, 20 kg)

## Basenji

Short-haired, tawny and white in color, or black and white or three-toned. This dog of Fox Terrier size appears in Egyptian frescoes dating from 3600 BC. But it was not until 1870 that the English discovered this breed: silky coat, pointed ears, tail rolled up across his back. Unusual, elegant and delicate, is highly appreciated in town, where he does not have the tendency to take off that he has in the country. His very weak voice—the Basenji does not bark, but coos or yelps—makes him an ideal apartment dog. Independent, stubborn—he does only what he wants—he has a fascinating character. Can he really be a dog when he washes himself like a cat, and when he perches as high as he can to observe those around him?

*AKC Group II*
16–17 in., 22–24 lbs.
(40–42.5 cm, 10 kg)

## Basset artésien normand (Normandy-Artois Basset)

Short fur, two-tone or three-toned. In the 19th century this breed was obtained by crossing Normandy Bassets with Artois Bassets. The result is a very long body with short limbs (twisted of half-twisted at the front), an elegant head. Independent, this very tonic dog gifted with patience is a good weekend companion.

10–14 in., 33–55 lbs.
(26–36 cm, 15–25 kg)

## Basset Hound

Of all the Bassets, this country-dweller, a hunter by trade, is the lowest, the longest, and the heaviest. Coat of two or three colors, head marked by folds and double folds, long, pendulous ears "in curlpapers," large well-developed flews: a physique like this could hardly escape the attention of breeders. It was the American who, importing from England this dog of pure French origin, revealed him to the general public in the 1950s. Cartoons and advertisements made a star of this astute animal, who trifles with his master as he does with a hare. Off-stage, this obstinate creature needs a firm and persevering education.

*AKC Group II*
14–15 in., 65 lbs.
(33–38 cm, 30 kg)

## Beagle Harrier

Merry and playful, this short-haired dog, generally three-colored, reaches his full potential only in the country. A few years ago he was the subject of a genetic reconstitution program. He is cross between Beagles and Harriers, which improves his performance compared to what it was initially. That goes back to the end of the 19th century, in the days when Baron Gérard was trying to develop the Beagle for hunting in horseback.

*AKC Group II*
19–21 in., 45 lbs.
(43–48 cm, 20 kg)

## Bearded Collie

Crossed with the Bobtail (Old English Sheepdog), this bearded dog is a cousin of the Collie nicknamed the Highland Collie. A sporty animal in love with the wide open spaces, but with a very flexible character and very precocious, this puppy can fit in anywhere, even in town, where he forgets his sheepdog origins.

He lends himself to any of the specialized training routines. With his rectangularly cut body and his long, curving tail, he looks like a well-combed bearcub. His fur, often gray and white, sometimes tawny, beige, black, or black with a touch of white, must be thoroughly brushed every week. His trump card: balance. His *bête noire:* solitude and indifference. Is that because he almost disappeared?

*AKC Group VII*
22–26 in., 65 lbs.
(51–55.6 cm, 20 kg)

## Beauceron

Short, close hair, little fringes across the abdomen and the back of the thighs, black coat with tawny red tips. This dog with his pastoral vocation is a native not only of Beauce but of Paris basin as well. On the huge farms, he led the herds and was also employed by the butchers at La Villette. Rustic and of strong build, this self-assertive dog needs a master capable of moderating ardor and channeling his guarding instinct. Patience and firmness are indispensable in the education of this shepherd with pricked-up ears, to be considered a working animal.

23–28 in., 75–95 lbs.
(61–70 cm, 35–45 kg)

## Bedlington Terrier

Closely clipped or with his fur cut with scissors, this dog who looks like a lamb has the silhouette of a charger: he was crossed with Greyhounds and Terriers from the north of England to hunt rabbits. His coat has blue-gray or tawny gray tones, sometimes blue and flame, his fur is soft like his gentle temperament; calm and affectionate, his apartment behavior is perfect.

*AKC Group IV*
16–17 in., 17–23 lbs.
(40 cm, 8–10 kg)

## Belgian Shepherd

This little fireball, who proves remarkable in all the disciplines planned for useful work, exists in several varieties: the Groenendael Shepherd, with long black hair; the Tervueren Shepherd, with long tawny and gray hair (for these two, grooming is a necessity); the Malines Shepherd, with short tawny hair; the Laeken Shepherd, with rough tawny hair. Though he's a shepherd dog, he shows equal brilliance in his work as watchdog and guard dog. Quick and vigilant, his worst enemy is inaction. Eager for affection, the dog cannot tolerate the slightest brutality in his education, which must be undertaken very early on. Training that is too repetitive does not suit him.

*AKC Group VII*
24 in., 66 lbs.
(60 cm, 30 kg)

## Bichon bolonais (a lapdog)

The rarest of the Bichons, with thick fluffy fur (which does not molt), was very popular from the 15th to the 18th century in Italy and in Spain. Catherine the Great of Russia was also extremely fond of this little white dog.

He is quiet, he has all the good qualities of an apartment dog, and he adapts perfectly to city life. Very calm and observant, he becomes very attached to his masters.

9–12 in., 6–10 lbs.
(25–30 cm, 2.5–4 kg)

## Bichon Frise

Cheery and bright, very adaptable (he can live in an apartment just as well as in the country), this dog with his proud bearing frequented the court of Francis I of France and later inspired the artists Fragonard and Goya. With his tail curled over his back and his drooping ears, children think he looks like a little clown. Exuberant and mischievous, he is easy to educate, but his woolly coat [the curls are 3–4 in., (7–10 cm) long] which could easily be mistaken for that of the Angora goat, requires a lot of upkeep. A difficult art, because no knots can be allowed to hide among the ringlets!

*AKC Group VI*
9.5–11.5 in., 10 lbs.
(24–29.5 cm, 4 kg)

## Bichon havanais (Havana lapdog)

Very fashionable in the 18th century, this mischievous little creature, a native of Cuba, is the joyous result of marriages between European Bichons and small Antillean dogs. Having emigrated to the United States in 1960s, he shows more interest in minding the poultry than in drawing-room life. Happy in the country, he does not enjoy fussy grooming. However, his fur—rarely white, more often beige, light brown, gray, all one color or splashed with white—must be regularly maintained.

*AKC Group VI*
9.5–11.5 in., 13 lbs.
(25–30 cm, 6 kg)

## Bloodhound (Saint Hutbert)

Short black and flame, or blue and flame, or tawny fur; a long wrinkled head, with dewlaps at the neck; very long curlpapered ears. His career started in the 8th century in an abbey in the Ardennes placed under the patronage of Saint Hubert, protector of hunters. Until the French Revolution this massive dog was the

*Polish Plains Shepherd (p. 231)*

pride of the kings of France. The monks made gifts of their best sleuth-hounds to their sovereign lords. The Saint Hubert would have had a gloomy future if it had not been suggested by the famous French hunting expert Le Coulteux de Canteleu that Great Britain take him on, at the end of the 19th century.

Thus he was able to pull his numbers up again as Bloodhounds. Very independent but very capable of obedience, he's a deterrent guard with a bass voice. A country-dweller, he is also a good friend for children.

*AKC Group II*
24–26 in., 90–110 lbs.
(60–70 cm, 40–48 kg)

### Bordeaux Mastiff

Despite more than 110 lbs.(50 kg) of muscle and bone, a broad head covered in stern wrinkles and surmounted by little ears, and a big tail, this watchdog in his tawny or mahogany coat is not vicious. He's a calm animal who keeps his voice down (except in front of other dogs). The French writer Buffon referred to him, however, as "an Aquitaine Mastiff used as a fighting dog with bears, donkeys, and lions.

That does not prevent this double-sized Boxer from being required in American movies.

His education as a puppy requires certain precautions: he needs to be around people in order to become sociable; from the time he's three years old he has to be careful so that he will not have heart problems later on.

22.5–26.5 in., 110 lbs.
(58–68 cm, 50 kg)

### Border Terrier

He originated in the Border country, where the north of England and Scotland meet, and where he used to flush otter out of their holts. Oddly enough, his head is like that river animal's: short square muzzle, crossed by a black mustache, and short, rough hair. A sporting animal at heart, he likes to frolic in the open air, but accepts city life well, provided that enough walks are organized for him.

*AKC Group IV*
14 in., 12–15 lbs.
(36 cm, 57 kg)

### Borzoi

He's one of the largest Greyhounds. He has an arched back, a flat, narrow ribcage, and a long, well-fringed tail. The Borzoi became a favorite with Russian nobility. In the 18th century the Boyards made him a great wolf hunter. He's a sporting dog and he needs a yard. Overflowing with affection this highly sensitive animal is very attached to his master and hardly ever thinks of taking off on his own. In town, if he goes out frequently, he fits in gladly, gracefully wearing his long silky coat with its waves and curls, which is of all colors and shades: gold, gray, flame umber, black and flame, tones splashed with white.

*AKC Group II*
26–28 in., 75–95 lbs.
(65–80 cm, 35–45 kg)

### Boston Terrier

A distinctly American creation, the Boston Terrier's roots can be traced back to the late 19th century. A cross between an English Bulldog and a white English Terrier, the Boston Terrier has an exceptional disposition, and interacts great with children. General appearance is that of a smooth coated, short-headed, compact dog carrying an expression of high intelligence. The tail is naturally short. Colors include brindle and white, and black

and white, with a white blaze over the head, neck, chest, and inner forelegs.

*AKC Group VI*
14–16 in., 15–25 lbs.
(36–41 cm, 7–11 kg)

### Bouvier bernois (Bern cattle-herding dog)

Black coat picked out with white and flame markings on the head, the ends of limbs, the neck and the chest. This dog is the only one of the Swiss Bouviers to have long, thick, slightly wavy fur (to be brushed regularly). Peaceful, he excels in his role as watchdog and a domestic pet. After a fairly easy education, he shows no aggressiveness, but demonstrates a fine protective instinct toward his family. To become the children's idol, the Dürrvach dog, as he is called in the neighborhood of Bern, merely needs to renew ties with tradition and pull a little cart, as he did in the past to convey milk from the farms to the cheese factories.

*AKC Group II*
24.5–27.5 in., 85–110 lbs.
(58–70 cm, 40–50 kg)

### Bouvier des Flandres

In the Netherlands, this thick-set, powerful dog is better known than the universal German Shepherd. In the 1920s, he became one of the most highly reputed, dogs in "police dog" competitions. With wiry, rumpled hair (he has to be combed) he is rough to the touch. He's a rugged animal with a balanced character—patience and rigorousness are the qualities required for his education—a hard worker and a good house dog. His preference goes to children, whom he protects and reassures.

*AKC Group VII*
23.5–27.5 in., 55–85lbs.
(60–69 cm, 27–40 kg)

### Boxer

With a broad, massive head, a flattened muzzle—his jaw projects forward—this dog with pricked-up ears, short tail, and short fur is deceptively like a Mastiff. A very good watchdog, he displays vigilance and courage. But he needs to have a healthy lifestyle, his weak point being his heart, from the age of 6 or 7 years onward.

*AKC Group III*
21–25 in., 55–75 lbs.
(53–63 cm, 25–35 kg)

**Braque du Bourbonnais (a Pointer)**
Of stockly build, this keen-nosed hunter (a good retriever) with a coat sprinkled with light brown, sometimes nuanced with purplish-red (a particular feature of this breed), is a native of the Allier district. Within the Pointer family, he is the equivalent of the Brittany Spaniel. A dog who makes a good pet, he has become rare.
20–22 in., 35–55 lbs.
(51–57 cm, 18–25 kg)

**Briard**
Robust and self-willed, this strong-boned dog has a nice face. With rounded ears, he has a beard and mustache. His eyebrows hang over his eyes. At an early age, he's an adorable plush toy—but his fur is dry to the touch—black, tawny, sometimes gray, and needing brushing twice a week. The puppy has a great future before him as guard dog (he is instinctively protective), but despite his generosity and kind heart, he needs to be directed with firmness and perseverance. Exercise and space contribute to his development and balance.
AKC Group VII
23–27 in., 60–85 lbs.
(56–68 cm, 30–40 kg)

**Brittany Spaniel**
A broad-backed silhouette, short tail, fringed coat found in white and orange, white and brown, white and black, three-toned, or with patches or flecks. This is one of the hunting dogs most used in North America. Active, very willful, he is often a field trials champion. With some English Setter blood, this trackhound has very great capabilities. While he is full of vitality, spirited and playful, he is also a very good domestic pet, quiet, sociable, and obedient.
AKC Group I
18–20 in., 35 lbs.
(45–51 cm, 15 kg)

**Bullmastiff and Mastiff**
Drooping ears, long tail, the Bullmastiff looks like a Boxer who has done some muscle development exercises; the Mastiff is even more massive, as regards both his head and his body. Cumbersome because of their size, victims of their own weight, these dogs often have wounds and calluses on their elbows. Their very British stolidness calls for some patience during their education. In the past, Mastiffs were castle watchdogs in Britain, and to amuse the nobility, hurled themselves madly into fights with wild animals. The Bull Mastiff, with short tawny or brindled fur, wears a black mask. He was an accomplice of the poachers who trespassed on lordly estates during the 19th century. Both dogs make people feel safe and are good watchdogs for country or suburban homes.
AKC Group III
Bullmastiff:
25–27 in., 100–130 lbs.
(61–68 cm, 41–59 kg)

AKC Group III
Mastiff:
27.5–30 in., 135–200 lbs.
(66–82 cm, 60–100 kg)

**Cairn Terrier**
He is the ancestor of all wire-haired Scottish Terriers. Short-legged, with a short tail, upright ears, tousled hair (just brush it) in tawny tones (beige to red), gray (steel to black) and brindled, with black muzzle and ears, he's an attractive imp but not very obedient. Stubborn as a mule, he is forgiven because of his good humor, vivacity, and roguishness. The countryside makes him happy and piles of rocky earth are his favorite playground. Easy to get along with on the whole, he also adapts to city life, but he resolutely waits for it to be time for his walk.
AKC Group IV
10 in., 14 lbs.
(25 cm, 6–7.5 kg)

**Cesky Terrier**
This feather-light Basset, with gray-blue or beige fur with white patches, was born of marriages between the Bohemian Terrier and British hunting Terriers, like the Scottish Terrier and the Sealyham. Recognized by the Fédération cynologique internationale in 1963, he's a great choice not only as a good domestic pet but also as a city dog. He has a well-groomed look, (his silky fur needs clipping every 2 months): attention is drawn to his mustache, eyebrows and beard.
10.5–13.5 in., 13–20 lbs.
(27–35 cm, 6–9 kg)

**Chihuahua**
Bright eyes, pointed ears, short or long hair. Always on the alert, the smallest dog in existence has a shrill voice. Excellent watchdog, this "miniature" native of Mexico has a very assertive temperament. Snarling when facing large dogs, peevish with strangers, he's afraid of nothing and nobody. Of strong constitution despite his small appetite, he needs to take walks in the open at to wear down his long claws.
AKC Group V
8 in., 4–6 lbs.
(20 cm, 1.3–1.8 kg)

**Chow Chow**
The Chow Chow's origins are traced back to China over 2,000 years ago. Believed to be a cross of the Tibetan Mastiff and the Samoyed, the Chow Chow was a formidable hunter, characterized by his trademark blue-black tongue. He was also employed as a temple guard, to drive off evil spirits. Imported into Britain around 1880, Chow Chows made their way to America by the turn of the century.

This "bear dog" has a large, broad head with erect ears. His compact, stocky body is complimented by a curled tail carried well over the back. Chow Chows come in a variety of colors, including red, black, cream, blue, and white. Extremely loyal to his master, the Chow Chow exhibits remarkable intelligence, and can be trained quite easily.
AKC Group VI
18 in., 40–55 lbs.
(46 cm, 18–25 kg)

**Cocker Spaniel**
Black, red, or gold coat, or maybe black and flame (regular care and grooming necessary), Long ears frame this hunter's mischievous head: he notes with displeasure the shrinking number of wild rabbits. As a result he has converted to the job of being a companion.

One of the world's most popular dogs is energetic and self-willed. But he needs to romp in the countryside, jump across streams, or else run along beaches. Getting wet is his favorite activity.
AKC Group I
14–15 in., 25 lbs.
(38–40 cm, 12 kg)

**Collie**
Delicate head, sumptuous fur with fringes and plume, luxurious mane, and satin jabot.

Brilliant when he takes up activities such as agility exercises, tracking, searching under wreckage or herding sheep, etc., the Collie will never be free of the heroic image of *Lassie,* based on the novel by Eric Knight. Did she not cross the whole of England looking for her master? This highly sensitive animal, found in a sable (gold picked out with white), three-tone (black, flame, and white) or silver-blue (silvery gray, on a white background with flame markings) coat, had already made an impression on 19th-century minds: in the summertime, Queen Victoria used to take her Collie with her to Balmoral Castle. Robust, fond of water, snow and wind, he is not difficult to educate.

*AKC Group VII*
22–26 in., 65 lbs.
(51–61 cm, 20 kg)

### Continental Miniature Spaniel (Papillon)

This little dog who was admitted to the courts of Henry III, Francis I and Louis XIV of France, is better known by the name of Papillon—because of his upright ears, similar to the wings of a butterfly—and Phalaena when we are dealing with a variety with drooping ears, reminiscent of the folded wings of a night-flying moth. The top of his head is marked with a white dividing line, and his fur is silky with an abundance of fringes. He compels recognition as a pleasant little apartment dog very sensitive to his master's state of mind. Very rare, he is also much sought after.

11 in., 6 lbs.
(28 cm, 2.5 kg)

### Coton de Tulear

This little dog, a native of Madagascar—he bears the name of a Malagasy port—having escaped from a shipwreck around 1500, is related to the Bichons. Like them, he has his tail lifted up over his back, which gives him a saucy look, a factor in his growing popularity since 1981. His vitality makes him a dog that loves the country (he watches herds, tracks rodents). But this nice little imp forgets that he's always dressed up in his Sunday best, in his lovely spotless coat. All tousled, with his long, atrundant hair, he requires ongoing care.

12 in., 8–10 lbs.
(30 cm, 3.5–4 kg)

### Crested Chinese Dog

Stark naked though he is, this dog, of whom it is unknown whether he came from Asia or from America, is not absolutely hairless. He has, on his head ornamented with large, delicate, upright ears, a crest of fine long hair. He has socks on his paws, fringes on his whip of a tail. This is a luxury dog that is exclusively an apartment dweller. His skin is more or less dark hued, marbled with pink. Quite sturdy (he is often allergic to wearing coats), he possesses a trump-card that has brought him great popularity: he reputedly cures masters crippled with rheumatism!

*AKC Group V*
11–13 in., 10 lbs.
(28–33 cm, 45 kg)

### Crossbreed

Born by accident of a mongrel and a blue-blood, this dog with soft or rough coat, nice and smooth or full of tufts, is found everywhere. He has the class of a Labrador, the charm of a Spaniel and the eyes of a Westie, but his all-purpose physique is not a criterion of choice. His intelligence charms you, his multiple capabilities make him a night watchman, a chicken keeper, a regular bodyguard when he's around children. As regards education, a crossbred puppy must be raised like a thoroughbred dog.

*No group; size and weight variable.*

### Dachshund

This is the most "basset" of the basset hounds. The drawback is that at ground level the Dachshund is very sensitive to cold and damp. Another detail: he tends to become as round as a ball, having a pronounced taste for treats. But well covered in the wintertime, and kept on a diet, this dog stays very healthy indeed. All by himself, he makes up a whole dog group.

The extended Dachshund family includes no fewer than 27 individuals! With their elongated, finely chiseled heads and slightly curved foreheads, they are divided into three types of size: (standard, miniature, and toy), three varieties of fur (short, wiry, long), three coats (single-color red or yellow-red, two-tone with flame tips, or harlequin patches).

They are all born hunters, with happy, willful dispositions and long for active lives. Yet individual traits can be distinguished in the Dachshunds, starting with the toy, the smallest and an excellent rabbit hunter. Generally speaking, the wirehaired is the most restless, the most stubborn, and the one preferred by hunters; the longhaired is the gentlest; the short-haired is also stubborn. A determined creature, capable of leading his master by the nose.

*AKC Group II*
*(Standard)*
8–10 in., 16–32 lbs.
(20–25 cm, 7.25–14.5 kg)

*AKC Group II*
*(Miniature)*
11 lbs. maximum
(5 kg maximum)

### Dalmatian

The largest of the ornamental dogs is known as the white wolf: he was present alongside the popes in the 18th century, and accompanied luxury carriages in Great Britain during the following century. His coat, ornamented with little black or brown spots, as round as coins, has been seen over and over again in Walt Disney's *101 Dalmatians.* Elegant and athletic, ears held high, lips pressed together, he is a bit stubborn in his youth. He likes sports and long rambles.

*AKC Group VI*
19–23 in., 45–55 lbs.
(56–61 cm, 20–25 kg)

### Doberman

Strong and well-muscled, this dog with short tail, with short, close, black and flame, brown and flame, or blue and flame fur, seems like the Pinscher's big brother. Crossed with German Bouviers around 1870, then with Manchester Terriers, this elegant animal has some rather rough ways of showing his affection.

Full of vitality, very active, taking his Cerberus-like watchdog role to heart (he has an innate feeling for protection), he needs a firm, fair master. In the Doberman two sorts of character are encountered: one tough and inclined to bite, the other easy to handle, affectionate, and a very good guard dog for children.

*AKC Group III*
24–28 in., 55–85 lbs.
(61.5–72 cm, 25–40 kg)

### English Bulldog

Big head, scowling face furrowed with wrinkles, massive body, broad at ground level; tawny, brindled, white-splashed of entirely white coat (it needs no upkeep). This dog became one of Winston Churchill's favorites. It's hard to believe that this peaceable, awkward little creature, whose sensitivity lies no more than skin-deep, was once a fighting dog! He's an adorable stay-at-home, made for indoor life (he loathes going out in the country). You can rely on this patient and obedient companion.

*AKC Group VI*
12–15.5 in., 40–50 lbs.
(30–40 cm, 22.7 kg)

### English Springer Spaniel

A compact outline, long low-seated ears, a stump of a tail, silky fringes.

He's the spitting image of the Cocker, but much larger. A black and white, brown and white, or even three-toned coat adds to his resemblance to the above-mentioned English dog whose vocation is hunting.

The English Springer Spaniel attracted particular attention at the time of the field trials (competitions reproducing hunting conditions) at the end of the 19th century, but was not recognized until 1906 by the English Kennel Club. His pleasant character opens the doors to a career as a domestic pet.

*AKC Group I*
19–20 in., 50–55 lbs.
(49–51 cm, 23–25 kg)

### Eurasier (Eurasian)

Recognized by the FCI in 1973, this dog brings together the qualities of the Chinese Chow Chow and the German Pomeranian blended with a touch of Samoyed talent. He was selected as early as 1950 according to the ideal of the ethologist Konrad Lorenz. His red, gray, or black coat needs little upkeep. He is a calm, sociable, and independent dog who has his place anywhere—except in a club.

19–23 in., 45–65 lbs.
(48–60 cm, 20–30 kg)

### Flat-coated Retriever

Shiny black or brown coat endowed with lovely fringes (easy upkeep). Like the Newfoundland and the Labrador, his peers, this energetic dog used to tramp back and forth along the wharves of Poole, England at the beginning of the 19th century. His distinguishing feature is that he has Setter blood in his veins. This dog, a native of Newfoundland, is appreciated for his friendly, docile character and his perfect adaptability. But what he really likes is a stretch of water!

*AKC Group I*
22–24.5 in., 55–65 lbs.
(56–61 cm, 25–30 kg)

### Fox Terrier

Laughter in his eyes, body and head of rectangular cut, tail held high, fur all white: very speedy, always on the watch for moles and badgers, always ready to romp with the children, the Fox Terrier is of one world's most popular dogs. He owes his fame to Snowy, Tintin's companion, who thanks to the cartoonist Hergé, barks in 33 languages! Like his brother the Smooth-haired Fox Terrier, he is restless, loves traveling and needs a strong, energetic master.

*AKC Group IV*
15.5 in., 18 lbs.
(40 cm, 8 kg)

### French Bulldog

A forbidding appearance, ears upright and rounded, a brindled coat or one endowed with brindled patches on a white background that is to say quail-toned, (his short hair requires no upkeep). The Bulldog has all the qualities of a watchdog. His unprepossessing physique hides a great heart, with many qualities. Calm and silent, he shines as a remarkable house dog, adopting a quiet, stay-at-home style. He does not get in the way in an apartment, because of his small size, and takes good manners so far that he even gets along well with the cat!

*AKC Group VI*
12 in., 19–22 lbs.
(30 cm, 8–14 kg)

### Gasceny Blue Griffon

Body close to the ground, this hunting dog, born on the dry terrain of southwestern France, wears a white coat with large black patches. Officially recognized in France 1963, he has aroused the interest of the Conservatoire du patrimoine biologique regional de Midi-Pyrénées [Organization for the preservation of the regional biological heritage of the South of France-Pyrénées], which offers hope for his future.

*17–20 in., 45 lbs.*
*(42–53 cm, 20 kg)*

### German Pointer and Weimaraner

Short fur, short tail, drooping ears. This sporty dog of athletic stature does not lack elegance, but he's not intended just for showing off. The same is true of the gray-coated Weimaraner, highly prized at the end of the 18th century, at the court of the Grand Duke of Saxe-Weimar. These two dogs are pure hunters at the same time as good companions for the family. Affectionate, blossoming in a climate where strictness is blended with affection (he shows great aptitude for education), the German Pointer also fulfills his role as guard dog.

*AKC Group I*
21–25 in., 55–70 lbs.
(56–59 cm, 25–37 kg)

### German Shepherd

This dog, with tawny fur, capable of braving danger, facing up to the unexpected, gifted with great logical and intuitive intelligence, is for ever associated with the image of Rin-tin-tin. His multiple capabilities have led him to be now a wartime sentinel, now a tracker dog, now a rescue dog—to the extent that he has become the reference standard among working dogs—and have propelled him to the front of the stage. Very disciplined—obedience being the quality that most endears him to his masters—this hero adapts to any setting and is really happy only when he perceives the usefulness of his task among human beings. From the age of 3 months, or even 6 weeks, the puppy shows great aptitude for learning his job.

*AKC Group VII*
22–26 in., 65–85 lbs.
(55–65 cm, 30–40 kg)

### German Wirehaired Pointer

His fleece of rough, untidy hair is good protection for him in his life in the countryside.

A born hunter and trained to become, in the 19th century, the first multiple-skilled trackhound in the whole of continental Europe, the German Wirehaired Pointer (French since 1918) is also a good house dog and watchdog. He has a long head, flat ears, a brown, roan or gray coat sprinkled with brown patches. His amber eyes have an intelligent expression, a detail that is noticed as soon as the puppy's education begins.

*AKC Group V*
12–24 in., 45–60 lbs.
(50–60 cm, 20–30 kg)

## Glen of Imaal Terrier

Medium-length fur (rough on the top, soft underneath), gray-blue or wheat-colored coat. He's one of the oldest of the Terriers of Ireland. Yet it was not until 1933 that the Irish Kennel Club recognized him. A country dog at heart, this basset likes to run through marshes and bogs. Though full of self-assurance and subject to fits of mischief, he's a fairly docile dog.

14 in., 35 lbs.

(35 cm, 16 kg)

## Golden Retriever

Thick coat, shading from burnished gold to pale beige. The silhouette of this dog is longer than the Labrador's, and so is his tail. He's a model of courtesy. Pleasant, calm, quiet, he goes around seeking to "immerse himself in nature" in the countryside and the marshes.

With a broad head, a powerful muzzle, a compact, square body, this "yellow dog" with his strong bone structure is built for sports and family walks. Sociable and very courteous, full of great sensitivity (to be taken into account during his earliest puppyhood) he detests being alone. As for being a watchdog, he neither cares for it nor has the gift for it.

*AKC Group I*

21.5–24 in., 55–75 lbs.

(51–61 cm, 25–34 kg)

## Great Dane (German Mastiff)

Elongated, narrow, sculpted head, ornamented with heavy flews and upright ears; fur that is yellow or brindled, steel blue or black, harlequin patched with black spots. The German Mastiff is a very calm animal. Very obedient, in times past he frequented the German princes, after operating as a large-game hunting Mastiff.

*AKC Group III*

28–32 in., 100–143 lbs.

(72–82 cm, 45–65 kg)

## Greyhound

Since the high Middle Ages, this elegant courser has occupied a choice place in Great Britain where he has been the privileged companion of the nobility. With his highly developed rib cage, his powerful muscles outlining his thighs, lower back, shoulders and neck, he had no problem becoming, as early as the 17th century, the first sporting dog and a coursing champion.

His presence is eagerly awaited these days at greyhound racing stadiums. The start of greyhound racing, a chase after a hare [artificial nowadays] on an enclosed track, confirmed him in first place. This high level sporting dog, whose education presents no difficulties (he obeys hand and eye signals) adapts well to a city environment. A model of gentleness and affection, he is very unobtrusive and shows no aggressiveness toward people he doesn't know. Disinclined to take off on his own, he is a dog whose suitability as a domestic pet has been overlooked.

*AKC Group II*

27–30 in., 65–70 lbs.

(68–76 cm, 25–35 kg)

## Hovawart

Wavy medium-length coat, which may be blond, black, or blond and black, drooping ears, a plumy tail. Large and massive like a mountain dog, full of vitality like a shepherd, in the 19th century he lived near the Black Forest and Wittenberg, Germany. The "Hofwart" had been known since the 13th century for his qualities, as his name implies, as a court guard dog. This quiet, docile dog gradually became very rare. He did not begin to make a comeback until 1945. He performs with distinction in many sports disciplines. A yard and long walks are indispensable for him.

22–28 in., 55–85 lbs.

(58–70 cm, 25–40 kg)

## Hungarian Pointer

With a Turkish hunting dog in yellow livery as ancestor, this trackhound with short, rough hair was bound to inherit the tawny color. Later contributions from the German Pointer have strengthened his performance. As a result, this perfectly well-balanced, active animal can perform a number of tasks.

*AKC Group I*

21–24 in., 50–65 lbs.

(52–61 cm, 22–30 kg)

## Jack Russell Terrier

Smooth, wiry hair, all white or with tawny or black patches. He is almost a dead ringer for the Fox Terrier. However, he is a little smaller, less square, and his head is less long. He owes his name to a fervent huntsman who in 1819 achieved through crosses a line of little terriers for foxhunting. Recognized in 1990 by the Kennel Club of the FCI, this dog has a future that is already marked out.

14–15 in., 20–22 lbs.

(30–35 cm, 9–10 kg)

## Japanese Spaniel

Flat head, high forehead, tail over his back, white and black fur. This little dog, ideal in an apartment, needs regular care. He has gone by the name of Chin since the 8th century, and yet he is an American. Very sociable, both playful and well behaved, he is not interested in sports, seeking out home comforts rather than walks in the fresh air. This long-limbed little Spaniel, robust and bursting with health, who was the favorite dog of Queen Alexandra, the wife of Edward VII, and is still the unbeatable favorite of the Rothschilds, is a very good pet.

*AKC Group V*

10 in., 22 lbs.

(25 cm, 3 kg)

## Kerry Blue Terrier

Black all over in the first months of his life, this large Terrier, a native of the county of Kerry (in southwestern Ireland) has a surprise in store for adulthood: he turns blue-gray. Used in the past for hunting, he is very fashionable today and has been shown in exhibitions since 1920.

*AKC Group IV*

17.5–19.5 in., 33–40 lbs.

(44–49 cm, 15–18 kg)

## King Charles Cavalier (a Spaniel)

The little favorite of Charles II of England in the 17th century and today of Princess Margaret is very engaging. This miniature English spaniel, with long ears, long silky coat (to be brushed twice a week), is easy to educate and to get along with. He likes quiet days spent sitting on a sofa just as much as he enjoys wild chases through the countryside. Overflowing with vitality, inexhaustible at play, enjoying a roll among the grasses and tracking snails, he can also stay calmly near his master.

*AKC Miscellaneous class*

12–14 in., 12–16 lbs.

(30–35 cm, 5.5–8.2 kg)

## King Charles Spaniel

He has kept his old name which reminds us of his great friendship with Charles II of

England. With the silhouette he has of a little luxury Spaniel, his apple-shaped head, his tip-tilted nose, his fringed coat (looking after it is not much trouble) in black and flame, three tones, or white and red (Blenheim) or pure red (ruby), he can't stand an outdoors life. He likes the padded atmosphere of an apartment where he can share luxury and convenience with the family cat. As concerns his education, it's art in its infancy: he brings himself up all on his own, and blossoms among children.

*AKC Miscellaneous class*
10–13 in., 9–14 lbs.
(26–32 cm, 3.6–6.3 kg)

## Kuvasz

This dog of large stature, elegant and proud, with all-white, wavy hair, is of Turkish origin. He came from Hungary in the 18th century: there he used to hunt bear and boar for the Magyar kings and princes, whose castles he also guarded. In the 20th century, changing his calling, he is hired by the Hungarian police. Active and alert, this faithful dog, with his deeply rooted protective instinct, is very receptive to training.

*AKC Group III*
26–30 in., 90–115 lbs.
(66–75 cm, 30–50 kg)

## Labrador Retriever

He is yellow (in shades from cream to tawny) or black, rarely brown; his coat is dense, his neck and withers powerful, his head broad, his muzzle square, and his tail short (an "otter-tail").

Almost everyone recognizes the Labrador silhouette. This beautiful dog, a native of the island of Newfoundland, was not, unlike the other retrievers, crossed with European dogs. He is a great charmer. He is the choice of political figures, the favorite of great ones of the world, and the great friend of ordinary families. Solitude is his *bête noire*. In whatever setting he happens to be, from marshy countryside to ministerial offices, he displays a noble bearing. But in his infancy, with his boisterousness and his mania for "fetching" everything he finds within reach, he is not entirely reliable.

*AKC Group I*
22.5–24.5 in., 60–75 lbs.
(51–59 cm, 30–33 kg)

## Leonberg

Big and strong, his head masked with black, this huge dog with thick smooth fur is named after the city of Leonberg in Germany. He is reminiscent of a "mountain lion" because he wears a fine golden-tawny mane with black shading.

Placid, he's a model of balance and gentleness. He has in him the qualities of the Saint Bernard and the Newfoundland, and in his role as family watchdog he always keeps one eye on the children, at the same time remaining suspicious of strangers.

28–30 in., 110–160 lbs.
(65–80 cm, 50–75 kg)

## Lhasa apso

A large head, long thick fur like that of a goat (*apso* in Tibetan), a golden or gray coat, or it might be black, white or brown tones. The Lhasa apso was not recognized in Europe until the 1930s.

A native of the capital of Tibet, where he was the sacred dog of high dignitaries—he was then considered a bringer of good luck—this sage of great character had proven his efficiency: he warned human beings of major events such as avalanches.

The watchdog of the temples of the Roof of the World has a highly developed sense of responsibility. He has but one desire: to accompany his masters wherever they go.

*AKC Group VI*
10–11 in., 11–15 lbs.
(25–28 cm, 5–7 kg)

## Lundehund

The smallest of the Nordic hunting dogs, a native of the Lofoten Islands (northern Norway), where he has became common since the 17th century, is a curiosity of nature. To hunt puffins, he dashes unhesitatingly into the water, his ears being closable on demand and watertight.

He is also blessed with extraordinary flexibility and agility, due to his two dozen digits. Very playful and obedient, he easily tackles inclement weather, and can get used to living in town.

12–14 in., 14 lbs.
(30–36 cm, 6 kg)

## Maltese lapdog

This dog, shown in paintings by Titian (16th century), has lived with human beings for a

*Eurasier (page 227)*

very long time. He has been known about since the days of Aristotle. Yet after the great popularity he enjoyed in the Italian Renaissance he almost disappeared. In the 19th century, didn't Landseer paint the portrait of the "last of the breed"? With his tail curled like a hunting horn, this very sociable and pretty little dog is forced, because of his white outfit that trails down to the ground, to live a drawing-room existence: his fur, which may exceed 15 in. (40 cm) in length (for a body size of 20 cm) has to be put up, lock by lock, in curlpapers.

*AKC Group V*
8–10 in., 7–10 lbs.
(20–25 cm, 3–4 kg)

## Mongrel

Born of unpedigreed parents, on both sides, he does still have a hint of the thoroughbred dog: a Boxer head, Schnauzer fur, Terrier shrewdness.... Finding a way to get by has been his strong point for centuries, and his resourcefulness is appreciated on farms and in sheepfolds. Sought after for his niceness, this intelligent dog is receptive to the rules of mannerliness.

*Variable size and weight, no group*

*Jack Russell Terrier (p. 228)*

### Neapolitan Mastiff
This dark-coated dog has a huge head, thick flews, deep wrinkles, short-cropped ears. A born guard, he has a past laden with combat. His ancestors were the Mastiffs used for Roman circus games. From 1415 to1712, he was crossed in Sicily with Spanish fighting dogs. The same warrior fate overtook him even after that (he was the bodyguard of Neapolitan underworld figures). He is considered a guard dog.
*AKC Group III*
25–30 in., 110–150 lbs.
(60–75 cm, 50–70 kg)

### Newfoundland
Black, brown or chocolate coat, oily fur, palmate feet. England was his land of asylum while the country that gave him his name classified him in 1815 as undesirable.

Celebrated by poets such as Byron, shown from every angle by painters, he was praised to the skies in 1864 by the Prince of Wales. His dense, impermeable coat (which must be brushed regularly) makes him a great expert in the water.

Impressive size, strong bone structure, broad, massive head: he has the features of the mountain Mastiff.

With specialized training, he excels in his role as water rescue dog.
*AKC Group III*
26–28 in., 100–150 lbs.
(66–71 cm, 45–68 kg)

### Norwich Terrier
Tousled, wiry hair (no grooming), in tawny, wheat-color, black and flame or grayish shades. This red-haired little imp with upright ears was selected for hunting in the English county of Norfolk (hence also the Norfolk breed, with drooping ears). He is among the smallest of the true Terriers. Very lively and bright, crazy about traveling, he is the darling of boisterous children.
*AKC Group IV*
10 in. maximum, 12 lbs.
(25 cm maximum, 45 kg)

### Old English Sheepdog ("Bobtail")
Bobtail means "tail cut short," but his real name is "Old English Sheepdog." Explanation: a medieval custom consisted of docking the dog's tail in order to avoid paying taxes on dogs! Very strong, this dog has a big head, small ears, filmy fur (a weekly brushing is indispensable), gray at the back and white in front. But this adorable plush animal, whose character is as good as gold and who is highly intelligent, needs an education that's all authority and perseverance.
*AKC Group VII*
22 in., 75 lbs.
(61 cm, 35 kg)

### Pekingese
Massive head, wide, wrinkled muzzle, long fur, mane, collar and a profusion of fringes (not much grooming, but regular care). This very refined little Chinese is the proud representative of the ancient sacred animal of the Buddhists: the "lion of fö," a dragon endowed with the intelligence of the monkey, the nobility of the lion, and the appearance of the dog. According to legend he was the result of a love affair between a lion and a female ape. It was not until the 19th century that the breeding of Pekingese was established in Europe, after he was discovered following the sack of the Imperial Palace in Beijing in 1860. He had just experienced his time of glory in the reign of Tao Kwang (1822–1851). An indoors dog with lordly attitudes, the Pekingese is very

independent. In an apartment, he hates to share his existence with other animals.
*AKC Group V*
10 in., 10–12 lbs.
(25 cm, 2–8 kg)

### Picardy Blue Spaniel
His black coat with grayish patches over a bluish skin is the result of crosses with the Gordon Setter. He has flat, wavy hair, silky fringes over his ears, legs and tail, ears that frame his cheeks, gentle-looking deep eyes, a broad head with a square muzzle, the body of an athlete endowed with endurance. This cousin of the Picardy Spaniel, to be appreciated in the country as well as in town (he loves playing with children), is found only in small numbers.
23.5 in., 45 lbs.
(60 cm, 20 kg)

### Picardy Shepherd (Berger Picard)
With his little beard, and a tail curled up like a huntsman's horn, this dog with medium-length bushy fur, encountered in tawny or gray shades, needs no grooming. He is bursting with energy and gaiety. As old as the Beauceron and the Briard, he is, however, the least well known of the shepherd dogs. An excellent watchdog and guard he must have adequate activity if you don't want to be subjected to freakish behaviors.
22–25.5 in., 41–50 lbs.
(55–65 cm, 19–23 kg)

### Pinscher
Much smaller than the Doberman, whose black and flame coat he has, he is the Doberman's ancestor and perfectly illustrates the German canine type. In the 18th century this little dog from the stables accompanied stage coach drivers. Very lively, even boisterous, he has a vital need for exercise. He is both a very good, vigilant watchdog and a domestic pet intent on sharing the life of the family. Exuberant, the Pinscher is happy in any biotope, and gets along well with an even-tempered master determined to educate him.
*AKC Group V*
*(miniature)*
10–12.5 in., 4–9 lbs.
(25–30 cm, 2–4 kg)

*AKC Group V*
*(standard)*
17.5–20 in., 26–35lbs.
(45–50 cm, 12–16 kg)

## Polish Plains Shepherd

Called "the valley shepherd" then "Nizinny" (part of his Polish name), this dog of strong constitution, endowed with an ample fleece, is born without a tail. Recognized in 1971 by the Fédération cynologique internationale, he first entered France in 1981. Very robust, with a rectangular silhouette, this good watchdog gives voice when strangers arrive. He has one small defect: greediness, which tends to be encouraged during his training, since treats are used as rewards for this very gifted student.

16–17 in., 40 lbs.
(40–52 cm, 18 kg)

## Pomeranian (German Spitz)

Though he has lived for 10,000 years on the shores of the Baltic, in Switzerland, and in England, this dog was declared German in 1960, as a native of Pomerania. Hence his other name of Pomeranian. Pointed muzzle and ears (*Spitz* means point), square body, tail curled over his back, fine mane. His sumptuous fur, wolf-gray in adults, black or orange in the young, is reputedly odorless, even in the rain! The companion of artists: Mozart, Michelangelo, Emile Zola; of crowned heads: Catherine of Russia; and of travel people: boatmen, he has a taste for discovery, visiting people, and going away on vacation. Educated with firmness, he gives voice to lay down the law in the neighborhood; the miniature, always on the alert, aligns himself extremely well with the bigger ones.

*AKC Group V*
*(toy)*
under 10 in. (25 cm)

## Poodle

With his curly fur, in ringlets or twists, he is clipped in the "lion" style (hindquarters sheared short), the puppy style, the English style, or the "lamb" style (finished with scissors). Very fashionable in the time of Napoleon I, this descendent of the Barbet once hunted duck in the marshes of his homeland, France. Becoming a city dweller, he is easy to raise and all he has on his mind is play. He jumps about, stands on his hind legs, spins around. A bringer of good humor for the children.

*AKC Group V*
12–14 in.

*AKC Group VI*
*(miniature)*
10–15 in. (25–38 cm)

*AKC Group VI*
*(standard)*
over 15 in. (38 cm)

## Pug

Apricot-colored coat, sometimes silver, black, or tawny; round wrinkled head, flat nose, ears shaped like buttons, tail making a double loop. This little lapdog was Napoleon I's rival for Josephine's attentions.

After enjoying great popularity, he fell from grace with the British gentry until in the 1960s the Duke and Duchess of Windsor made him their favorite. This mini-mastiff does indeed present a lot of problems in his youth. Very lively, dynamic, and boisterous, but always amiable in spite of his scowling look, he is the opposite of what he will be in adulthood: a quiet, steady, even stay-at-home little barrel, to whom it is not advisable to give too many treats, for he tends to grow chubby!

*AKC Group V*
12–14 in., 14–18 lbs.
(30–35 cm, 6.3–8 kg)

## Pyrenean Mountain Dog

White coat splashed with gray, yellow, yellow with black marks or orange, requiring upkeep. We must mention the famous "Patou," brought to the court of the Louis XIV of France by Madame de Maintenon, who had just accompanied the young Duc du Maine to take the waters at Barèges. In the high valleys of the Pyrenees, his native territory, this noble-looking dog, with his black-rimmed brown eyes full of nostalgia, used to protect the herds. He's the bear dog of the Pyrenees. He also officiated as guardian of the castles at Foix and Lourdes in the 14th century. A very good companion for children, provided he plays in the open air, has wide open spaces to run in, and receives a very consistent education starting at the age of three months. A broad knowledge of psychology is needed to dominate this independent animal.

28–32 in., 132 lbs.
(70–80 cm, 60 kg)

## Pyrenean Shepherd

Long hair, tawny or gray, harlequin patches, or more rarely black. Every day this native of the Hautes Pyrénés needs to run 10–12 mi. (15–20

*Afghan (p. 221)*

km) in order to keep his shape. He cannot deny his past as a leader of herds, standing out as the oldest French dog in this discipline. Motivated by enjoyment of sports, he is also endowed with a remarkable sense of smell and is very brilliant in his tracking work. A faithful animal, he would follow his master to the ends of the earth. A very pleasant pet, this shepherd full of life and mischief needs to be educated with firmness. Very attached to his home, which he guards with great seriousness, is suspicious of people he doesn't know.

16–20 in., 35 lbs.
(38–50 cm, 15 kg)

## Rottweiler

Broad chest, compact body, strong head: destined to be a watchdog or a guard dog, this respect-inspiring dog has a great reputation in the United States. He began to arouse interest in 1910, on the information that he could be enrolled in the police force. It is to Rottweil (at the foot of the Alps), an old crossroads in the Wittenberg area and home to a huge and famous animal market in the 18th century, that this Mastiff owes his name. This former butcher's dog with short, strong jaws, short black and flame fur, short ears and tail must be educated with a firm hand.

*AKC Group III*
22–27 in., 85–110 lbs.
(55–68 cm, 40–50 kg)

### Saint Bernard

Voluminous wrinkled head, short muzzle, drooping flews, thick, short or long (two varieties exist), flat or wavy fur. The fine old image of the rescue dog is owed to Barry, who died at Bern in 1814 performing his assistance work. But this dog, who resembles the Mastiff as much as the mountain dog, is no longer required for his avalanche dog mission. That was not, in any case, his first job: he had earlier been a pack dog for the herdsmen monks of the Mont Saint Bernard Hospice in Switzerland. An efficient watchdog, this robust dog is a nice creature, but his niceness does not mean he doesn't need a strict education.

*AKC Group III*
25.5–27.5 in., 135–170 lbs.
(65–70 cm, 60–80 kg)

### Samoyed

The slightly upturned corners of his mouth give this white dog a "Samoyed smile." His voluminous fur requires constant care. Happy in the snow, he's a sports-loving animal who excels in *pulka* competitions and has passed his tests on polar expeditions. His exploits in the Antarctic with the explorer Robert Scott made him famous at the beginning of the 20th century. Having come from western Siberia, between the Venisei river and the White Sea [an arm of the Barents Sea], he was used as a sled dog. Having become a domestic pet, he must not lapse into inactivity nor be kept within four walls, or he will make his voice heard!

*AKC Group*
19–23.5 in., 55–65 lbs.
(50–60 cm, 25–30 kg)

### Schapendoes (Netherlands Shepherd)

The herd dog instinct is very much alive in this lively and flexible but stolid dog. Recognized in 1989 by the Confédération cynologique internationale after almost disappearing during the Second World War, this hirsute dog—he has huge eyebrows—is good natured and successful in his career as a domestic pet. In his chosen province, Drenthe in the Netherlands, he has to jump through woods and heaths and

stride over ponds. Capable of agility exercises, he is fairly easy to educate, though he has more than one trick up his sleeve!

17–20 in., 33 lbs.
(43–50 cm, 15 kg)

### Schipperke

His name means "little shepherd" in Flemish. He is the image, but smaller, of Groenendael, a Belgian Shepherd with long black fur. Queen Marie Henriette made him her favorite dog and opened up a career for him as a lapdog or domestic pet. Full of vitality, wide awake (he understands everything) this little dog, well adapted to urban life, is also a very good watchdog.

*AKC Group VI*
9–11 in., 10–18 lbs.
(23–30 cm, 3–8 kg)

### Schnauzer

Beard, eyebrows, mustache; salt-and-pepper coat (black and silver for the miniature) all three brothers—giant, standard, and miniature—need to be clipped.

As straightforward in temperament as they are square in outline, these dogs of German origin are made for guard work: an utter curse for burglars! The Schnauzer is afraid of nobody and feels at ease everywhere. He loves to go on weekend trips and walks; wide open spaces, games, and chasing moles and field mice fill him with joy. The smallest of the three musketeers is not the least of them in this. However, the little treasure needs to he taken in hand from the very beginning if you don't want him to turn into a tyrant.

*AKC Group III*
*(Giant)*
24–27 in., 75–100 lbs.
(60–70 cm, 35–45 kg)

*AKC Group III*
*(Standard)*
18–19 in., 30 lbs.
(40–50 cm, 15 kg)

*AKC Group IV*
*(Miniature)*
12–14 in., 9–15 lbs.
(30–35 cm, 4–7 kg)

### Scottish Terrier

Short, narrow back, long head; that's a very graphic silhouette. This Scottish dog has wiry fur, to which clipping has been applied since

the period between World Wars I and II: neck, back, and top of head exposed, setting off the fringes on limbs and abdomen and the eyebrows, beard, and mustache. He was very much in fashion at that time.

In the 1950s he became very popular in the United States, having earlier been made famous by President Roosevelt.

Equally at home in town and in the country, neither jealous nor sulky, he is quite ready to join in the mischievous games of children, provided that he has been properly schooled!

*AKC Group IV*
10 in., 19–22 lbs.
(25 cm, 9–10 kg)

### Setter

This trackhound has great training capabilities. He is brave, has a good nose, stamina, obedience, and great presence. Each breed has its own nationality and its own characteristic coat or coats.

The Irish Setter with his red coat (the red and white, more unusual, constituting a separate breed) is held to be the most elegant. The Gordon Setter, with black and flame coat, is the strongest: he is also much appreciated for guard work. The English Setter is extremely well provided for. Four coats distinguish him from his cousins: Blue Belton (city in UK), three-toned, lemon Belton, and liver Belton. Lively and enterprising in adulthood, he's in no hurry as a puppy: up to the age of three years, he lacks maturity, has no self-control as yet, and needs to receive a strict upbringing.

*AKC Group I*
*(English Setter)*
24–25 in., 55–65 lbs.
(25–35 cm, 25–35 kg)

*AKC Group I*
*(Gordon Setter)*
24–27 in., 50–80 lbs.
(62–66 cm, 29 kg)

*AKC Group I*
*(Irish Setter)*
25–27 in., 60–70 lbs.
(52–62 cm, 20–25 kg)

### Shar Pei

A hippopotamus muzzle, small ears, deep-set eyes, a purple tongue, a well built body covered with short wiry hair. This Chinese dog has one special feature: the folds in his "sable coat," of which there are many when he is a puppy. His popularity after his arrival in France in 1972 was restricted only by his price (for a long time he was costliest of dogs). Very calm and easy to get along with, he makes you forget his origins as a fighting dog, during the Han period (202 BC to 220 AD). His willful and domineering temperament toward his peers must not be overlooked in educating him.

*AKC Group VI*
15.5–19.5 in., 35 lbs.
(40–51 cm, 15 kg)

## Shetland

Head shaped like an elongated quince, almond-shaped eyes, half-upright ears, a plumy tail, a thick jabot. Both a luxury dog and a small shepherd—he has been crossed with Spitzes and working Collies in his region of origin, the Shetland Islands—this elegant animal has a heavy steel blue or golden coat. He's efficient at giving the alarm and suspicious of strangers, yet he's an easy-going companion. Docile and calm in the house, he watches over children out of a sense of duty.

*AKC Group VII*
13–16 in., 20–25 lbs.
(35–39 cm, 7–8 kg)

## Shiba Inu

Broad head, pointed muzzle, thick coat colored black, black and flame, tawny and white or brindled, small ears, tail curled over his back. This Nordic dog was saved from extinction: protected by the Japanese government since 1936, he belongs to an ancient breed expert in tracking the *yamadori* or mountain pheasant. Silent, he is cat-like in his independence and displays restful calmness.

14–16 in., 13–18 lbs.
(35–41 cm, 6–8 kg)

## Shih Tzu

A well-proportioned figure, an apple-shaped head decorated with a white blaze, a plumy tail, sumptuous fur that requires meticulous care. Until 1908, the Shih Tzu led a golden existence in China at the empress' side, having the freedom of the palace from the day in 1643 when the Dalai Lama made a gift of him to the Emperor of China. He then became the darling of wealthy Chinese, before conquering England in 1930 and then France in 1970. This little prince has far too beautiful

a coat to go running through the mud: he's a city dog.

*AKC Group V*
8–10.5 in., 9–16 lbs.
(20.5–27 cm, 7.25 kg)

## Siberian Husky

He looks like a medium-sized wolf. With his close-growing medium length fur, sometimes two-toned, and forming a cap over the top of his head, his straight ears and the "spectacles" over his pale blue eyes, he is impressively equipped for taking part in competitions in the Far North. In 1925 the breed became famous in the United States: indeed it was thanks to a Husky sled-team relay that it was possible to bring an antidiphtherial serum to the inhabitants of Nome, in Alaska. Granted AKC recognition in 1930, this dog has the hunting instinct (something not to he overlooked in his education) and barks so little he is almost silent.

*AKC Group III*
20–23.5 in., 45–60 lbs.
(50–60 cm, 15–28 kg)

## Skye Terrier

Decked with long fringes, ears upright or drooping, this highly temperamental dog, cherished by Queen Victoria has become famous. Praised to the skies because of the story of the London dog Bobby, who was faithful to his master even beyond death. He probably inspired the jolly dog Pollux who charmed French television audiences. This Scottish terrier has great abilities: he can also guard the house.

*AKC Group IV*
10 in., 12–15 lbs.
(25 cm, 5–7 kg)

## Small Lion-dog

Clipped in a lion style, like the Poodle, (tail plumed, pompons on the legs) this miniature dog with long wavy fur was stated in 1966 to be the rarest breed in the world. A very French luxury dog, with a relaxed and sparkling nature, he looks for a master in town, preferably a whimsical and cheery one.

8–9.5 in., 9–14 lbs.
(20–25 cm, 4–6 kg)

## Small Vendean Griffon Basset

Very lively, this good hunter is descended from one of the most prestigious branches of

*Rottweiler (p. 231)*

French courser dogs: the old "Kinss Whites," and the Greffiers. With wiry, bushy fur, bowed or half-bowed forelegs, he is shaped like a basset and has every chance of being found pleasing in his hare's-fur color and grayish white coat. Easy to get along with, he overflows with affection for his master.

14–15 in., 35 lbs.
(34–38 cm, 15 kg)

## Staffordshire Bull Terrier

Short hair and modest size, an imposing voice: this dog seems to have come straight out of English pictures showing dogs being tossed into the air by enraged bulls. He is a descendent of the English Pit Bulls trained to attack, but nowadays his fighting dog role consists of appearances in exhibitions ring in the United States.

*AKC Group VI*
14–16 in., 24–38 lbs.
(35–41 cm, 11–17 kg)

## Tatras Mountain Shepherd

With his totally reliable hardiness, this mountain Mastiff, whose coat is long and smooth (give it an occasional brushing), immaculate and thick the better to deal with

*Pomeranian (p. 231)*

bad weather, comes from the high plateaus of central Turkey. He was recognized as a purebred dog in 1989. With his domineering temperament, this independent animal was not meant to be inactive. Rustic, made for life in the open air, he is outstanding as a watchdog.
24–27.5 in., 75 lbs.
(60–70 cm, 35 kg)

### Tibetan Mastiff

Large head, slightly wrinkled, square muzzle, nice flews, long thick coat, black and flame, or blue and flame, or solid black, brown, gray, or golden tawny; plumy tail and mane. His gigantic size amazed Marco Polo, who thought he was looking at a donkey!

Reaching France in the 1980s after being selected at the beginning of the 1970s in the United States, Switzerland, the Netherlands, and Germany, this watchdog is loved for his profound gaze and his balance. But this independent animal needs to feel his master's authority very early.
*AKC Group III*
25–27.5 in., 110 lbs.
(65–70 cm, 50 kg)

### Tibetan Spaniel

A long silky coat (requiring regular care), long body, small head, drooping ears, tail curled over his back. This sulky-faced Asian, who looks like that because of his prognathous lower jaw, which extends beyond the upper jaw, retains all his enigmatic looks.

He does not bond with just anyone, and those whom he does approach are spellbound by his personality. Undemonstrative, he makes little noise. His great agility has earned him the nickname "monkey-cat-dog."
*AKC Group VI*
10 in., 9–15 lbs.
(25 cm, 4–6.8 kg)

### Tibetan Terrier

Known for 2,500 years in Tibet where he was a shepherd or a companion of the monks and guardian of the monasteries, this "mini-Bobtail" [Old English Sheepdog] expected to be very much in fashion in the next few years, cannot be comfortable just anywhere.

Not that he is a nuisance or difficult—he can lead an urban existence if he goes out frequently—but his long coat (which exists in all colors except chocolate) requires him to live with an extremely patient master. His fur, somewhere between wool and silk, requires frequent careful untangling and combing. In addition, this luxury dog does not tolerate solitude well.
13.5–15.5 in., 18–30 lbs.
(35–40 cm, 8–13 kg)

### Volpino

Nothing has changed since the Renaissance. In Italy, this little dog with the pointed muzzle—half fox, half wolf—with white or red fur is still the artists' favorite. A native of Tuscany, this Spitz was the faithful companion of princes and popes. City life suits him perfectly: in a full-size apartment or a studio (the Volpino is tiny) he brings all his good humor to mounting the guard.
10–12 in., 9 lbs.
(25–30 cm 4 kg)

### Welsh Corgi

Short-haired, short-legged, all the better to bite the cows' legs, this dog with his rustic past exists in two varieties: the Cardigan, with brindled or black coat, with the tail held up like a scimitar, and the Pembroke, in tawny or black and flame coat. It was the latter that captivated

Queen Elizabeth II of England, from the day her father made her a gift of one in 1936. Overflowing with vitality, this royal dog enjoys making the rounds of a garden as if he were its owner, and he guards it with great conviction.
*AKC Group VII*
10–12 in., 22–30 lbs.
(25–30 cm, 10–13 kg)

### Welsh Terrier

He looks as if he's related to the wire-haired Fox Terrier, but he is stockier, broader headed, and like the Airedale has a black and flame coat. Recognized as a purebred in 1885, this dog enchanted the general public in England in the 1950s.
*AKC Group IV*
15 in., 20–35 lbs.
(39 cm, 9–14 kg)

### West Highland White Terrier

White all over (his coat must be groomed) and with a sparkling, exuberant look, this little imp is highly visible since he has been involved in television advertising.

He was already well known before that: James I of England had given one as a present to the king of France in 1600. "White Terrier reputedly from the West Highlands" and simply known as the "Westie" in France, he's a boisterous domestic pet who often needs to stretch his legs and throughout his infancy be put back on the right road by his master.
*AKC Group IV*
10–11 in., 15 lbs.
(27–31 cm, 7 kg)

### Whippet

Short hair, ears laid back, rat-like tail. A little athlete endowed with a powerful musculature, he is supposed to be the result of a marriage of Terriers and Greyhounds very much in fashion at the end of the 19th century, in the North of England, where rag races used to be held. His name comes from the shouted order "Whip it!" (made to a coachman). Impelled by a spirit of competition—he is febrile before the test, shines, fidgets, becomes suddenly irritable—he excels in racing, is lightning-fast, having the advantages of a very light skeleton and endurance. This loving, unobtrusive dog is extremely sociable and gets along well with cats. Easy to educate, he causes no trouble. In town, he adapts; in the country he is not obsessed by the desire to run off on his own.

*AKC Group II*
18–22 in., 25 lbs.
(44–51 cm, 10 kg)

## Wirehaired Pointing Griffon

Blunt muzzle, tousled fur, he was featured as a stableyard Griffon in Renaissance paintings. Robust, great in an apartment, this affectionate and lively dog gets along well with children, who have the following colors to choose from: steel gray with brown markings, white and brown, and white and orange (to name a few varieties).

*AKC Group V*
11 in., 8–10 lbs.
(28 cm, 3–6 kg)

## Yorkshire Terrier

Short muzzle, pointed ears, silky steel-blue or tawny coat. Unconstrained, this miniature Terrier, a native of the country of Yorkshire, is not afraid of people or of mastiffs, which he provokes with his loud voice. He's a strong animal with a powerful jaw, and always has the last word. Sports loving, very lively, he hides a will of iron under a velvety glance! A barrette on his head to hold back the fur between his ears, pajamas and haircurlers to get ready for shows make him a delightful-looking dog, but no stay-at-home. He's a stubborn little creature that needs controlling.

*AKC Group V*
8 in. maximum, 7 lbs.
(20.5 cm maximum, 3.1 kg)

## Yugoslav Shepherd (Charplaninatz)

This large gray dog, half wolf, half feline, is known as the Charplaninatz, from Sar Planina, a mountain located on the borders of Albania, of which he is a native. His ancestors were Tibetan Mastiffs, which arrived in Europe thousands of years ago: hence his great corpulence and strength.

In France since 1980, this courageous dog, very attached to family life, is a very gifted learner and appreciated for his watchdog instincts. Well protected as he is by his long, bushy fur (to be curry-combed every week), high winds or snow do not harm him at all.

24 in., 110 lbs.
(60 cm, 50 kg)

# Contents

All of the photographs in this book have been provided by the Cogis Agency:

Alexis: 83, 129

Amblin: 17, 98, 116, 139, 166

Beroule: 132

Français: 49, 73, 74, 155, 156, 173 right, 175 left, 175 right, 233

Gissey: 19, 119, 194

Hermeline: 113, 128, 130 top

Labat: 6, 11, 20, 23, 58, 66, 71, 77, 86, 91, 92, 105, 146, 149, 178 top, 178 bottom, 189 top, 193, 198, 210, 218, 234

Labat/Lanceau: 61, 65, 120

Lanceau: 9, 12, 16, 44, 63, 68, 75, 76, 78, 80, 84, 85, 88, 103, 104, 106, 108, 117, 118, 127, 135 141, 144, 152, 154, 159, 165, 176, 179 bottom, 182, 186, 189 bottom, 191, 213, 220, 231

Lepage: 25, 56, 95, 109, 115, 130 bottom, 145, 188, 203, 209

Nicaise: 13, 81, 82, 124, 179 top, 196, 199, 229, 230

Testu: 123

Varin: 97, 100, 130 center, 157, 181, 185, 190, 192, 200, 224

Vedie: 4, 14, 24, 48, 50, 52, 55, 64, 89, 96, 101, 111, 112, 136, 142, 173 left, 180, 217

Vidal: 162

Front and back cover: Labat


The photographs of the echogram on page 47 were kindly provided by Dr. Nudelmann
of the Reproductive Services of the Veterinary School at Alfort.


The photograph on page 214 was supplied by the SCC (Société centrale canine) photograph library.


The color illustrations on pages 26 to 43 were drawn by Jeane Montano-Meunier and were
originally published in l'Inventaire des animaux domestiques en France, Éditions Nathan, Paris, France, 1993.


The illustrations on pages 53, 57, 90, 96, 97, 110, 114, 122, 131, 150, 151, 160, 161, 164, 168,
169, 170, 171, 172, 174, 187, 197, 198 were provided by Kéna/Watorek Illustration.


Paste-up by Carmèle Delivré


Design by
Studio François Mutterer & Associés
Composition, Georges Bréhier
Page make-up, Sophie Goldring and Dimitra Bréhier